Education Today

ABOUT THE AUTHOR

Dr.R.Annadurai is working as Director-in-Charge in Centre for Educational Research at Madurai Kamaraj University in Madurai, Tamil Nadu. He was served Fourteen years in College of Education and University, Experience in field of Education. He is Editor in Chief for International Journal of Educational Research, Development and Extension (IJERDE) at Centre for Educational Research-MKU- He has served as member in the visiting team conducted by NCTE, Bangalore. He was presented the research papers in many National and International conferences and organizing many Conference, Seminar and Workshop related to academic Activities.

ABOUT THE BOOK

In Education Today, we study about E-learning technology in Classrooms, Audio-visual aids used by the Teachers, Digital Techniques in Classroom Teaching. This book also emphasizes the teaching method of Economics digitally. Nowadays English has become very famous, popular and essential language in every field therefore teachers are using technique of teaching English Grammar through Computers. Moreover, this book also throws light on learning process through Cloud Computing. Last but not the least I hope that this book will be helpful to the teachers as well as students.

❐

Education Today

Dr. R. Annadurai
Director-in-Charge in Centre for Educational Research
Madurai Kamaraj University
Madurai, Tamil Nadu

AMIGA PRESS INC.

AMIGA PRESS INC.
H.O:- 28-A, Indra Park, St.No-9
Near-Chander Nagar, Krishna Nagar
Delhi: - 110051 (India)
Tel: - 011-22504028, +91-98736-57000
Email: - amigapress@gmail.com
info@amigapress.co.in
amigaeditorial@gmail.com
amigapub@gmail.com

Website: - www.amigapress.co.in

This edition is published by Amiga Press Inc.

ISBN: 978-93-84533-57-1

First Published 2020

Printed and bound in India by Replika Press Pvt. Ltd.

Contents

1. **Utilizing Cell Phone among Students** 1
Review of literature; Objectives of the study; Hypothesis of the study; Samples for the study; Tool used for the study; Disscussion; Conclusion.

2. **Audio-visual Aids used by the Teachers** 7
Review of literature; Objectives; Methodology; Hypothesis; Analysis and interpretation; Conclusion; Findings of the study; Discussion; Educational implications; Suggestions; Conclusion.

3. **Utilizing Cell Phone among Students** 17
Technology based teaching in geography; Need for social sciences; Important role of the geography teachers; Need for technology based instruction; Objectives of teaching geography; Innovative methods; Need of the study; Objectives of the study; Statement of the problem; Hypothesis; Selection of the media for the study; Design Sample; Construction of tool Analysis and interpretation; Hypotheses testing; Findings of the study; Educational implications; Suggestions for further research; Conclusion.

4. **Attitude on the use of ICT** 25
Role of the teacher in ICT; Computer as tutor; Statement of the problem; Objectives; Delimitation of the study; Methodology; Research design; Objectives; Research tool; Validity of the tool; Reliability of the tool; Sample; Collection of data; Analysis and interpretation; Differential analysis; Findings; Summary and findings; Conclusion.

5. E-Learning in Classroom Instruction **32**

Types of e-learning; Hypothesis of the study; Methodology of the study Scope of the study; Limitation of the study; Analogy of the studies; Selection of the population and sample for the study; Stages in the construction of tool; Statistical techniques used in the study; Hypothesis testing; Analysis of data and interpretation; Major findings of the study; Educational implications of the study; Recommendations of the present study; Suggestions for further research study; Conclusion.

6. Digital Techniques in Classroom Teaching **42**

Rationale of the study; Statement of the problem; Objectives of the study; Method and materials; Analysis the collected data was analysed by using different statistical technique like mean, sd and't' test.;The results are given in the following tables; Results and discussion; Recommendations for policy makings; Conclusion.

7. Awareness on Educational Media **47**

Objective; Methodology; Method of data collection; Sample; Data collection; Statistical tools for analysis; Analysis and interpretation; Hypothesis; Suggestions; Conclusion.

8. Educational Television **54**

Introduction; Audio-visual aids; Educational television; Types of educational television programmes; Television as a means of extending children's experience; Etv in india: a historical perspective; Secondary school television project (1961); Delhi agriculture television (datv) project-krishi darshan (1966); Indian national satellite project - insat (1982); Ignou-doordarshan telecast (1991); Statement of the problem; Operational definitions of the terms; Objectives of the study; Methodology; Research procedure; Sample for the study; Selection of the tool' Collection of data Analysis of data; Major findings of the study; Suggestions and recommendations; Suggestion for further research; Conclusion.

9. Effectiveness of Blended Learning **64**

Objectives of the study; Hypotheses of the study; Sample; Tools used Testing of hypotheses; Findings of the study; Conclusion.

10. Effectiveness of Educational Software on Chemistry **69**

Objectives of the study; Hypotheses; Nature of the research; Sample selection; Development of tool; Data analysis; Findings & discussion; Conclusions.

11. **Edu-Digital Skill** 78
Objectives; Methodology; Population; Attitude scale towards multimedia programme; Scoring; Data collection; Hypothesis; Administration of retention test; Analysis and interpretation; Conclusion.

12. **Multimedia in Teaching Economics** 84
Objectives; Methodology; Sample; Data collection; Statistical tools for analysis; Analysis and interpretation; Findings; Conclusion.

13. **Multimedia in Teaching Human Anatomy** 91
Objectives; Methodology; Sample; Data collection; Analysis and interpretation; Suggestions; Conclusion.

14. **Task Oriented Language Teaching of English** 97
Need and significance of the study; Statement of the problem; Scope of the study; Objectives of the study; Hypothesis of the study; Limitation of the study; Research design; Statement of the problem; Limitation of the study; Research method; Research tool; Samples of the study; Pilot study; Validity of the tool; Reliability of the tool; Collecting the data; Statistical techniques used; Analysing and interpretation of data; Findings of the study; Suggestion for the study; Recommendation of the study; Conclusion.

15. **English Grammar through Computer** 110
Aims of teaching english in india; Methods of teaching grammar; Teaching of english; Need for teaching english grammar; Statement of the problem; Background of the problem; Objectives; Hypothesis; Scope of the study; Delimitations; Methodology; Design; Selection of the subject; Selection of the topic; Pilot study; Blue print of the achievement test; Research methods; Tool used for the study; Sample; Procedure; Pre-test and post-test; Personal data sheet; Scoring key; Statistical measures used Statistical analysis of data and interpretation; Major findings; Educational implication; Recommendations for further study; Conclusion.

16. **ICT Competency and Performance** 118
Objectives of the study; Hypotheses of the study; Sample; Tools; Data collection; Statistical analysis; Analysis of the data; Hypothesis testing; Findings of the study; Conclusion.

17. **E-Learning in Class-Room** 124
Electronic learning -e- learning concepts; Types of e-learning; Objectives of the study; Methodology of the study; Methodology of the study; Statistical techniques used in the study; Analysis and interpretation of data; Statistical analysis used for the present study; Hypothesis testing; Analysis of data and interpretation; Summary of findings, conclusions, suggestions and recommendations; Major findings of the study; Educational implications of

the study; Recommendations of the present study; Suggestions for further research study; Conclusion.

18. **Need and Significance of Multimedia** **135**
Concept of technology enabled learning (tel); Educational radios; Educational television; Television and higher education; Statement of the problem; Objectives of the study; Hypotheses of the study; Methodology Methodology; Research design; Construction of the tool; Findings and conclusions of the study; Suggestions and recommendations; Conclusion.

19. **Teachers Attitude of New Technology** **143**
Objectives; Methodology; Sample; Data collection; Analysis and interpretation; Correlation analysis; Suggestions; Conclusion.

20. **Computer based Learning** **149**
Objectives; Sampling technique; Analysis and interpretation; Conclusion.

21. **Importance of Teaching English Language** **157**
Conclusion.

22. **Economics Influence in Education** **165**
Need of the study; Objectives; Findings of the study; Major findings of the study; Conclusion.

23. **Students Attitude towards Audio-Visual Aids used by the Teachers** **174**
Conclusion,

24. **Learning Style of Higher Secondary Students in Biological Science** **184**
Hypothesis; Conclusion.

25. **Transitive Cloud Computing for Teaching-Learning Process** **192**
Conclusion.

26. **Effectiveness of Edu-Digital Skill among Higher Secondary Students** **197**
Conclusion.

27. **Educational-Digital Skill** **205**
Conclusion.

Bibliography **217**

❒

1

Utilizing Cell Phones among Students

Nine in ten people around the world are carrying a powerful computing device in their pockets and purses. They don't realize it, but today's mobile phones have the computing power of a personal computer from the mid-nineties, while consuming a fraction of the energy and are made at significantly lower cost. In India, the mobile phone has revolutionized communication and India is now one of the faster growing markets for mobile phone service, with growing usage and increasing penetration. According to TRAI, there are 286 million wireless subscribers in India, June 2008, of which 76 million were capable of accessing data service. The increasing ubiquity of the mobile phone begs for it to be used as a learning tool. Internet browsers are now built into an increasing number of phones, especially those that take advantage of 3G or enhanced data networks such as GPRS. The BijuPatnaik University of Technology started a service in collaboration with SMS GupShup called the BPUTALERT, which distributes information, academic notice and calendars through SMS to students. Voice tap is another service using which people can send their queries through SMS, and the company messages back names of experts on the subject, and then users can connect to the right expert. The field mobile learning is in its infancy, and developers are still fumbling with products.

The invention of the fixed telephone in the late 19th century in the United States changed the way that people interacted and communicated. This has been paralleled in the early 21st century by the advent of the mobile phone. The mobile phone was originally created for business use. In the last few years extraordinary growth has taken place worldwide Information and Communication Technologies (ICT) and especially in the ICT sector tied to mobile communications, as evidenced by the more than two billion mobile phones handsets sold around the world in 2013. Mobile and light weight devices that are sometimes small enough to fit in a pocket or in the palm of one's hand are part of everyday life. The new mobile technologies can be used in mediate the relationships between schools and parents. The discourses of the participants for what regards the new mobile technologies have been analyzed in order to mediate the relationships between the school and the parents, leaving the possibility of discussing more general topic to the parent school relationship.

1. Scope of the Study
2. To Study the attitude of teenagers towards cellular phones.
3. Enumerate the usage patterns and arrive at peculiarities.

Examine the way young people relate to the functionality of mobile phones as well as asses observable phenomena.

In this context the investigator attempts to study the influence and awareness towards utilizing cell phones among the higher secondary school students.

Need of the Study

Most of the people are using mobile phones in their daily life. Mobile phones are using to send the message and communicate the information's easily. Also college students are using the mobile for clearing the doubts on their subjects from teachers and pears. Hence this study is most important to identify the awareness of the mobile phones among the higher secondary school students.

REVIEW OF LITERATURE

According to Guerra (2007), although most of the people are frequent textures, not all of them apply shorthand texting when writing. She said that students say it does affect their writing proficiency, and it has no impact at all. Nevertheless, texting is still a problem to most people.

Edwards (2009) said that texting contributes to people's indolence when it comes to writing. In his own experience, he himself developed changes on his writing abilities ever since he engaged in text messaging. According to him, it helps in speeding up communication. And because of frequent usage of shortened messages in texting, it becomes a “habit”. He sometimes caught himself using the shorthand method of writing even in doing his projects in school, which goes to show that text messaging has really affected his writing ability. When he researched in the internet, he discovered that many people also believed that texting affects the writing skills of students. Edwards always feel that using the “original way” of writing when doing his school project is more difficult than using the “text messaging language”. Because of this, he became lazier. He also said that most people are hooked up to texting that they send text messages even when they’re doing several activities like driving, when in a funeral, or in a graduation ceremony. Myhra (2010) concluded that frequent sending of text messages could affect the student’s way of writing. Students have developed the habit of writing in shorthand form, which caused them to write informally. Texting has affected the students writing and grammar proficiency negatively.

OBJECTIVES OF THE STUDY

1. To find out the level of significant difference between Boys and Girls higher secondary school students among the awareness towards utilizing Cell phones.
2. To find out the level of significant difference between Rural and Urban higher secondary school students among the awareness towards utilizing Cell phones.
3. To find out the level of significant difference between Government, Government Aided and Private higher secondary school students among the awareness towards utilizing Cell phones.

HYPOTHESIS OF THE STUDY

The null hypotheses were made with above objectives of the study.

Methodology

Normative survey method was used for the present study.

SAMPLES FOR THE STUDY

The investigator used random sampling technique for the selection of sample. 160 students were selected as sample of the present study. Out of these 160 students 75 of them are boys and 85 of them are girls.

TOOL USED FOR THE STUDY

To assess the awareness of utilizing cell phones among the students the tool ATUCP (Awareness towards Utilizing Cell Phones) was consists of 50 statements with four point rating scale was used. This was developed and standardized by the investigator.

Scoring Procedure

The students were asked to show their responses by placing (✓) tick marks. The tool consists of 28 positive statements and 22 negative statements. The negative statements were scored as 1/2/3/4 and positive statements were scored as 4/3/2/1 they are Strongly Agree, Agree, Disagree and Strongly Disagree.

Statistical Techniques Used

For the analysis of data following statistical techniques were adopted. They were,

1. Arithmetic Mean
2. Standard Deviation and
3. 't'-test Analysis of the Data

The result of the Analyzed Data is presented below.

TABLE.1.1: Significant Difference between Boys and Girls Higher Secondary School Students' on the Awareness Towards Utilizing Cell Phones

Gender	N	Mean	S.D	't' Value	Significance at 0.05 Level
Boys	75	77.85	7.07	1.56	1.97**
Girls	85	79.70	7.84		

**No Significant

The above table-1 shows that the calculated't' value is less than the tabulated't' value at 0.05 level of significance. Hence the null hypothesis is accepted, so there is no significant difference between Boys and Girls higher secondary school students' on the awareness towards utilizing cell phones.

TABLE.1.2: Significant Difference between Rural and Urban Higher Secondary School Students on the Awareness Towards Utilizing Cell Phones

Locality	N	Mean	S.D	't' Value	Significance at 0.05 Level
Rural	90	77.72	8.35	2.09	1.97*
Urban	70	80.07	6.12		

* Significant

The above table-2 shows that the calculated 't' value is more than the tabulated 't' value at 0.05 level of significance.Hence the null hypothesis is not accepted. So there is significant difference between Rural and Urban higher secondary school students on the awareness towards utilizing cell phones.

TABLE.1.3: Significant Difference between Government and Private Higher Secondary school Students on the Awareness towards Utilizing cell Phones

Types of School	N	Mean	S.D	't' Value	Significance at 0.05 Level
Government	50	75.70	9.05	3.77	1.98*
Aided	50	81.50	6.02		
Aided	50	81.50	6.02	1.82	1.98**
Private	60	79.35	6.32		
Private	60	79.35	6.32	2.41	1.98*
Government	50	75.70	9.05		

* Significant ** No Significant

The above table-3 shows that the Government and Aided schools students and Government and Private schools students are differed on the awareness towards utilizing cell phones. But Aided and Private schools students 't' value is less than the table value. So there is no significant difference between Aided and Private Students.

Major Findings of the Study

1. There is no significant difference between Boys and Girls and Aided and Private Higher Secondary School Students on the awareness towards utilizing Cell phones.
2. There is significant difference between Rural and Urban, Government and Aided and Private and Government Higher Secondary School Students on the awareness towards utilizing Cell phones.

DISSCUSSION

1. Awareness towards Utilizing Cell phones are more by the Girls than the Boy Students. Because, the Girls are more enthusiastic to work and use of cell phones.
2. Awareness towards Utilizing Cell phones are more by the urban students than the rural students. Because, the urban students are having more opportunities to use the Cell phones. But, the rural students are having less opportunities to use the Cell phones.
3. Awareness towards Utilizing Cell phones are more among Aided and Private School students. Because most of the Aided and Private Schools are mostly connected with the Parents on the progress, fees, results, attendance and relevant information's. So they have more awareness than the Government School students.
4. Regarding the review of literature past research's are in using the cell phones. But this research is known about awareness on the utilizing cell

phones. So it is different from the review and the results are also new one.

Educational Implication of the Study

1. More measures are to be taken at Rural and Government School Students to create awareness of utilizing cell phones.
2. More programmes are to be conducted to create awareness of using cell phones for the benefit of higher secondary school students, parents and teachers.
3. The Teachers may be trained to teach their lessons by using the cell phones.
4. Government should introduce the curriculum about awareness of utilizing cell phones.

CONCLUSION

In the past three years, we have gone from a smattering of mobile to an abundance of useful information. But there's still a long way to go, there are still huge gaps in our knowledge to utilize the cell phones. It has been predicted that by the end of 2014 the number of mobile phone users in India will reach 1 billion. In the world every 100 citizens 97 are have mobiles. In India 90.47 have mobiles. In future M - teaching and learning is a new creative approach and technique to apply in Education for futuristic developments and requirements of the society.

❐

2

Audio-Visual Aids Used by the Teachers

Audio Visual aids or Graphic aids are the form of visuals that are represented on plane surface. The subject matter areas that are represented in Audio Visual aids or Graphic aids are in an abridged and easily understandable form. They convey meaning mainly through relatively conventionalized symbols that are nearer to reality perceptually than verbal symbols. They secure the attention of the pupils by their attractive format and simplicity of layout. They convey the expected message by combination of visual and pictorial message made meaningful by suitable captions. Pictures and words blended in harmony deliver the required information. The idea conveyed by any graphic aid should be a single concept. The layout and words should not be complicated so as to puzzle the viewer and make him lose interest in the same. The statement "one good visual which can secure and maintain attention and educate the viewer in the desired area is worth a thousand words" is quite correct. Graphics could be truly considered as the shorthand language of the idea presented. The criteria for good graphics are that they should be simple, bold, legible brief and have adequate margins. Graphics are only two-dimensional and should be carefully planned to offset the limitation. An Audio Visual aids or a graphic aid by eliminating non–essentials and by using bold symbolic representations with attractive portrayal should be able to create interest and secure the attention of the pupils.

Since the message to be conveyed pertains to a single concept and hence brief, the viewer will not get perplexed on being exposed to the visual but will try to read and understand what is implied (visual and words).Audio Visual aids or a graphic aids could easily be prepared by and teacher using simple materials that are easily available and stored for future use. Making graphics should form an integral part of the teacher's preparation for teaching. Almost any material involving illustrations is basically graphic in nature. There can be an infinite variety of graphic materials. It is difficult to give a rigid list of these materials. The present study aims to find out the students attitude towards audio-visual aids used by the teachers in Coimbatore district. A samples of 100 respondents selected randomly were studied. An interview schedule method of survey was used to find out the attitude towards audio-visual aids. Primary data were collected by using a structured interview scheduled. All the respondents were asked the same questions in the same fashion and they were informed the purpose of study. ANOVA, t-test and regression analysis were applied to test the hypotheses. The data collected through questionnaires have been tabulated. The findings and observations are the result and outcome of the interpretations made during the study of analysis.

Graphs, Diagram, Posters, Maps, Comics, Cartoons, Charts, Globes, Display Board, Peg Boards, Hook and loop board, felt board, magnetic board, marker board, chalk board, bulletin board, models, Epidiascope, slight projector, over head projector (OHP), fields trips, excursion, exhibition, museums, radio, Television, Tape recorder, Video Caste Record VCR and Computers. By using audio visual materials in accessible process, materials givens objects changes in time, speed and space could easily be brought to the class. Audio visual aids can helps to imaginative teachers to solve the communication problems. It also helps to extend human experience. Use of audio visual aids results in greater acquisition of knowledge of facts and ensures longer retention of the information gained. It can provide effective substitutes for direct contact of students with environment-social and physical. It also adds an expected change in attitude and behaviour of the students. It can provide integrated experiences varying from abstract to concrete. It helps in to secure and retain to attention as well as develop the communication skills. It could be used to motivate and stimulate interest of students to gain further knowledge. Lastly, in a conventional teaching method teacher is the centre of attention and the primary sources of information.

An attitude is a mental state of readiness exerting directive or dynamic influence upon individual's response to all objects and situations with which it is related. Therefore if we can have some judgement about the attitude of an individual towards a specific thing or activity then we can have a fair idea as to whether the individual can be persuaded to participate in a particular thing or activity and whether he shall adopt it with interest and sincerity or not.

The attitude is the degree of positive or negative effect associated with some psychological objects namely institution, ideal, symbol, phrase, slogan, job or idea towards which people can differ with respect to positive or negative effect (Thurstone, 1946). The attitude is a dispositional readiness to respond to certain situations, persons, objects in a consistent manner which has been learnt and has become one's typical mode of response (Free Mann, 1950). According to Guild (1950) attitude is a tendency of individual to favour or not to favour some type of situation. The attitude may be considered as motivational perceptual states, which direct perceptions and predispose a person to act in accordance with perceptions (Allport, 1955). The attitudes are learnt pre-dispositions to respond positively to certain objects, situations, institutions, concepts or other persons (Aiken, 1979).

REVIEW OF LITERATURE

Glee Harrah Cady and Pat Mc Gregor (2005) describes that "Internet is a network of network and the internet mostly connects network of computers".

Barry (2006) studied the relationship between student's perceptions of their science class room learning environment and attitude to four different scores of scientific information experiments, books, promote positive attitude towards experiment as a source of information, while less favorable environment promoted more positive attitude to the more authoritarian sources of information.

Schafer (2007) compared third and fourth grade students using ESS units with students using laid low science serious on classification skills, science achievements and science attitudes. No achievement or classification skill different were noted but ESS students had more favorable attitudes.

Williams (2008), "Attitude of high school pupils towards general science and its relationship with achievement and its subjects". In her study it is found to examine if there are any differences among the different groups of students such as boys and girls. Rural school pupil and Urban school pupils in respect of their achievement in science, attitude towards science and attitude forwards science education.

Martis Anandi (2009) developed the test on scientific attitudes (TOSA), taking the point of view that attitudes must be inferred from the behavior of students. They developed a multiple – choice format test. The developed behavioral definitions of eight attitudes: (1) critical mindedness, (2) suspended judgment (3) Respect for evidence (4) Honesty, (5) Objectivity, (6) Willingness to change opinions, (7) Open – mindedness and (8) Questioning attitude. The behavioral definitions to these eight attitudes were used to develop items.

Mohanty Ajay Kumar (2010) investigated attitudes towards education, critical thinking ability and specific effective behavious of (1) Students who had studied, the BSCS environmental models “Investing your Environment” (IYE), (2) Those students using one of BSCS biological science version and (3) Those studying models of Biology. He found that the ability of students who had experienced BSCS Biological science was significantly increased but no other differences were found among the students on any of the other variables.

OBJECTIVES

The present study attempts to investigate the attitude towards Audio-visual aids used by the teachers.

METHODOLOGY

Methodology is an important aspect of any research work. There are different methods followed at various stages of any investigation. The details of methods followed in this study such as selection of tools, sample frame, collection of data, and analysis of data are involved in this research paper. The study has been designed with the student’s attitude towards Audio-visual aids used by the teacher’s achievement. The major aim of the present study is to determine the student’s Audio-visual aids used by the teacher.

Method of data collection

The investigator personally distributed the questionnaires to each member of the randomly selected sample. They were requested to answer the items in the booklet as per the instructions provided at the beginning of each questionnaire. Confidentiality of response was assured. The questionnaires were collected by the investigator from the employees. The responses were scored as per the scoring key of the respective questionnaire. Then the results were tabulated, analysed and discussed.

Sample

A sample is a finite number of observations (or) cases in a particular universe of which it is a pat (Good 1952). The investigator prepared a representative random sample of students studying VIII & IX standard in different schools at Coimbatore District. A sample of 100 students was finally selected

HYPOTHESIS

Students have favorable attitude towards use of Audio Visual Aids in Coimbatore district school.

Nature of the Tool

The inventory contained general instruction for the students and information about bio data. In addition to that the specific instruction ware given to on the first page of the inventory. Space for collecting personal data like students name type of school, locality of the school, class, gender, community, religion, group, medium of instruction, birth order of the child and parental literacy.

Data Processing

The collected data were analysed using appropriate statistical techniques. The descriptive statistics such as mean and S.D, t-ratio were computed. In order to study the functional dependencies to indicate the likelihood of causal relationships between the variables, inferential statistical techniques of ANOVA and Percentage analysis were computed.

ANALYSIS AND INTERPRETATION

TABLE.2.1: Showing Mean, SD and t-test for Respondent about Students Attitude towards Audio Visual Aids used by the Teachers on the basis of Type of the School.

Types of the school	N	Mean	SD	t-value	LS
Government	62	70.48	6.50	2.78	0.01
Private	38	73.30	10.33		

Hypothesis 1: Students do not differ in their student's attitude towards audio visual aids used by the teachers on the basis of types of the school.

The calculated t-value (2.78), which is significant at 0.01 level, confirms that there is a significant difference in student audio visual aids on the basis of type of the school. Hence the stated hypothesis is rejected. So government students have high level of audio visual aids than private school students.

TABLE.2.2: Showing Mean, SD and t-test for Respondent about Students Attitude Towards audio Visual aids used by the Teachers on the basis of Locality of the School.

Locality of the school	N	Mean	SD	t-value	LS
Urban	74	72.24	8.11	1.07	NS
Rural	26	71.14	9.19		

Hypothesis 2: Students do not differ in their student's attitude towards audio visual aids used by the teachers on the basis of locality of the school.

The calculated t-value (1.07), which is not significant at 0.05 level, confirms that there is no significant difference in their audio visual aids on the basis of locality of the school. Hence the stated hypothesis is accepted.

TABLE.2.3: Showing Mean, SD and t-Test for Respondent about Students Attitude towards Audio Visual Aids used by the Teachers on the basis of Gender.

Gender	N	Mean	SD	t-value	LS
Male	74	70.97	7.41	1.85	NS
Female	26	72.90	9.89		

Hypothesis 3: Students do not differ in their student's attitude towards audio visual aids used by the teachers on the basis of gender.

The calculated t-value (1.85), which is not significant at 0.05 level, confirms that there is no significant difference in their audio visual aids on the basis of gender. Hence the stated hypothesis is accepted.

TABLE.2.4: Showing Mean, SD and t-Test for Respondent about Students Attitude Towards Audio Visual Aids used by the Teachers on the basis of Group.

Group	N	Mean	SD	t-value	LS
Arts	56	69.19	5.37	5.58	0.01
Science	44	74.58	10.37		

Hypothesis 4: Students do not differ in their attitude towards audio visual aids used by the teachers on the basis of group.

The calculated t-value (5.58), which is significant at 0.01 level, confirms that there is a significant difference in student audio visual aids on the basis of group. Hence the stated hypothesis is rejected. So science students have high level of audio visual aids than art students.

TABLE.2.5: Showing Mean, SD and F-Ratio for Students Attitude Towards Audio Visual aids used by the Teachers on the basis of Medium of Instruction.

Medium of instruction	N	Mean	SD	F-ratio	LS
Hindi	50	70.20	9.64	6.49	0.01
English	30	71.75	4.19		
Kannada	20	75.00	11.60		
Total	100	71.78	8.58		

Hypothesis 5: Students do not differ in their attitude towards audio visual aids used by the teachers on the basis of medium of instruction.

The calculated F-ratio (6.49), which is not significant at 0.05 level, confirms that there is a significant difference in students attitude of audio visual aids on the basis of medium of instruction. Hence the stated hypothesis is rejected.

TABLE.2.6: Regression for Student Demographic Characters and their Attitude Towards Audio Visual Aids used by the Teachers.

Model Summary

Model	R	R Square	Adjusted R Square	Std. Error of the Estimate
1	.436[a]	.190	.159	7.87

a. Predictors: (Constant)

ANOVAb

Model	Sum of Squares	df	Mean Square	F	Sig.
Regression	.4189.756	11	380.887	6.155	.000[a]
Residual	17821.724	88	61.881		
Total	22011.480	99			

a. Predictors: (Constant)
b. Dependent variable

Coefficientsa

Model	Unstandardized Coefficients		Standardized Coefficients	t	Sig.
	B	Std. Error	Beta		
Name of the school	58.979	4.376		13.477	.000
Type of the school	2.387	1.116	.139	2.139	.033**
Locality of the school	-1.000	1.005	-.058	-.995	.320
Class	-.500	1.046	-.028	-.478	.633
Gender	1.989	1.052	.115	1.891	.060
Community	-1.365	.422	-.190	-3.233	.001**
Religion	.757	.627	.068	1.208	.228
Groups	5.255	.947	.306	5.548	.000**
Medium of instruction	2.183	.649	.191	3.365	.001**
Birth order of the child	-9.11	1.032	-.001	-.009	.993
Parental literacy (Father)	-.143	1.003	-.008	-.143	.887
Parental literacy (Mother)	-.585	.955	-.033	-.612	.541

a. Dependent Variable: Attitude towards Audi visual aids
**Significant at 0.01 level

According to the regression result it is known that the demographic variables are influenced nearly 19 per cent to measure their attitude towards audio visual aids. This is proved by the obtained r square value (0.19).

Further the calculated F-value (6.15) also significant at 0.01 level. It indicates that there is a significant influence between students demographic characters and their attitude towards audio visual aids.

Also from the obtained t- values the demographic variables such as type of school, community, group studied and medium of instructions the students studied are significant at 0.01 level. So it is concluded that there is a significant difference regarding attitude towards audio visual aids on the basis of these variables.

CONCLUSION

Audio Visual aids or graphic aids are the form of visuals that are represented on plane surface. The subject – matter areas that are represented in Audio Visual aids or graphic aids are in an abridged and easily understandable form. They convey meaning mainly through relatively conventionalized symbols that are nearer to reality perceptually than verbal symbols. They secure the attention of the pupils by their attractive format and simplicity of layout. They convey the expected message by combination of visual and pictorial message made meaningful by suitable captions. Pictures and words blended in harmony deliver the required information. The idea conveyed by any graphic aid should be a single concept. The layout and words should not be complicated so as to puzzle the viewer and make him lose interest in the same. The statement "one good visual which can secure and maintain attention and educate the viewer in the desired area is worth a thousand words" is quite correct. Graphics could be truly considered as the shorthand language of the idea presented. The criteria for good graphics are that they should be simple, bold, legible brief and have adequate margins.

FINDINGS OF THE STUDY

1. Based on the results that students do not differ in their audio visual aids on the basis of types of the school
2. From the calculation that students do not differ in their audio visual aids on the basis of locality of the school
3. Based on the results that students do not differ in their audio visual aids on the basis of gender
4. Based on the results that students do not differ in their audio visual aids on the basis of group
5. From the analysis that students do not differ in their audio visual aids on the basis of medium of instruction

DISCUSSION

Audio visual aids a process of inward journey to unravel the hidden potentialities of a being. It helps an individual to develop ones personality. A systematic approach of Audio visual aids helps an individual to see the all around development at physical, mental, intellectual and emotional level. The practice of use of audio visual aids makes an individual perfect. It removes the unwanted elements in the mind of the learner. It improves concentration and brings mental stability. Audio visual aids is an essential tool for students to achieve higher score in their studies as if improve concentration, memory and skills. The present study clearly indicates and recommends the students to use of audio visual aids as to develop positive attitude towards everything in their life which helps to excel themselves in their studies. The entire study concluded reveals that the use of audio visual aids have high achievement and expressed more favourable attitude.

EDUCATIONAL IMPLICATIONS

Audio-visual aids are very important and useful aids for teaching. As well as it creates high interest among the students to learn the subjects. So, the department of education shall take a steps to implement the latest audio-visual aids to all the school and colleges for teaching purpose.

For self-learning, these type of aids are very helpful to the students. Also students are very much interested in using latest technologies such as computers and internet. In internet lot of facilities are there to learn new information with visual appearance. From that students are also get more interest to use that.

In the case of teaching, in older days teachers follow interactive methods and oral demonstration. But these are not creating much interest. In order to create interest and attention audio-visual aids are highly useful. So, the concerned educational institution try to provide these facilities. So that teachers and students get benefited.

SUGGESTIONS

The following suggestions are arrived from the research findings. Research found that use of audio visual aids will contribute more in students achievement. Also the result reveals that use of audio visual aids increases the memory power, concentration. Further it sharpens the intelligence. Apart from that it reduces misconception in learning. Further due to use of audio visual aids the sensory expression would be more exercised. So, the present research suggested that in all schools and colleges, the students advised to use of audio visual aids compulsory. The education department form a rule for that and advise the educational institutions make a step to establish separate infrastructure for this one. Also the Government take a step to use audio visual aids effectively students in their academic. This will definitely help the students to be a good learner imbibing the concepts.

CONCLUSION

The present study attempted to identify the students attitude towards audio-visual aids used by the teachers. For that the researcher framed some objectives. On the basis of objectives, a questionnaire is framed. After framing the questionnaire, these are circulated to the selected samples. 100 samples were selected randomly. The responses were collected and coded using computerised. To test the hypotheses and characteristics of the data, some standard statistical tools were used. The statistical tools such as t-test, F-ratio and correlation were used. From the analysis the result concluded that the students have positive attitude towards audio-visual aids used by the teachers.

❐

3

Technology Based Teaching in Geography

Education appeared as old as the human race. In course of time its meaning has undergone many changes. As a result of these periodical changes in the meaning of education is now considered as the instrument of making one's life experiences completed and rich. The impact of changes is described as 'modernization'. Both Geography and Social studies must be accurate and reliable- only then they can be useful. Geography and social studies are different from each other in a number of ways. It is not expected of a text-book in Civics or History meant for children in schools to report new knowledge; it just summarizes and interprets what has already been ascertained. Children's learning is the focal point of concern among these who plan and implement the social studies curriculum. In contrast to the concentrated careful research orientation that is the hall mark of the social sciences, the central purpose of social studies is to provide easy, useful and learnable material.

Tool and techniques we have used to impart education must cater to the needs of our younger generation. Unless our educational instruments in particular and the education technology in general have given due attention in instructional strategies. Modernization will have no meaning. The teachers must concentrate on the Utilizing Technology must initiate the learners to involve themselves in learning more.

NEED FOR SOCIAL SCIENCES

"Geography is the advanced studies of human society to be taught the high school and college level. Social studies are simplified portions of Geography selected for instructional purposes" to be taught at primary level. In the words of Maurice P.Moffat "The Geography are those broad areas of know edge dealing with man and society in the development of civilization. The social studies may be considered in terms of knowledge drawn from the Geography and contemporary life for instructional purposes in aiding youth to understand to growth modern civilization." Take the case of Political Sciences and Civics as subjects. The former being an advanced scholarly subject is taught at graduate level, the latter being a simplified version is meant for children in schools.

IMPORTANT ROLE OF THE GEOGRAPHY TEACHERS

The teacher of Geography has a responsible role to fill. His tasks are many and varied. He transmits knowledge, directs social research, censors information collected by pupils and may also advise them in choosing their career and generally act as their guide, philosopher and friend. The teacher of Geography must become the leader of the local community, its interpreter and reformer. He must be able to transform the school into a centre of social reconstruction for a new social order.

The success of education for world citizenship depends on the daily work to the teacher in general and of the Geography in particular. Education reforms something have their beginnings in the classroom and sometimes out of it, but always must they be approved by the teacher and uses in the class-room before they can take effect, Therefore, the civilization of the future must inevitably look to the teacher of Geography for much help in the effort to end war before war ends humanity. As a matter of fact, the teacher of citizens of the future is one of the most important agents for promoting good will and preventing chaos.

NEED FOR TECHNOLOGY BASED INSTRUCTION

Education today is more than teaching and learning. Now we are in a world of technologies. The society needs quality in every sphere of work. Technology continues to move forward. Therefore, the field of education is also needs technology for better teaching-learning process. Mc. Kenzie stated the following as the major need for technology in education.

1. To reach out to maximum number of students.
2. To provide improved range of learning materials.
3. To provide greater opportunities for independent study.
4. To permit at least a limited student response.

OBJECTIVES OF TEACHING GEOGRAPHY

1. The acquaint the students with their past and present geographical and social environment.
2. To enable the students to appreciate India's rich cultural heritage as to recognize and get rid of what is undesirable and antiquated, especially in the context of social change.
3. To build intelligent demo critic citizenship.
4. To help the students gain insight into spiritual, economic and political values as forces in human behaviour and human relationships.
5. To develop desirable qualities for an all round development of a rich personality.
6. To foster attitudes to knowledge, life and learning relevant to the present and to promote understanding of all history and all human experience as a process of change and development.

INNOVATIVE METHODS

It is method that determines the quality of result. Geography is the subjects that mould the character development of the individuals. Necessary efforts must be taken to devise innovative methods in teaching Social Science.

NEED OF THE STUDY

Today the role of the teacher is also changed. The teacher has to provide individualized self paced learning experiences while teaching social sciences. These are all possible with the help of technology. So there is a need for studying the technology based geography teaching among school teachers.

OBJECTIVES OF THE STUDY

1. To study the utilization of Technology for geography teaching among high school teachers.
2. To study the nature of utilization of technology for geography teaching among high school teachers.

STATEMENT OF THE PROBLEM

Taking into consideration of the above discussion the title of the thesis is *"study of technology based teaching of geography among high school teachers in karur taluk"*.

HYPOTHESIS

1. There is significant Gender difference among high school teachers in the Nature of Utilization of technology for teaching Geography.

2. Medium of Instruction in the schools has significant influence among high school teachers in the nature of utilization of technology for teaching Geography with reference to.
3. Government and Private High School teachers differ significantly in the nature of utilization of technology for teaching Geography.
4. Urban and Rural High School teachers differ significantly in the nature of utilization of technology for teaching Geography.

SELECTION OF THE MEDIA FOR THE STUDY

While the media contains many, the investigator had chosen the following as the media for this study: (i) Map (ii) Chart (iii) Models (iv) Slide Projector (v) OHP (vi) Radio (vii) Tape Recorder (viii) Television (ix) Computer (x) Internet (xi) Demonstration (with gadgets) (xii) Field Trip.

DESIGN

Survey method is concerned with the present attempts to trace the status of phenomenon under investigation. No category of education research is more widely used than the type known variously as the survey, the normative study and descriptive research. Surveys are oriented towards the isolation of factors. Survey most does more than merely uncover data, they must interpret, synthesis and integrate these data and point to implications and inter relationships. The survey approach to educational problems is one of the most commonly used approaches. It is followed in studying local as well as state, national and international aspects of education.

SAMPLE

By using the random sampling technique, 100 geography teachers of various Govt. and Private school in Karur Taluk was taken as the sample for the study.

CONSTRUCTION OF TOOL

The check list, to investigate the nature of utilization of Technology based teaching was developed by the investigator. The checklist was given to the experts in the field of Educational Technology to obtain their opinions. Necessary corrections were made on the basis of the opinion of the experts. Thus face validity for the tool was established.

ANALYSIS AND INTERPRETATION

TABLE.3.1: Percentage of Utilization of Technology among high School Teachers

Sl.No	Instructional Aids	Percentage of Use
1.	Map	70
2.	Chart	60
3.	Models	63
4.	Slid Projector	52
5.	OHP	60
6.	Radio	32
7.	Tape Recorder	31
8.	TV	56
9.	Computer	66
10.	Internet	63
11.	Demonstration (with gadgets)	49
12.	Field trip	74

HYPOTHESES TESTING

Hypothesis-1

There is significant gender difference among high school teachers in the nature of utilization of technology for teaching Geography with reference to:

i) Map
ii) Chart
iii) Models
iv) Slide projector
v) OHP
vi) Radio
vii) Tape recorder
viii) Television
ix) Computer
x) Internet
xi) Demonstration
xii) Field trip

TABLE.3.2: Test of Significance of Gender Difference in the Nature of Utilization of Technology among High School Teachers for Teaching Geography.

Sl. No.	Facilities of Technology	Gender		df	χ^2	Level of significance at 0.05 level
		Male	Female			
1.	Map	53	17	3	3.64	NS
2.	Chart	45	15	3	4.20	NS
3.	Models	50	13	3	2.80	NS
4.	Slide Projector	38	14	2	2.24	NS
5.	OHP	45	15	3	1.12	NS
6.	Radio	25	7	3	0.28	NS
7.	Tape Recorder	23	8	3	0.84	NS
8.	Television	38	18	2	7.84	** 0.05 level

9.	Computer	45	21	3	2.80	NS
10.	Internet	44	19	3	2.52	NS
11.	Demonstration	42	7	3	1.68	NS
12	Field trip	57	17	2	1.40	NS

NS =No significance

Hypothesis-2

Government and Private high school teachers differ significantly in the nature of utilization of technology for teaching Geography with reference to:

TABLE.3.3: Test of Significance of Difference in the Nature of Utilization of Technology among High School Teachers for Teaching Geography on the basis of Type of Schools.

Sl.No.	Facilities of Technology	Institution		df	χ^2	Level of significance at 0.05 level
		Govt.	Private			
1.	Map	24	46	3	4.29	NS
2.	Chart	31	39	3	4.95	NS
3.	Models	15	48	3	3.30	NS
4.	Slide Projector	22	34	2	2.64	NS
5.	OHP	24	36	3	1.32	NS
6.	Radio	10	22	3	0.33	NS
7.	Tape Recorder	10	21	3	0.99	NS
8.	Television	15	41	2	9.24	** 0.05 level
9.	Computer	22	44	3	1.98	NS
10.	Internet	20	43	3	2.97	NS
11.	Demonstration	9	40	3	1.98	NS
12	Field trip	23	51	2	1.65	NS

Hypothesis-3

Urban and Rural High School teachers differ significantly in the nature of utilization of technology for teaching Geography with reference to:

TABLE.3.4: Test of Significant of Differences in the Nature of Utilization of Technology among High School Teachers for Teaching Geography on the basis of Locality of the Schools.

Sl. No.	Facilities of Technology	Locality of schools		df	χ^2	Level of significance at 0.05 level
		Urban	Rural			
1.	Map	25	42	3	5.20	NS
2.	Chart	23	37	3	6.00	NS
3.	Models	24	39	3	4.00	NS

4.	Slide Projector	18	34	2	3.20	NS
5.	OHP	24	36	3	1.60	NS
6.	Radio	11	21	3	0.40	NS
7.	Tape Recorder	11	20	3	1.20	NS
8.	Television	22	34	2	11.20	** 0.05 level
9.	Computer	30	36	3	4.00	NS
10.	Internet	22	41	3	3.60	NS
11.	Demonstration	16	33	3	2.40	NS
12	Field trip	29	45	2	2.00	NS

NS = No Significance

FINDINGS OF THE STUDY

1. Multimedia, Teleconferencing, Video conferencing and Video Assisted and Instruction were not utilized by high school teachers of geogrpahy.
2. There is no significant Gender difference among high school teachers in the nature of utilization of technology for teaching geography.
3. There is gender difference among high school teachers in the nature of utilization of Technology for teaching Geography with reference to 'Television'.
4. Medium of Instruction has significant influence among high school teachers in the nature of utilization of technology for teaching Geography with reference to T.V.
5. Government and Private high school teachers do not differ significantly in the Nature of utilization of Technology or teaching Geogrpahy with reference to: (i) Map (ii) Chart (iii) Models (iv) Slide Projector (v) OHP(vi) Radio (vii) Tape Recorder (viii) Computer (ix) Internet (x) Demonstration (with gadgets) (xi) Field trip.
6. Government and Private high school teachers differ significantly in the nature of utilization of technology for teaching Geography with reference to 'Television'.
7. Urban and Rural high school teachers differ significantly in the nature of utilization of technology for teaching Geography with reference to 'Television'.

EDUCATIONAL IMPLICATIONS

Utilization of technology for teaching ensures the use of maximum senses. Even than the utilization of technology among geography teachers in the Karur Taluk is not found satisfactory. Even though chart is a very cheap instructional aide only 60% of teachers are making use of it. The number of teachers who make use of the advanced technologies like recorder etc.

SUGGESTIONS FOR FURTHER RESEARCH

The following suggestions are put forward keeping in view of the findings of the present study as well as that of related literature.

1. A study may be attempted to relate to Technology Based teaching and achievement of the students.
2. A study may be attempted to investigate the factors that affect teachers utilizing Educational Technology in enhancing teaching learning process.
3. A study may be attempted to investigate the cost effective factors of the institutions in equipping the classroom with modern technological aids like video conferencing, teleconferencing, Video Assisted learning etc.
4. A study may be attempted to evolve the strategies to evaluate the technology Based teaching in school and college level.

CONCLUSION

Science and technology have occupied almost all spheres of human life. The wonderful achievement of the science and technology has glorified the modern world. Since science is included with, sociology, economics, history, psychology and geography, one has to realize the need for up-to-date knowledge of teaching social sciences. For the successful dissemination of benefits of technology based teaching among the high school teachers, it is imperative that every teacher has to be exposed various possibilities of utilizing technology in their teaching process.

❒

4

Attitude on the Use of ICT

We are living in a society where rapid changes are occurring due to the advancement of Science and Technology. As a result, the learning tools at the command of the children are getting more effective and sophisticated. At the root of this revolution are the personal computer, the television set, video cassettes, and the satellite network. Educational Technology is an innovative way to design, deliver, facilitate, and manage instruction for learners of all ages, whether it is face-to-face in a classroom, online, or a combination of methods. In Educational Technology at Boise State, you'll take courses in technology integration into the classroom, web design, flash, theory and skills of multimedia development. ICT has become an invaluable tool for children with special education needs. Teacher's skill and training are the important components of the whole educational process, which can be effectively used for improving the educational status. As education is the fundamental basis for a country, the quality of education lies under the teacher's ability and skill.

Using the Internet has far reaching effects. As well as facilitating communication, it develops skills of searching, interpreting and organizing information often defined as 'Network Literacy'. Communication through email improves students, writing skills as they take more care in grammar, spelling, punctuation and conveying meaning to an audience which isn't their teacher. ICT enables pupils with reading difficulties to find different ways in to the curriculum and raise the status of visual and aural illiteracies to the level of literacy acquisition through text.

ROLE OF THE TEACHER IN ICT

The teacher's role within an ICT-rich environment must necessarily change to help students learn in the best way they can by recognizing different learners' needs, and support students in to making choices about how and where they access new knowledge. The role of the teacher is broadened beyond the classroom and he school. As school and home boundaries start to blur, the teacher's role will be to support learners through alternative means to traditional face to face experiences. Teachers will have to learn how to teach at a distance through virtual learning spaces, e-mail, web-based discussion forums, and computer conferencing systems.

COMPUTER AS TUTOR

One orientation is 'computer as tutor'; and he compares this with the transmission model of teaching or the 'stuffing in' of knowledge. Take for example Integrated Learning Systems (ILS) that is increasingly gaining popularity for teaching literacy and innumeracy. This software coaches students in basic skills, assessing their performance on items and taking them to a higher level if they are succeeding or to more reinforcement if not. Often it is shortcomings in current educational practice that are cited as justification for using this technology.

STATEMENT OF THE PROBLEM

In present scenario, it is important to know and apply the ICT and its applications by the teachers in their classrooms. Some Mathematical problems, graphs, geometer's, and three dimension picture cannot be explained clearly in normal classroom. With the help of ICT we can show it very clearly and easily. In order to make them to know the level of these conditions, the investigator has taken the problem. This statement of the problem is titled "A Study on Attitude of Higher Secondary School Teachers on the Use of ICT in Education at Erode District".

OBJECTIVES

The following are the objectives of the study,

1. To identify the ICT skills among the higher secondary school teachers.
2. To find out the purposes of using computer resources among the higher secondary school teachers.

DELIMITATION OF THE STUDY

The investigator has attempted to collect data from a representative and manageable sample of 150 teachers from 25 higher secondary schools at Erode District.

METHODOLOGY

The heartthrob of any research activity is the research procedure adopted by the investigator. The method used in the study is dictated by the nature of the problem and the type of data required. The present study, which aims at finding out A Study on Attitude of Higher Secondary School Teachers on the use of ICT in Education at Permbalur District", has been designed by using the methodology as survey method. This study describes the design of the study in detail. The tool, sampling technique, data collection are presented in this study.

RESEARCH DESIGN

1. Nature of the study is the survey method.
2. Variable of the study is Attitude of Higher Secondary School Teachers on the Use of ICT.
3. The Researcher adopted the Tool questionnaire type.
4. The Samples are 150 higher secondary schools at Erode District.
5. The investigator used mean, Standard Deviation and "t" test techniques for analyzing the data.

OBJECTIVES

The following are the objectives of the study,

1. To identify the basic computer knowledge among the higher secondary school teachers.
2. To find out the purposes of using computer resources among the higher secondary school teachers.

RESEARCH TOOL

The investigator developed and used a Questionnaire, rating scale as a research tool for this study to find out the uses of ICT in Education at Higher Secondary level.

VALIDITY OF THE TOOL

Validity is one of the important aspects in measuring device. Validity of tool refers to the tools quality to measure what is extended to measure. The highly discrimination items are included in the scale. The content validity has been established by the experts in the field of ICT using Education.

RELIABILITY OF THE TOOL

The investigator has established the reliability. The split half reliability (correlating the odd and even items) of the attitude scale by applying the spearman Brown prophecy formula is found to 0.68. Since, the reliability value of 0.68 is above normal, the test is said to have high reliability.

SAMPLE

The investigation decided to collect the data from Erode District High School Teachers. Stratified Random sampling technique was adopted for the present study. The sample of school Teachers were selected in the simple random manner. This sample was used for the collection of data it consist of 150 Higher Secondary Teachers.

TABLE.4.1: Distribution of the Sample

Variable	Sub-Variable	Samples	Percentage Value	Total
Gender	Male	86	57.33	150
	Female	64	42.66	
Locality	Rural	40	26.66	150
	Urban	110	73.33	
School Type	Government	76	50.66	150
	Aided	74	49.33	
Qualification	B.Ed	87	58	150
	M.Ed	63	42	
Experience	Below 15	77	51	150
	Above 15	73	49	

COLLECTION OF DATA

Data for the study can be collected through observation, interviews; questionnaires schedules etc., for the present study are investigator has collected the data through the questionnaire method.

ANALYSIS AND INTERPRETATION

The collected data are known as 'Raw data', analysis of data means to make the raw data meaningful. The analysis and interpretation of data represent the application of deductive and inductive logic to the research process. The analysis of the sample in term of gender, students, caste and school.

DIFFERENTIAL ANALYSIS

Different analysis was also applied to analysis the data apart from descriptive statistics. The group was large and independent, so the critical ratio was computed.

TABLE.4.2: Analysis of the Gender

S. No.	Gender	N	Mean	SD	*"t" Value*	Significant at O.O1 Level
1	Male	64	91.375	10.449	3.679	S**
2	Female	86	85.779	7.237		

**S- Significant

Critical value: 2.61

This table shows that the mean values if male and female teachers arc 91.375 and 85.779 respectively. The corresponding standard deviations are 10.449 and 7.237.

The calculated "t" value is 3.679 which is higher than the table value 2.61 for df =148 at 0.01 level of significance. Therefore it is concluded that the male and female higher secondary school teachers different significantly in their Attitude of ICT uses.

The following figure showing in (4.1) of analysis male and female higher secondary school teachers different significantly in their Attitude of ICT uses.

TABLE.4.3: Analysis of the Locality

S. No.	Caste	N	Mean	SD	't' Value	Significant O.O1 Level
1	Rural	40	96.225	9.2555	6.77	S**
2	Urban	110	85.3	7.132		

**S- Significant

Critical value: 2.61

This table shows that the mean values of rural and urban schools are 96.225 and 85.3 respectively. The corresponding standard deviations are 9.2555 and 7.12 respectively.

TABLE.4.4: Analysis of the Management

S. No	Income	N	Mean	SD	't' Value	Sisnificant at O.O1 Level
1	Government	76	84.0395	5.608	6.356	S**
2	Aided	74	92.5	10.03		

**S-Significant

Critical value: 2.61

This table shows that the mean values of government and aided school teachers are 84.039 and 92.5 respectively. The corresponding standard deviations are 5.608 and 10.03 respectively.

TABLE.4.5: Analysis of the Qualification

S.No.	Qualification	N	Mean	SD	't' Value	Significant at O.O1 Level
1	B.Ed	87	87.77	9.36	2.473	
2	M.Ed	63	87.63	9.09		

*S- Significant

Critical value: 1.98

This table shows that the mean values if B.Ed qualified teachers and M.Ed qualified teachers are 87.77 and 87.63 respectively. The corresponding standard deviations are 9.36and 9.09.

FINDINGS

1. The distribution of sample in terms of gender. As seen from the above table 57.33percentage of the sample is male and the remaining 42.66 percentage are female.
2. The distribution of sample in terms of locality. As seen from the above table 26.66 percentage of the sample is rural and the remaining 73.33 percentage are urban.
3. The distribution of sample in terms of management. As seen from the above table 50.66 percentage of the sample is government school and the remaining 49.33 percentage are aided.

SUMMARY AND FINDINGS

In this study, the focus of attention is on the results or outcomes of the research and implications. The outcomes of any research are to be judged on the purpose or objectives are restated, followed by the whole procedure of the study which is helpful to conceive the outcome from its absolute essence.

CONCLUSION

The recommendations offered by the investigator, if implement would lead to the increase levels of higher secondary school teachers mastery of ICT skills. This will result in more wide spread and better applications of ICT into the teaching learning process so as to increase the quality of Education at large. ❐

5

E-Learning in Classroom Instruction

The modern Information and Communication technologies are technological tools and resources used to communicate, and to create, disseminate, store and manage information. ICT enables self-paced learning to help all students to achieve high academic standards. It also helps to provide immediate feedback, enhancing active participation in the learning process, sharing ideas and information. Hence investigator sorted out the utilization of e-learning which is one of the resources of ICT's in Classroom Instruction which has become more result-oriented in improving the teaching learning process. Educational Technology is the communication process resulting from the application of scientific methods to the behavioural science of teaching and learning. E-Learning is an environment in which the lessons and lecture notes are deployed on CD's or Web servers. A complete Learning Management System (LMS) helps the learners in the process. E-Learning is considered a more effective way of teaching to a large group of students, thereby providing consistency in educational quality. e -Learning is considered a more effective way of teaching to a large group of students, thereby providing consistency in educational quality. One of the main resources of Educational Technology is e-learning. The concepts of e-learning features are discussed elaborately below. E-Learning is defined as a learning environment supported by continuously evolving, collaborative processes focused on individual and organizational performance. The "e" in e-learning stands for Evolving or everywhere or enhanced or extended.

The root meaning of education is given as bringing up or leading out or making manifest the inherent potentialities in a pupil. Education refers to any act or experience that has a formative effect on the personality of an individual. Education in broad terms means, "The life-long process of acquiring new knowledge and skills through both formal and informal exposure to information, ideas and experiences". Education in narrow terms means, "Systematic planned instruction that takes place in school". Education has a very important role to play in the present set up of world.

TYPES OF E-LEARNING

The following are few of the most common types of e-Learning,

1. Technology -Based Learning (TBL)
2. Web- Based Training (WBT)
3. Computer- Based Training (CBT)
4. Synchronous e-learning
5. Asynchronous e-learning
6. Role of teachers IN e-Learning

A shift form teacher-centered instruction to learner-centered instruction is needed to enable students to acquire the new dimension knowledge and skills. This new environment also involves a change in the roles of both teachers and students. Therefore Teacher should be made aware of various tools and advantages of on-line teaching in order to bring about great changes in the field of education in the country at large. The creation of virtual classrooms i.e. classrooms in the cyber space.

Provision of Web-based learning materials.

Communication through e-mail and electronic discussion groups such as mailing lists and news groups.

Need for the study

One of the main tasks of education in a modern society is to keep pace with the advancement of Technology in acquiring the related information from the reliable e-Resources. The rapid development of information and communication technologies during the past two decades has had many points of contact with education and training. The development of technology is placing new demands on expertise and it is also leading to the increasing use of information technology in teaching and learning.

The Attitude on e-Learning in Classroom Instruction is important factor among B.Ed. Students in order to implement the usage of it in a productive way. Therefore the present study attempts to assess the Attitude on e-Learning in Classroom Instruction among the B.Ed. Students at the colleges of Education.

Statement of the problem

Technology in education is an unavoidable element in present age. In this developing state, the preparation and presentation of the content by the Teachers should have an expertise's skills towards the reach ability of students especially in the Classroom situation. The Investigator identified most common utilization of e-learning resources in the Classroom Instruction by the Teacher-Educators at colleges of education.

This experience will help them to integrate e-Learning in Classroom Instruction when they are becoming Teachers in the schools. In this backdrop, the present study attempts to find out the "Attitude on e-learning in Classroom Instruction among B.Ed. Students in Salem District, Tamil Nadu."

Objectives of the study

The Major objective of the study is to find out the Attitude on e-Learning in Classroom Instruction among the B.Ed. Students at Colleges of Education. The Specific objectives of the study are:

1. To measure the level of different component of e-Learning such as Multimedia, WEB, Video Conferencing and CCTV towards the Attitude by the B.Ed. Students in Classroom Instruction at Colleges of Education.
2. To measure the priority pattern of e-Learning Attitude for the Classroom Instruction in the Colleges of Education.
3. To measure the influence of Demographic variables such as gender, age, parent's qualification and occupation with respect to the Attitude on e-Learning in Classroom Instruction.
4. To measure the level of Attitude by the B.Ed. Students with respect to the different types of Management Institutions.

HYPOTHESIS OF THE STUDY

1. There is no significant difference in mean values of level of Attitude with respect to the e-learning in Classroom Instruction.
2. There is no significant difference in mean values on the influence of Demographic variables such as gender, age, parent's qualification and occupation with respect to the Attitude on e-Learning in Class-room Instruction.

3. There is no significant difference in mean values of Attitude on e-Learning in Classroom Instruction with respect to the B.Ed. Students in their subject.

METHODOLOGY OF THE STUDY

As the present study is descriptive by nature, a Normative Survey technique was adopted. As many as 203 B.Ed. Students from 3 colleges were chosen as sample using simple random sampling technique. A questionnaire, aimed at assessing the B.Ed. Student's Attitude on e-Learning in Classroom Instruction was developed by the investigator himself for the purpose of collecting and interpreting data. The collected data were subjected to "t" and percentage analysis.

SCOPE OF THE STUDY

The investigator attempted to know the attitude of B.Ed. Students towards e-Learning in Classroom Instruction. This study will be of great help for the educationists to adopt to integrate e-Learning features which is one of the main resources of Information and Communication Technologies (ICT) in Classroom Instruction.

LIMITATION OF THE STUDY

Though e-Learning is a vast subject the investigator restricted himself only to limited area of his study. The investigation is only on Attitude on e-Learning in Classroom Instruction among B.Ed. Students which is restricted to 3 Colleges which includes 3 Self-Aided colleges only. Also other various resources of Information Communication Technology which can be utilized in the Classroom Instruction cannot be accessed due to time constraints and cost-factors.

ANALOGY OF THE STUDIES

All the reviewed studies were related to E-learning awareness and attitude towards the teaching-learning Process. Mean, Standard Deviation,'t' test and Percentage analysis were the Statistical Technique followed in the majority of the studies. Other Statistical Techniques used in some of the studies were ANOVA, ANCOVA, Correlation Co-efficient, Chi-square.

The findings of the various studies conducted in India revealed that Educational Technology such as the Effect of E-learning, Multimedia Approach and Computer Aided Instruction showed positive effect. From the analysis of studies conducted abroad, the results of all the studies were in support of learning through Computer Assisted Instruction, Computer Mediated Instruction and Multimedia Instruction and so on.

SELECTION OF THE POPULATION AND SAMPLE FOR THE STUDY

The population was entirely covered with regard to all the colleges in the Salem district. From that 3 Colleges from Self-Aided were selected as Sample for the present study.

The present descriptive part of the research adopts the survey techniques for data collection. Questionnaire was the tool used to collect the data for this descriptive study.

STAGES IN THE CONSTRUCTION OF TOOL

Establishing Reliability and Validity

"Reliability and Validity are tools of an essentially positivist epistemology" Walting as cited in Winter (2000). Reliability is a concept used for testing or evaluating quantitative research. This idea is most often used in all kinds of research.

The face validity of the present tool was established by the fact that the test was constructed by methods suggested and endorsed by eminent people and experienced teachers in the field. The content validity was also established since an analysis was the first make of the skill itself and decisions were made on what dimensions of the skills need to be tested, and in what proportions. As the analysis and the resultant tests accord with the views of recognized authorities in the skills area, the tests can be said to have content validity.

Collection of data

The e-Learning Attitude Questionnaire developed for the purpose of collecting data for the present study was administered to as many as 203 B.Ed. Students randomly selected from 3 Self-Aided colleges.

STATISTICAL TECHNIQUES USED IN THE STUDY

As the present study is descriptive in nature, the data collected through the questionnaire were subjected to descriptive statistical analysis. To find out solutions to the problems Mean, Standard Deviation and "t" test were used to analyze the Significant Difference between the Mean scores of the Attitude on e-Learning in Classroom Instruction with respect to the B.Ed. students in the Colleges of Education. The Percentage Analysis was used to find out the priority pattern of the various components of e-Learning perspectives towards the attitude among the B.Ed. students.

HYPOTHESIS TESTING

Hypothesis formulated in this study were tested on the basis of results obtained through analysis of the data using the statistical procedure and the level of significance.

The following is the hypothesis framed for this study

1. There is no significant difference in mean values of level of Attitude with respect to the e-learning in Classroom Instruction.
2. There is no significant difference in mean values on the influence of Demographic variables such as gender, age, parent's qualification and occupation with respect to the Attitude on e-Learning in Class-room Instruction.
3. There is no significant difference in mean values of Attitude on e-Learning in Classroom Instruction with respect to the B.Ed. Students in their subject.

ANALYSIS OF DATA AND INTERPRETATION

Measuring the Level of B.Ed. Students attitude towards e-learning in Class-room Instruction

TABLE.5.1: B.Ed. Students' Attitude towards E-Learning in Class-Room Instruction

N	Minimum %	Maximum %	Mean	SD
203	50	200	157.89	13.48

Table 5.1 shows the mean and standard deviation towards Attitude on e-Learning in Classroom Instruction among the B.Ed. Students at Colleges of Education. The mean attitude towards e-Learning in Classroom Instruction is 157.89. The attitude towards e-Learning in Classroom Instruction score varies from 50 to 200. The percentage of attitude on e-Learning in Classroom Instruction among the B.Ed. Students is 78.94%. Since the percentage score is greater than 50%, the hypothesis "Attitude on e-Learning in Classroom Instruction among the B.Ed. Students at Colleges of Education" is accepted.

To Measure the influence of Demographic variables such as gender, age, parent's qualification and occupation with respect to the Attitude on e-Learning in Class-room Instruction.

TABLE.5.2: Mean, Standard Deviation and 't' Value of B.Ed. Students Attitude towards E-Learning in Class-Room Instruction with Respect to their Age.

Age	N	Mean	S.D.	't'	Level of Significance at 0.01 Level
Below 25	176	158.28	13.314	1.0076	Significant
25-35	27	155.29	14.51		

From the table 5.2 indicates that the calculated 't' value 1.0076 is less than the table value 1.96 for df = 201 at 0.01 level of significance. Hence the null hypothesis, "There is no significant difference between the mean attitude of B.Ed. students towards e-learning in class-room instruction with respect to Age" is accepted. It is concluded that the B.Ed. students below 25 years and 25-35 years have equal attitude towards e-learning in class-room instruction. It is good to note that B.Ed. Students of all ages have attitude towards e-Learning.

To measure significance of mean scores of B.Ed. students attitude towards e-learning in Class-room Instruction with respect to their Gender

TABLE.5.3: Gender wise M, S.D. and "t" Value of B.Ed. Students Attitude towards E-Learning in Classroom Instruction

Gender	N	Mean	S.D.	't'	Level of Significance at 0.01 Level
Male	57	157.77	14.3	0.0777	Significant
Female	146	157.94	13.196		

The above table 5.3 indicates that the calculated 't' value 0.0777 is less than the table value 1.96 for df = 201 at 0.01 level of significance. Hence the null hypothesis namely "There is no significant difference between the mean scores of the attitude of B.Ed. students towards e-learning in class-room instruction with respect to Gender" hence the hypothesis is accepted. It is concluded that the B.Ed. students of male and the B.Ed. students of female have equal attitude towards e-learning in class-room instruction.

To measure significance of mean scores of B.Ed. students attitude towards e-learning in Class-room Instruction with respect to their Locality of Residence.

TABLE.5.4: Locality of Residence -wise M, S.D. and "t" Value of B.Ed. Students Attitude towards E-Learning in Classroom Instruction.

Residence	N	Mean	S.D.	't' Value	Level of Significance at 0.01 Level
Rural	159	157.949	13.226	0.1108	Significant
Urban	44	157.68	14.518		

Table 5.4 indicates that the calculated 't' value 0.1108 is more than the table value 1.96 for df = 201 at 0.01 level of significance. Hence mean scores of the B.Ed. students attitude towards e-learning with respect to the locality of residence is significant and hence the null hypothesis is accepted. It is inferred that B.Ed. students belonging to urban area and B.Ed students of Rural area have equal attitude towards e-learning in class-room instruction.

To measure the level of significance of the mean scores B.Ed. students attitude towards e-learning in Class-room Instruction with respect to their Academic Qualification.

TABLE.5.5: The mean, Standard Deviation and 't' Value of B.Ed. Students Attitude towards E-Learning in Class-room Instruction with Respect to their Academic Qualification.

Academic Qualification	N	Mean	S.D.	't'	Level of Significance at 0.01 Level
U.G.	164	157.689	13.565	0.4443	Significant
P.G.	39	158.743	13.254		

Table 5.5 indicates that the calculated 't' value 0.4443 is more than the table value 1.96 for df = 201 at 0.01 level of significance. Hence mean scores of the B.Ed. students attitude towards e-learning with respect to Academic qualification is significant and hence the null hypothesis is accepted. It is inferred that the Academic qualification of P.G. students and U.G. students have same attitude towards e-learning in Classroom Instruction.

MAJOR FINDINGS OF THE STUDY

The major findings which have emerged from the study are as follows:

1. The percentage level of attitude on e-Learning in Classroom Instruction among the B.Ed. Students is 78.94%. The study reveals that the B.Ed. Students have attitude on e-learning in Classroom Instruction with higher percentage factor.
2. In measuring the influence of Demographic variables such as gender, age, Parent's qualification and occupation, the study reveals that there was no significant difference between the mean scores of the B.Ed. students attitude on e-learning in classroom instruction of the ages below and 25-35 years.
3. It was found out there is no significant difference between the mean scores of the attitude of B.Ed. students towards e-learning in classroom instruction with respect to Gender.

EDUCATIONAL IMPLICATIONS OF THE STUDY

The study revealed that the attitude on e-Learning in Classroom Instruction among the B.Ed. students having 78.94%. It is a higher factor, which implies that the B.Ed. students have higher attitude towards e-Learning in their classroom instruction. On another aspect, it is good to note that the B.Ed. students of all ages having the attitude on e-learning in classroom instruction as there was not much difference between the students of ages below25 and 25-35 years. In measuring the influence of Demographic variables such as locality of Residence, it implies that the B.Ed. students belonging to urban area and rural area were same. In the case of discipline of their subject both had same attitude. There is no significant difference between the mean scores of attitude on e-learning towards Parent's Qualification and their occupation. It is clear to note that the students are not dependent towards their Parent's factor. In the case of Academic Qualification P.G. students and U.G. students have same attitude.

RECOMMENDATIONS OF THE PRESENT STUDY

1. The attitude on e-Learning can be used to enhance both the theoretical knowledge and practical knowledge.
2. The attitude on e-Learning is found to be more effective in Classroom Instruction since simulation, 3D images, experiments, dissections, phenomena etc can be presented effectively.
3. Teachers and Professors should be trained to produce e-Learning material at various levels. In-service training and orientation courses can be provided.
4. Since e-Learning is a self instructional method it encourages active participation and able to cater all needs of the students with full satisfaction. It is a motivating factor in their learning process.
5. The attitude on e-Learning perspectives among B.Ed. students is needed to improve. As they are future teachers they should be well-versed with concepts of e-Learning and have the ability to utilize them in their teaching.

SUGGESTIONS FOR FURTHER RESEARCH STUDY

1. As the study is limited to study the attitude on e-Learning in Classroom Instruction among the B.Ed. students, it can be enhanced to find out the effectiveness of e-learning material and other e-Resources.
2. The study can be also conducted for the students of other Professional colleges such as Engineering, Medical, Management and Agriculture.

3. Since e-Learning is the emerging field of Instructional technology, there is a wide horizon of possibilities for further researchers in this area of study.
4. The study also suggests carrying out research in terms of level of utilization of e-Learning components in the Classroom Instruction among the B.Ed., M.Ed., and M.Phil. students in the colleges of education.

CONCLUSION

A notable feature is that in the extensive literature reviewed in the present study, there has been no recorded evidence of any research work having been carried out on Attitude on e-Learning in Classroom Instruction among the B.Ed. Students at Colleges of Education. It is in this context that the present study becomes important and essential as endorsed by the specific concerns of earlier researchers both in its aims of the study and its procedures. The research design of the present study included the selection of problem, selection of sample, construction of appropriate tool, administration of the tool for collection of data and analysis and interpretation of data. The collected data were subjected to appropriate statistical analysis as shown in this study. It is inferred that the B.Ed. Students have attitude on e-learning in Classroom Instruction with the lesser percentage. The present study is the first of its kind with its specific reference to Attitude on E-learning in Classroom Instruction towards B.Ed. Students. The findings of the study would be of immense use to the Teacher-Educators. Only on ethical teacher can create an efficient student. In the training period of the B.Ed. Students itself, it is important to impart the need and value of Attitude on e-learning and its various applications. They have to possess awareness, knowledge and skills with regard to e-Learning.

❐

6

Digital Techniques in Classroom Teaching

Modernization is generally regarded as a process of change of traditional society into a society based on technology. As Teaching has entered the Digital age over the last several years, Technology in the Classroom is an area that all Teachers and Students are Embracing. For Teachers who have taught many years before this can be a challenging one. There are many Computer lesson plans, CDs, DVDs, audio e -books and videos available that will help in the transition. Digital Technology in the Classroom involves a lot of time and focus in its infancy, but with the Computer Lesson plans mentioned, it will develop into a fun and creative learning experience for Students and new and exciting challenges for Teachers. The incorporation of Digital technology in the education sector is important to meet the challenges presented by new trends, especially with the Global Communication of Knowledge. It is essential that the Students become familiar with the concept and use of Computer Technology in order to equip them for future job market. Similarly, the teacher can achieve better quality in Teaching Methodology.

RATIONALE OF THE STUDY

Computer plays key role in Education. Learning through Computer is an interesting affair. Now–a-days Digital Technology in Education has become the essential part of the system. In fact Teacher must well aware of the potentiality of the Digital Technology. Government is very much interested in introducing Computer Technology in Class Room instruction in Teacher Education. Hence the Investigator was interested to know the level of Awareness on Digital techniques applying in classroom teaching for present generation among Teacher Educators.

STATEMENT OF THE PROBLEM

The important key words used in this problem were i) Awareness: Alertness, New Idea. ii) Digital Technology: The Technology which is used to change the method of Class Room Teaching with the help of Electronic machines and Computer, iii) Teacher Educators Teachers who are working in the Colleges of Education.

OBJECTIVES OF THE STUDY

The objectives of the study were i)To measure the level of Awareness on Digital Technology among Teacher Educators. ii) To measure the level of significant difference on the Awareness on Digital Technology among Male and Female, Rural and Urban, Science and Arts group Teacher Educators.

METHOD AND MATERIALS

It is the Normative Survey method. Investigator constructed a Tool Awareness on Digital Techniques applying in Classroom Teaching for present generation among Teacher Educators. That consists of 40 statements with different dimensions such as Computer in Teaching Learning, Power point Presentation and Internet, which have four point scale such a Strongly Agree, Agree, Disagree and Strongly Disagree. After the Development of the Questionnaire, the Investigator distributed it to Teacher Educators for validation. Their valuable ideas were taken care. Then the questionnaire was given to 10 Teacher Educators by Test - Retest method. The obtained r value 0.84 reveals that the tool is reliable one. Investigators randomly selected 100 Teacher Educators from various Colleges of Education in Perambalur and Trichy Districts.

ANALYSIS

The collected data was analysed by using different statistical technique like Mean, SD and't' test. The results are given in the following Tables

TABLE.6.1: Significant Difference on the Mean Scores of Male and Female Teacher Educators

S.No	Dimension	Gender	Mean	SD	t test	Remarks
1.	Total	Male Female	64.3 63.0	0.74 0.92	7.38	S
2.	CTL	Male Female	60.54 61.62	1.19 1.41	1.48	NS
3.	PPT	Male Female	65.04 61.24	3.89 0.98	6.43	S
4.	INT	Male Female	71.07 69.58	1.92 3.35	2.38	S

CTL – Computer in Teaching Learning **PPT** – Power Point Presentation
INT – Internet NS - Not Significant **S** – Significant

From the above Table it is noted that the 't' values are significantly difference at 5% level of the Teacher Educators for Total, PPT(Power Point Presentation) and INT(Internet). Total, PPT (Power Point Presentation) and INT (Internet) the Mean score of Male Teacher Educators are higher than the Female Teacher Educators. In CTL (Computer in Teaching Learning) there is no significant difference at 5 % level of the Teacher Educators.

TABLE.6.2: Significant Difference on the Mean Scores of Rural and Urban Teacher Educators

S.No	Dimension	Locality	Mean	SD	t test	Remarks
1.	Total	Rural Urban	64.7 63.07	0.837 0.823	5.46	S
2.	CTL	Rural Urban	60.74 63.18	1.61 0.989	1.69	NS
3.	PPT	Rural Urban	62.90 63.07	0.78 0.65	1.06	NS
4.	INT	Rural Urban	74.53 70.93	1.72 1.68	3.62	S

From the above Table, the calculated 't' values are revealing that there is no significant difference at 5% level for the dimensions CTL and PPT. But there exists significant difference at 5% level with respect to Total and INT. In the Total and INT the Mean score of the Rural Teacher Educators are higher having higher awareness on Digital Technology than the Urban Teacher Educators.

TABLE.6.3: Significant Difference on the Mean Scores of Science and Arts Teacher Educators.

S.No	Dimension	Subject	Mean	SD	t test	Remarks
1.	Total	Science Arts	63.83 64.31	0.929 0.779	1.21	NS
2.	CTL	Science Arts	62.43 61.28	1.06 1.11	4.79	S
3.	PPT	Science Arts	63.02 60.34	4.22 0.934	3.27	S
4.	INT	Science Arts	71.94 73.38	1.19 1.02	6.03	S

The Mean scores and the calculated 't ' values from the above table shows that there is significant difference in all the mean score of CTL, PPT and INT at 5% level except Total. It can be understood that the level Awareness on Digital Technology among Teacher Educators are good in CTL, PPT and INT.

RESULTS AND DISCUSSION

The salient findings of the study are i) All the Teacher Educators are having good Awareness on Digital Technology. ii) The Mean score of Male Teacher Educators are higher than the Female Teacher Educators towards Awareness on Digital Technology with respect to the dimensions such as Total, PPT and INT. iii) With regards to Locality, the Mean score of Rural Teacher Educators are higher than the Urban Teacher Educators towards Awareness on Digital Technology in Total and INT. iv) The Mean scores of Teacher Educators with respect to Science Subject are higher in CTL, PPT and Arts Teacher Educators are higher in INT.

The result shows that Gender, Locality and Subject of Teacher Educators were not the influencing factor in determining Awareness on Digital Technology. While considering the Gender, Male Teachers are having higher Awareness on Digital Technology than the Female Teachers. This is because Male Teacher Educators may have more time to work in the Computer but the Female Teachers have the commitment to look after their family. By this way Rural Teachers are having Good Awareness on Digital Technology than the Urban Teachers. This is due to the fact that Rural Teachers may show more interest to know about the new things. As well as Science Group Teacher Educators are show more awareness than Art Group Teacher Educators. It may be due to their subject knowledge.

RECOMMENDATIONS FOR POLICY MAKINGS

The result of this study shows that the Teacher Educators are having Good awareness on Digital Technology. Hence the usage of Computer must be increased to develop their practical knowledge. They are having more involvement in using Digital Technology in their class room Teaching. Effective teaching to promote better learning, proper orientation training Programme must be provided them to develop their knowledge in Digital Technology. The Government must ensure proper training to Teacher Educators to maintain Computers and Electronic things. Educational Authorities should create, improve and sustain the Awareness of Teacher Educators about Computer Knowledge. Teacher Educators should be encouraged by Administrators to use the stand alone Computer Applications in their Teachings. Using Internet application should be given special concentration, because, it empowers and enhance creativity. Digital Technology acts as a catalyst to support change in Teacher Pedagogy.

CONCLUSION

The Good Awareness on Computer Technology among Primary and Middle School Teachers will show the Conducing Climate towards Educational Technology. The Instruction through Computer has been making wonders in the Class Room Activities. Hence Teachers must have Awareness on Computer Technology to get success and enjoy their Professions.

❐

7

Awareness on Educational Media

Perception refers to "the way in which man senses or becomes immediately aware of his environment". Although knowledge about the world is gained through the senses, sensory impressions themselves are not enough to given a suitable understanding of the object perceived. It is the brain that receives and interprets them, which then become organized into meaningful understanding. Thus any given perceptual event is the result of multiple sensory messages. Perceptual events do not occur in isolation, they are continuous. As result of constant sensory stimulation, experiences are arranged and rearranged, shuffled and reshuffled, selected and reselected and organized into a convenient combination of patterns. This process finally leads the formation of concept. In general, understanding of the things and events of the world is based on sensory experiences and the physical objects, as the human beings known them are products of their own sensory perceptions. The present study aims to find out the awareness of educational media among Higher Secondary teachers of Thiruvannamalai district and their perception of media based education. A samples of 200 samples selected randomly were studied. A questionnaire method of survey was used to find out the awareness of educational media among Higher Secondary teachers. The data were collected by using questionnaire as an instrument. Primary data were collected by conducting direct structured interview using questionnaire. All the respondents were asked the same questions in the same fashion and they were informed the purpose of study. t-test, One way ANOVA analysis, correlation analysis were applied to test the hypotheses. The findings and observations are the result and outcome of the interpretations made during the study of analysis. The result found that the average level of awareness of educational media among Higher Secondary teachers.

The present era is an information technology era. Now-a-day the students are more aware of latest technological advancement. In olden days, teachers generally used oral method of teaching as well as they used black board for writing purpose. But these things were not given much more concentration to the students. Teachers faced a lot of problems to create attention among the students. Even though teachers used these aids but there is a necessity to measure the teachers awareness of educational media and their perception of media based education. Only by knowing the teachers can enhance their method of teaching. In this concept, the present research title is significant and needed for the study.

OBJECTIVE

To find out the awareness of educational media among Higher Secondary teachers of Thiruvannamalai District and their perception of Media based Education of the entire and its sub samples.

METHODOLOGY

The methodology adopted for the study is explained in detail. The sampling technique, size of the sample, variables of the study, description of the tool used and administration of tool are elaborated.

METHOD OF DATA COLLECTION

The investigator personally distributed the questionnaires to each member of the randomly selected sample. They were requested to answer the items in the booklet as per the instructions provided at the beginning of each questionnaire. Confidentiality of response was assured. The questionnaires were collected by the investigator from the teachers. The responses were scored as per the scoring key of the respective questionnaire. Then the results were tabulated, analysed and discussed.

SAMPLE

The investigator prepared a representative random sample of Higher Secondary teachers in different schools at Thiruvannamalai District. A sample of 200 teachers was finally selected.

DATA COLLECTION

Primary data, required for the present research work were collected by conducting direct interviews using questionnaire. All the respondents were given sufficient information about the study. These respondents were provided with the same questionnaires. They were also informed that they have to answer in the same fashion.

STATISTICAL TOOLS FOR ANALYSIS

The following tools statistical tools were used for the analysis of data. t-test, ANOVA analysis and correlation analysis.

ANALYSIS AND INTERPRETATION

TABLE.7.1: Showing Mean, SD and F-test for Respondent about Educational Media Awareness among Higher Secondary Teachers on the basis of Academic Qualification

Academic qualification	N	Mean	SD	F-value	Level of Significance
M.A. B.Ed.	54	72.26	9.37	3.24	0.01
M.Sc. B.Ed.	48	72.89	8.84		
M.Com. B.Ed.	98	69.00	7.08		
Total	**200**	**71.78**	**8.58**		

Hypothesis

Teachers do not differ in their educational media awareness among higher secondary teachers on the basis of Academic qualification.

The calculated F-value (3.24), which is significant at 0.01 level, confirms that there is a significant difference in their educational media awareness among higher secondary teachers on the basis of Academic qualification. Hence the stated hypothesis is rejected.

TABLE.7.2: Showing Mean, SD and t-Test for Respondent about Educational Media Awareness among Higher Secondary Teachers on the basis of Designation

Designation	N	Mean	SD	t-value	Level of Significance
PG Teachers	132	72.08	9.22	2.34	0.01
BT Teachers	68	69.33	5.18		

Hypothesis

Teachers do not differ in their educational media awareness among higher secondary teachers on the basis of Designation.

The calculated t-value (2.34), which is significant at 0.01 level, confirms that there is a significant difference in educational media awareness among higher secondary teachers on the basis of Designation. Hence the stated hypothesis is rejected. So PG Teachers have high level of educational media awareness than BT teachers.

TABLE.7.3: Showing Mean, SD and F-Test for Respondent about Educational Media Awareness among Higher Secondary Teachers on the basis of Type of Institution

Type of Institution	N	Mean	SD	F-value	Level of Significance
Govt.	58	70.31	4.09	3.42	0.01
Govt. Aided	68	71.30	9.56		
Self-Financing	74	74.29	9.75		
Total	**200**	**71.78**	**8.58**		

Hypothesis

Teachers do not differ in their educational media awareness among higher secondary teachers on the basis of Type of Institution.

The calculated F-value (3.42), which is significant at 0.01 level, confirms that there is a significant difference in their educational media awareness among higher secondary teachers on the basis of Type of Institution. Hence the stated hypothesis is rejected.

TABLE.7.4: Showing Mean, SD and F-Test for Respondent about Educational Media Awareness among Higher Secondary Teachers on the basis of Teaching Experience

Teaching Experience	N	Mean	SD	F-value	Level of Significance
Below 10 years	67	69.20	9.64	3.62	0.01
11 – 20 years	88	71.75	4.19		
Above 20 years	45	75.00	8.60		
Total	**200**	**71.78**	**8.58**		

Hypothesis

Teachers do not differ in their educational media awareness among higher secondary teachers on the basis of teaching experience.

The calculated F-value (3.62), which is significant at 0.01 level, confirms that there is a significant difference in their educational media awareness among higher secondary teachers on the basis of Teaching experience. Hence the stated hypothesis is rejected.

TABLE.7.5: Showing Mean, SD and F-Test for Respondent about Media Perception Evaluation among Higher Secondary Teachers on the basis of Academic Qualification

Academic qualification	N	Mean	SD	F-value	Level of Significance
M.A. B.Ed.	54	92.42	9.69	3.42	0.01
M.Sc. B.Ed.	48	92.24	9.24		
M.Com. B.Ed.	98	99.00	8.24		
Total	**200**	**91.81**	**7.24**		

Hypothesis

Teachers do not differ in their media perception evaluation among higher secondary teachers on the basis of Academic qualification.

The calculated F-value (3.42), which is significant at 0.01 level, confirms that there is a significant difference in their media perception evaluation among higher secondary teachers on the basis of Academic qualification. Hence the stated hypothesis is rejected.

TABLE.7.6: Showing Mean, SD and T-Test for Respondent about Media Perception Evaluation among Higher Secondary Teachers on the basis of Designation

Designation	N	Mean	SD	t-value	Level of Significance
PG Teachers	132	92.26	9.48	2.22	0.01
BT Teachers	68	98.42	5.36		

Hypothesis

Teachers do not differ in their media perception evaluation among higher secondary teachers on the basis of Designation.

The calculated t-value (2.22), which is significant at 0.01 level, confirms that there is a significant difference in media perception evaluation among higher secondary teachers on the basis of Designation. Hence the stated hypothesis is rejected. So BT Teachers have high level of media perception evaluation than PG teachers.

TABLE.7.7: Showing Mean, SD and F-Test for Respondent about Media Perception Evaluation among Higher Secondary Teachers on the basis of Type of Institution

Type of Institution	N	Mean	SD	F-value	Level of Significance
Govt.	58	90.24	4.29	3.92	0.01
Govt. Aided	68	91.29	9.29		
Self-Financing	74	94.65	9.36		
Total	**200**	**91.81**	**7.24**		

Hypothesis

Teachers do not differ in their media perception evaluation among higher secondary teachers on the basis of Type of Institution.

The calculated F-value (3.92), which is significant at 0.01 level, confirms that there is a significant difference in their media perception evaluation among higher secondary teachers on the basis of Type of Institution. Hence the stated hypothesis is rejected.

TABLE.7.8: Showing Mean, SD and F-Test for Respondent about Media Perception Evaluation among Higher Secondary Teachers on the basis of Teaching Experience

Teaching Experience	N	Mean	SD	F-value	Level of Significance
Below 10 years	67	99.22	9.24	3.94	0.01
11 – 20 years	88	91.24	5.29		
Above 20 years	45	95.21	7.21		
Total	**200**	**91.81**	**7.24**		

Hypothesis

Teachers do not differ in their media perception evaluation among higher secondary teachers on the basis of teaching experience.

The calculated F-value (3.94), which is significant at 0.01 level, confirms that there is a significant difference in their media perception evaluation among higher secondary teachers on the basis of Teaching experience. Hence the stated hypothesis is rejected.

The above table shows correlation between educational media awareness and media perception evaluation among Higher Secondary teachers. Result shows that there is a positive and significant correlation between educational media awareness and media perception evaluation.

SUGGESTIONS

The following suggestions are arrived from the research findings. Research found that use of educational media will contribute more in student's achievement. Also the result reveals that use of awareness educational media increases the memory power, concentration. Further it sharpens the intelligence. Apart from that it reduces misconception in learning. So, the present research suggested that in all schools and colleges, the students advised to use of educational media compulsory. The education department forms a rule for that and advises the educational institutions make a step to establish separate infrastructure for this one. Also the Government take a step to use media based teaching effectively students in their academic. This will definitely help the students to be a good learner imbibing the concepts.

CONCLUSION

The present study awareness of educational media among Higher Secondary teachers of Thiruvannamalai district and their perception of media based education. For that the researcher framed some objectives. On the basis of objectives, a questionnaire is framed. After framing the questionnaire, these are circulated to the selected samples. 200 samples were selected randomly. The responses were collected and coded using computerised. To test the hypotheses and characteristics of the data, some standard statistical tools were used. The statistical tools such as t-test, F-ratio and correlation were used. From the analysis the result concluded that the Higher Secondary teachers have favourable of educational media and their perception of media based education. ❐

8

Educational Television

Educational Television (ETV) is a system that presents learning content in various subjects produced by an agency. It is a means of providing direct instruction (formal) as well as continuing education (non-formal). Educational inequality is a persistent problem in most countries, from both economic and socio-cultural viewpoints. ETV can promote the concept of equalization of educational opportunities by providing instructional actions that are so universal that they become specific to every viewer and are effective regardless of sex, race, ethnic background or economic condition. EDUSAT is the first exclusive satellite for serving the educational sector. It is specially configured to meet the growing demand for an interactive satellite based distance education system for the country through audio-visual medium, employing direct to home (DTH) quality broadcast. The ISRO scientists claim "the satellite will bring education to home (ETH) nearer". While scientists, economists, politicians and the common public talk so much about EDUSAT and its potentials, it is disheartening that it failed to create the much-needed sensation among the teaching community. In this aspect, this study is of great importance, as its findings will throw light on the Diploma level teacher trainees' ETV awareness, based on which decision with far-reaching implications can be taken to ensure effective utilization of the services in India. Besides, the study will give the necessary input for the planners and designers of pre-service training programmes and in-service training programme for the professional development of primary level teachers.

INTRODUCTION

It has been a little over a decade since a television set became a part of the equipment of many Indian homes. And it became the part and parcel of our life within no time. When television began, there were great hopes and great fears concerning its possible effects. The optimists believed that it could educate children in the widest possible sense, giving them an opportunity to learn about science and human life in such a fascinating way that learning would be a joy instead of labour. And now, it's the time to think over the topic that whether this powerful medium is being utilized effectively in educational field or not.

AUDIO-VISUAL AIDS

"Audio-visual aids are the different types of tools that appeal to the senses of learning and vision and are used in classrooms for presentation of abstract information". Today it has been proved beyond doubt by research and classroom experience that audio-visual aids can contribute effectively in learning.

EDUCATIONAL TELEVISION

Educational Television (ETV) is a system that presents learning content in various subjects produced by an agency. It is a means of providing direct instruction (formal) as well as continuing education (non-formal).

TYPES OF EDUCATIONAL TELEVISION PROGRAMMES

ETV programmes are made available to the students in a variety of modes. Some of the most important types of ETV programmes are

1. **Monologue:** A narrator narrates the aspects, interlacing it with visuals the illustrations.
2. **Dialogue:** Conversation between two people.
3. Interviews
4. Panel Discussion
5. Quiz
6. Dramas
7. Stimulated Classrooms
8. Virtual Classrooms

TELEVISION AS A MEANS OF EXTENDING CHILDREN'S EXPERIENCE

TV in the classroom is truly what UNESCO has often called it "a window on the world". The programmes allow students to transcend the boundaries to space and time and to see society in new and diverse ways. The rural child sees life in the city and the urban child sees life in the country, various patterns of consumptions and economic structure, alternative religious forms, cultural patterns and sexual role models are made available on the television. ETV can promote the concept of equalization of educational opportunities by providing instructional actions that are so universal that they become specific to every viewer and are effective regardless of sex, race, ethnic background or economic condition.

ETV IN INDIA: A HISTORICAL PERSPECTIVE

Television first came to India [named as Doordarshan (DD)] on September 15, 1959 as the National Television Network of India. The first telecast started on Sept. 15, 1959 in New Delhi.

SECONDARY SCHOOL TELEVISION PROJECT (1961)

This project was designed for the secondary school students of Delhi. With an aim to improve the standard of teaching in view of the shortage of laboratories, space, equipment and dearth of qualified teachers in Delhi, this project started on experimental basis in October 1961 for teaching Physics, Chemistry, English and Hindi for the students of Class XI.

DELHI AGRICULTURE TELEVISION (DATV) PROJECT-KRISHI DARSHAN (1966)

This project, one of the largest techno-social experiments in human communication, was commissioned for the villagers and their Primary School children of selected 2330 villages in six states of India. It started on August 1, 1975 for a period of one year in six states namely Rajasthan, Karnataka, Orissa, Bihar, Andhra Pradesh and Madhya Pradesh.

INDIAN NATIONAL SATELLITE PROJECT - INSAT (1982)

As a part of INSAT project, ETV broadcasts were inaugurated and continued through terrestrial transmission from 15th August 1982 in Orissa and Andhra Pradesh. Later, other states namely Bihar, Gujarat, Maharashtra and Uttar Pradesh were covered under INSAT service using INSAT-1B in June 1983. As of today, these ETV programmes are offered in five languages - Oriya, Telugu, Marathi, Gujarati and Hindi- for a large population of primary school children. Programmes telecast in Hindi are being received in all Hindi-speaking states in the northern belt (IGNOU, 2000).

IGNOU-DOORDARSHAN TELECAST (1991)

The IGNOU-Doordarshan telecast programmes, designed mainly for Distance learners started in May 1991. Initially they were telecast on Monday, Wednesday and Friday from 6.30 to 7.00 am through the national network of Doordarshan with an aim to provide tele-counselling to students of open universities in remote areas. Owing to the encouraging response from viewers, the frequency of this project was increased to five days a week.

STATEMENT OF THE PROBLEM

The present study has been taken up to find out the level of awareness of ETV among the Diploma Level Teacher of Karur district. Hence, the problem of the study is stated as "ETV Awareness among the Diploma Level Teacher Trainees of Karur District.

OPERATIONAL DEFINITIONS OF THE TERMS

The term 'ETV Awareness' includes information regarding Educational Television channels, the type of ETV programmes and the role of EDUSAT in Indian ETV experience and the knowledge of methods of utilizing ETV programmes for qualitative improvement in the teaching – learning process. The term 'Diploma Level Teacher Trainees' refers to the student Teachers with +2 qualification who are undergoing pre-service Teacher Training at Teacher Training Institutes and who would be qualified to teach at the primary level of school education.

OBJECTIVES OF THE STUDY

The main objectives of the study are:

1. To find out the awareness of ETV among the Diploma Level Teacher Trainees of Karur District and
2. To suggest measures to create, sustain and improve the Diploma Level Teacher Trainees' Awareness of ETV.

METHODOLOGY

As the present study is descriptive by nature, normative survey technique was adopted. As many as 140 Student Teachers from Diploma level Teacher Training Institutes were chosen as sample using simple random sampling technique. A questionnaire, aimed at assessing their awareness of ETV used for the purpose of collecting data. The questionnaire was administered by the investigator in the respondents' respective institutions of work. The collected data were subjected to descriptive analysis.

RESEARCH PROCEDURE

Selection of a particular research procedure depends on the objectives of research and suitability of the particular research procedure.

SAMPLE FOR THE STUDY

The present study aims to find out the ETV awareness among the Diploma Level Teacher Trainees of Karur District. As many as 140 (One hundred and forty) student teachers have been chosen to form the sample using simple random sampling technique. The student teachers who formed the sample were drawn from two Diploma Level Teacher Training Institutions, one Government and other Self financing.

SELECTION OF THE TOOL

Data regarding general information, details of television viewing and educational television awareness were collected from **Diploma Level Teacher Trainees of Karur District** who formed the sample through the questionnaire.

COLLECTION OF DATA

The ETV Awareness Questionnaire was administered to as many as 140 **Diploma Level Teacher Trainees** randomly selected from two Diploma Level Teacher Training Institutions.

ANALYSIS OF DATA

The data obtained from the sample through the administration of the developed tool have been subjected to descriptive analysis in tune with the stated objectives. The data were analyzed through simple percentage analysis, this being descriptive research using normative survey technique. The analysis of data are presented in the form of tables below and further discussed after the tables.

TABLE.8.1: Analyses of Sample in Terms of Gender, Locality and Medium of Instruction

Gender	No. of Candidates	%
Male	47	33.57
Female	93	66.43
Locality	No. of Candidates	%
Rural	102	72.86
Urban	38	27.14
Medium of Instruction	No. of Candidates	%
Tamil	130	92.86
English	10	7.14

The table (Table No. 8.1) presents the distribution of sample in terms of their gender, Level of Locality and Medium of Language. As seen in the table, out of the total sample (140 Student Teachers), 33.57 per cent are males and the remaining 66.43 per cent are females. From the table, it is clear that 72.86 per cent of the Student Teachers who formed the sample are Rural while the remaining 27.24 per cent hold Urban formed. As the table shows, among the 140 Student Teachers, 92.86 per cent belong to English medium and 7.14 percent belong to Tamil medium category.

TABLE.8.2: Analyses of Sample in Terms of (Domicile) and Age

Locality	No. of Candidates	%
Day Scholar	65	46.43
Hosteller	75	53.57
Age	No. of Candidates	%
18-20	106	75.71
21-23	20	14.29
24-25	14	10.00

The table (table no.8.2) presents the distribution of sample in terms of their Domicile and age. As evident from the table, 53.57 per cent of the Diploma Level Teacher Trainees who formed the sample are from Hosteller, while the remaining 46.43 per cent are from Day Scholar. As the table shows, among the total sample (140 Student Teachers), 75.71 percent are in the age group of 18-20, 14.29 percent are in the age group of 21-23 and the remaining 10.00 percent are in the age group of 24-26.

TABLE.8.3: Analysis of Sample in Terms of Frequency of TV Viewing

Frequency of TV Viewing	No. of Candidates	%
Daily	66	47.14
Alternate days	34	24.29
Once in a fortnight	26	18.57
Never	14	10.00

The above table (Table No. 8.5) presents the distribution of sample in terms of the frequency of television viewing. It is evident from the table that 47.14 per cent of the total sample (66 Student Teachers) has the habit of watching television daily; 24.29 per cent of the Student Teachers have the habit of watching television on alternate days;18.57 percent in a week; only (Teacher Trainees 10.00%) watch television never. There is none who does not have the habit of working TV.

TABLE.8.4: Analysis of Sample in Terms of Length of TV Viewing

Length of TV viewing	No. of Candidates	%
1 – 3 years	39	27.86
4 – 6 years	31	22.14
7 – 9 years	23	16.43
More than 10 years	47	33.57

The table (table no. 8.6) represents the distribution of sample in terms of their length of TV viewing. It is evident from the table that all the 39 Student Teachers who formed the sample have 1-3 years of experience in 27.86 percent, 31 Student Teachers who formed the sample have 4-6 years of experience in 22.14 percent watching 23 Student Teachers who formed the sample have 7-9 years of experience in 16.43 percent and 47 Student Teachers who formed the sample have more than 10 years of experience in 33.57 watching following.

TABLE.8.5: Analysis of Sample in Terms of their First Preference for Medium of Programs

Medium of Programme	No. of candi-dates	%
Tamil	125	89.29
English	13	9.29
Hindi	1	0.71
Others	1	0.71

The above table (Table No. 8.7) shows the distribution of students in terms of their first preference for medium of programs. It is evident from the table that a majority (89.29%) of the Student Teachers prefers to watch programs in Tamil. The next rating is for English programs, with 13 (9.29%) Student Teachers preferring it to others; as many as (0.71% Student Teachers) prefer to watch Hindi programs and 0.71% one Student Teachers to watch others programs.

TABLE.8.6: Analysis of Response to Questions on ETV Awareness

Question No	Question	Response			
		Right	%	Wrong	%
1	ETV refers to *Educational Television*	92	65.71	48	34.29
2	Programs of Educational importance are available on *ETV Channels*	72	51.43	68	48.57
3	The Indian satellite for education is *EDUSAT*	108	77.14	32	22.86
4	An exclusive educational satellite has been launched by *India Only*	55	39.29	85	60.71
5	An ideal ETV Program is of duration.	24	17.14	116	82.86
6	ETV programs can be best used as *Complementary to Class Room Teaching.*	58	41.43	82	58.57
7	EDUSAT has paved the way for *Radio Stations, Television Channels, Audio & Video conferencing and all the above.*	72	51.43	68	48.57

8	ETV channels provide *Video Programs with multimedia elements, video lectures and video recordings of classroom instruction.*	64	45.71	76	54.29
9	ETV channels in India broadcast *Programs of Educational Importance*	40	28.57	100	71.43
10	The channel Gyandarshan caters to the academic needs of the students in *School Education.*	26	18.57	114	81.43
11	EMMRCs (Educational Multi Media Resource Centers) produce television programs on *College Subjects.*	52	37.14	88	62.86
12	EDUSAT is a*n Exclusive Educational Satellite*	38	27.14	102	72.86
13	CIET (central Institute of Educational Technology) produces television programs on *School Subjects.*	35	25	105	75
14	On ETV channels, one can watch *No Advertisement.*	29	20.71	111	79.29
15	ETV channels in India are Co-coordinated by *UGC-CEC.*	22	15.71	118	84.29
16	Subject based Educational programs are available *On other Doordarshan Channels also.*	43	30.71	97	69.29
17	The channel Vyas caters to the academic needs of the students in *Higher Education*	72	51.43	68	48.57
18	ROT with regard to EDUSAT services refers to *Receive only Terminal*	24	17.14	116	82.86
19	Vyas Higher Educational is available *Round the Clock on all Days.*	42	30	98	70
20	UGC – CEC refers to UGC's *Consortium for Educational Communication*	47	33.57	93	66.43
21	ETV channels provide *General Programs on Various Subjects; Syllabus based programs and Enrichment Programs.*	33	23.57	107	76.43
22	The channel Ekalavya caters to the academic needs of the academic needs of the students in *Technical Education.*	49	35	91	65
23	SIT with regard to EDUSAT services refers to *Satellite Interactive* Terminal.	41	29.29	99	70.71

24	Through EDUSAT services, one can *interact with other connected centers through video conferencing.*	79	56.43	61	43.57
25	The life of EDUSAT with its full potential on the orbit is *12 years.*	44	31.43	96	70.71
26	ETV Programs are best received when they are given through…..	54	38.57	86	61.43

**As the respondents were given the freedom to give multiple responses, data are presented separately.*

MAJOR FINDINGS OF THE STUDY

The following are the major findings that emerged from the descriptive analysis and interpretation of the data.

1. The ETV awareness of the Diploma Level Teacher Trainees of Karur District is below average
2. A majority of the women's students of Karur District are aware of the concept called Educational Television (ETV).
3. Only 50 percent of the samples of Diploma Level Teacher Trainees know about Educational TV channels and their programmes.
4. Only 75 percent of the Diploma Level Teacher Trainees who formed the sample are aware of EDUSAT as an exclusive educational satellite.
5. Only 39 percent of the Teacher Trainees are aware of the fact that India is the only country which has launched an exclusive satellite for education and the majority remaining is quite unaware of this fact.

SUGGESTIONS AND RECOMMENDATIONS

Based on the above given findings and conclusions, the present study offers the following suggestions and recommendations:

1. Steps must be taken to increase the awareness, Educational Television and its potentials among the Student Teachers.
2. Watching ETV programmes should be included as compulsory component in the Diploma level Teacher Trainees programmes.
3. Interesting programmes should be telecast in the form of edutainment on ETV channels so as to gain the attention of the teaching-learning community.

SUGGESTION FOR FURTHER RESEARCH

The findings of the present study open up a few areas for further investigation. They are as follows:

1. As this study has been taken up with only Diploma Level Teacher Trainees of Karur District as sample, studies with Diploma level student

teachers and B.Ed level student teacher of other areas as sample may be taken up.

2. The same study can be replicated with more advanced statistical analyses in terms of gender, locality and other relevant variables.
3. Comparative studies can be taken up to compare the ETV awareness of the Diploma Level Student Teachers of Karur District with the Diploma Level Student Teachers of other Teacher Training Institutions.

CONCLUSION

Though it is specifically about the Diploma Level Teacher Trainees of Karur District, it presents a general view of the awareness of ETV among the Teacher Trainees by including the various aspects related to ETV in the purview of the study. The findings of the study would be of immense use to policy makers at the NCTE and state agencies of teacher education and curriculum planners for in-service training programmes.

❒

9

Effectiveness of Blended Learning

The technology is an integral part in the lives of young people who are direct beneficiaries of the educational process. This was often made argument for the need to develop learning methods that use modern technology in the formative and educational. By such methods students are responsible for their own learning, on which they themselves have control and manage it according to their interests and needs. The specialists' researches reveal that the methods which combine the traditional education with the modern technologies (blended learning) have increased the effectiveness. Blended Learning is a strategy which integrates the teaching learning process with different learning environments like face-to-face, online, social networking etc. Its rapid growth has been facilitated by the Internet and other emerging technologies like cloud computing, social networking etc. This paper provides a view about the effectiveness of blended learning programme in teaching biology at higher secondary school students.

Blended learning provides platform to attract the senses of the learner for easy and happy learning. Blended learning is a programme which integrates teaching learning process with different leaning environment. Its rapid growth facilitated by the internet and other emerging technology cloud computing and social networking. "Blended learning is the thoughtful fusion of face-to-face and online learning experiences. The basic principle is that face-to-face oral communication and online written communication are optimally integrated such that the strengths of each are blended into a unique learning experience congruent with the context and intended educational purpose." Blended learning – an instructional practice that combines teaching methods from both face-to-face instruction and online learning, gives to educational institutions new approaches and strategies for addressing the challenges they face and for taking advantage of the exciting new learning opportunities that are now available.

OBJECTIVES OF THE STUDY

The objectives of the study as follows:

1. To find out the effectiveness of blended learning programme for the teaching of biology at higher secondary level.
2. To compare the effectiveness of blended learning programme in the teaching of biology with conventional method of teaching biology.

HYPOTHESES OF THE STUDY

The following null hypotheses have been formulated

1. There is no significant difference between the experimental group and control group in the achievement of biology at pre-test level.
2. There is no significant difference between the experimental group and control group in the achievement of biology at post-test level.
3. There is no significant difference between the pre-test and post-test in the achievement of biology for the experimental group.
4. There is no significant difference between the pre-test and post-test in the achievement of biology for the control group.

SAMPLE

The sample of the study consists of 100 students studying in XI standard under State Board syllabus at perambalur district. The sample includes both boys and girls.

TOOLS USED

The following tools had been used for the present study:

An achievement test in biology constructed and validated by the investigators Blended learning programme was developed by the investigator for the teaching of the concepts in biology topics included in the XI standard biology syllabus.

The progrmme was arranged logically based on the psychological principles of learning. Experimental design was adopted. For the experimentation pretest was conducted and sample was divided into two groups. The students of the experimental group were taught with the blended learning progrmme and the control group through the conventional method. After the treatment period the posttest was administered. The collected data were subjected to statistical analysis and the results obtained were interpreted.

TESTING OF HYPOTHESES

Hypothesis 1

There is no significant difference between the experimental group and control group in the achievement of biology at pre test level.

The‘t’ test applied to test the significance of difference between the mean achievement test scores of the experimental group and control group of pretest level.

TABLE.9.1: Mean Achievement Test Scores of the Experimental Group Compared with that of the Control Group at Pretest level

Groups	N	Mean	S.D	‘t’ value	Level of Significance at 0.05 level
Experimental	30	20.43	2.09	0.46	Not significant
Control	30	19.63	1.87		

The table indicates that the ‘t’ value is not significant at 0.05 level. The students of the experimental group do not differ significantly from the students of the control group in the mean achievement test scores at pre test level.

Hypothesis 2

There is no significant difference between the experimental group and control group in the achievement of biology at posttest level

The ‘t’ test applied to test the significance of difference between the mean achievement test scores of the experimental group and control group of posttest level.

TABLE.9.2: Mean Achievement Test Scores of the Experimental Group Compared with that of the Control Group at Posttest level

Groups	N	Mean	S.D	‘t’ value	Level of Significance at 0.01 level
Experimental	30	36.40	3.96	15.08	significant
Control	30	20.10	5.14		

The table indicates that the ‘t’ value is significant at 0.01 level. Hence there is there is a significant difference between the two groups. As indicated by the mean value, it can be concluded that the students of the experimental group fared better in the achievement test than the students of the control group. This shows that learning with the help of blended learning programme will increase the achievement of the students better than learning through the conventional method.

Hypothesis 3

There is no significant difference between the pretest and posttest in the achievement of biology for the experimental group.

The 't' test applied to test the significance of difference between test scores of the pretest with that of the posttest for the experimental group.

TABLE.9.3: Mean Achievement Test Scores of Pretest Compared with that of the Posttest for the Experimental Group

Groups	N	Mean	S.D	't' value	Level of Significance at 0.01 level
Experimental	30	20.43	2.07	20.52	Significant
Control	30	37.40	3.96		

Table 9.3 indicates that the't' value is significant at 0.01 level. Hence, it could be concluded that there is a significant difference between the mean achievement test scores of the pretest and posttest for the experimental group. The higher mean value in the posttest shows that the students fared better in the posttest than in the pretest. This shows that the blended learning programme has helped the students to score more in the posttest.

Hypothesis 4

There is no significant difference between the pretest and posttest in the achievement of biology for the control group.

The 't' test applied to test the significance of difference between the mean achievement test scores of the pretest with that of the posttest for the control group.

TABLE.9.4: Mean Achievement Test Scores of Pretest Compared with that of the Posttest for the Control Group

Groups	N	Mean	S.D	't' value	Level of Significance at 0.05 level
Experimental	30	19.76	1.87	0.034	Not significant
Control	30	20.00	5.06		

Table 9.4 indicates that the 't' value is not significant at 0.05 level. Hence, it could be concluded that there is no significant difference between the mean achievement test scores of the pretest and posttest for the control group.

FINDINGS OF THE STUDY

1. There is no significant difference between the experimental group and control group in the achievement of biology at pre-test level.
2. There is a significant difference between the experimental group and control group in the achievement of biology at post-test level. The students leaning with the help of blended learning programme fared better in biology than in students learning through the conventional method.

3. There is a significant difference between the mean achievement test scores of the pre-test and post-test for the experimental group. This shows that the blended learning programme has helped the students to score more marks in the post-test.
4. There is a significant difference between the mean achievement test scores of the pre-test and post-test for the control group. This shows that the conventional method of teaching will not help the students to score more marks in the post-test.

CONCLUSION

In the field of education is not possible to equip the teaching leaning in higher and higher secondary level because most of the higher secondary schools suffering from lack of modern methods of teaching, they still follow the conventional method of teaching in higher secondary level. This should be change in the modern era; they should follow the blended learning methods in their teaching learning methods because it supports the education department well in advance.

❒

10

Effectiveness of Educational Software on Chemistry

The instruction through Educational Software has been making wonders in the class room activities. 'Eureka Educational Software' has developed Educational Software in the name of "Designmate" for different subjects such as Mathematics, Physics, Chemistry and Biology for the Standards from VI to XII. More animations and interactions are incorporated in this Software. The Investigator wanted to know, the effectiveness of the Eureka Educational Software on the Achievement in Chemistry. Hence the Investigators were aimed to study the Effectiveness of Educational Software on Achievement in Chemistry among the Students of Standard XI. The study belongs to an Experimental Research. The sample of the study based on the half – yearly performance of the students, they are divided into two groups. The total number of students 79, of which 37 belonged to Control Group and 42 belonged to Experimental Group. The Eureka Educational Software "Designmate" was the Dependent Variable and the Achievement in Chemistry was the Independent Variable. The developed Achievement Test in Chemistry by the Investigator was conducted before and after the treatment for both Control and Experiment Groups.

Computer Assisted Instruction (CAI) has emerged as an effective and efficient media of instruction in the advanced countries of the world. CAI is being used in the formal and non- formal educations at all levels. In India too computer has been introduced in most of the areas such as data processing, decision making, etc., It has impact on the working methods of research and development in the field of Science and Technology. First CAI attempt was made around 1961 when University of Illinois produced Programmed Logic for Automatic Teaching Operation (PLATO). Hence, the use of computer in general education started from early sixties. The Computer Assisted or Aided Instruction may be defined as the use of computer as an integral part of an instructional system, the learner generally engaging in two – way interaction with the computer via terminal."Designmate', is a Educational Software developed by Eureka Educational Software which is a 17 years old Multimedia Production House, involved into various activities like making of interactive presentation, animated films, music videos, special effects. They are the first people in India to do a full four minute animated music video where a live character interacts and dance with a computer generated character Anaida's" HooHallaHoo". They received an award for Best Animation from Autodesk. Eureka Educational Software developed 'Designmate', which were converting the entire textbooks into colourful 3D animated movies with interactive games and puzzles. This Education Software was distributed to Schools via Server and LAN. This Education Software covers Science and Mathematics subjects from class VI to XII.

OBJECTIVES OF THE STUDY

The objectives of the study are:

1. To find out the significant difference between the Pre – Test Scores of the Control and Experimental group.
2. To find out the significant difference between the Post – Test Scores of the Control and Experimental group.
3. To find out the significant difference between Control and Experimental group at the Pre – Test and Post – Test Scores.
4. To find out the effect of Educational Software on Achievement in Chemistry with respect to different variables such as of Gender, Caste and Science Marks secured in Standard X.

HYPOTHESES

The following hypotheses were formulated to realize the above objectives.

1. There is no significant difference between the Pre- Test and Post – Test Scores of the Control group and Experimental group.
2. There is no significant difference between the Control group and Experimental group at the Pre – Test and Post – Test Scores.
3. There is no influence of Gender, Caste and Science Marks secured in Standard X (SMSX) over the effect of Educational Software on Achievement in Chemistry.

NATURE OF THE RESEARCH

The present investigation is Experimental in nature, because the investigators aimed to compare the Effectiveness of Teaching Chemistry to the XI Standard Students through Teaching and through Eureka Educational Software.

SAMPLE SELECTION

The investigators selected XI Standard Students of Periyar Centenary Memorial Matriculation Higher Secondary School, K.K. Nagar Trichy to carry out the Experiment because the School has been posed with well-equipped computer facilities. Based on the half – yearly performance of the Students, they are divided into two groups. The total number of students 79, of which 37 belonged to Control Group and 42 belonged to Experimental Group.

DEVELOPMENT OF TOOL

The Eureka Educational Software, 'Designmate' was the Dependent Variable and the Achievement in Chemistry was the Independent Variable. The Eureka Educational Software was given to the Post Graduate Teachers who are handling Chemistry in the nearby schools for content validity. The opinion of them was highly satisfactory.

The developed Achievement test questionnaires were framed by the investigators with the guidance of the subject experts covering the following items such as Knowledge, Understanding, Application and Skill. These questionnaires were validated by Test – Retest method among the Student of XI Standard. The obtained 'r' value 0.74 shows that the tool is highly valuable. Thus the Validity and Reliability of the tool were established. The developed Achievement Test in Chemistry was conducted before and after the treatment for both Control and Experiment Groups. Then the Investigators taught Chemistry through Educational Software to the Experimental Group. Similar topics in Chemistry were taught through Lecture Method to the Control Group.

After the finalization of the tool, the investigators had given 40 items to the Students. Each item was in the form of multiple choices with an incomplete statement. For each item four alternative answers were given. Only one was the correct answer. The Students were requested to write the response in the form of correct alpha bate a, b, c and d. Each × responses carry 1 mark.

DATA ANALYSIS

Thus the data collected in this manner undertake analysis by using different statistical technique. Mean and SD were calculated for each Variables to calculate ‘t’ values which is the test of significance of the difference between two means. The following tables contained the data regarding the Control group and Experimental group with the following variables such as Gender, Caste and SMSX.

TABLE.10.1: Mean and SD of the Student towards Achievement Score for different Category of Control Group

Sl.No	Variable	Category	Sample Size	Mean		SD	
				Pre-Test	Post-Test	Pre-Test	Post-Test
1.	Gender	Boys	18	20.83	65.97	9.09	13.31
		Girls	19	15.53	62.5	12.05	17.37
2.	Caste	OC/BC	23	22.07	65.43	11.48	16.57
		MBC/SC/ST	14	11.61	62.14	6.09	13.69
3.	SMSX	Above 70%	21	21.55	68.21	10.73	11.34
		Below 70%	16	13.59	62.66	9.72	16.31
4.	**Total**		37	18.11	64.19	11.03	15.63

From the above table1 it is revealed that the average Mean Score of the Student towards Achievement Score for different category is 18.11 at Pre-Test level and 64.19 at Post-Test level which show the effectiveness of Lecture Method. Moreover at the Pre-Test level the minimum score is 11.61 and the maximum score is 22.07. At the Post-Test level 62.14 is the minimum score and 68.21 is the maximum score.

TABLE.10.2: Mean and SD of the Student towards Achievement Score for different Category of Experimental Group

S. No	Variable	Category	Sample Size	Mean		SD	
				Pre-Test	Post-Test	Pre-Test	Post-Test
1.	**Gender**	Boys	21	25.6	81.67	9.66	10.24
		Girls	21	13.81	70.12	7.82	10.62
2.	**Caste**	OC/BC	26	21.63	76.44	10.56	11.99
		MBC/SC/ST	16	16.56	74.68	9.84	12.58

3.	SMSX	Above 70%	18	18.89	78.89	10.28	9.33
		Below70%	24	19.9	73.65	11.24	13.11
4.	**Total**		**42**	**19.70**	**75.89**	**15.63**	**11.93**

Above table 10.2 shows that the average Mean Score of the Student towards Achievement Score for different category is 19.70 at Pre-Test level and 75.89 at Post-Test level which show the Eureka Educational Software has considerable effect in Teaching Chemistry. Moreover at the Pre-Test level the minimum score is 13.81 and the maximum score is 25.6. At the Post -Test level 70.12 is the minimum score and 81.67 is the maximum score.

TABLE.10.3: Significant Difference between the Mean Scores of Control Group and Experimental Group at Pre -Test level

Group	N	Mean	SD	t value	Remarks
Control	37	18.11	11.03	0.661	NS
Experimental	42	19.70	10.58		

NS: Not significant

The above table 10.3 reveals that the obtained mean Student Achievement Scores in Chemistry of the Control group and Experimental group are more or less same. The calculated 't' value also indicates there is no significant difference at 5% level between Control group and Experimental group at Pre-Test level. Hence the stated Null Hypothesis is that, there is no significant difference between the mean Student Achievement Scores in Chemistry of the Control group and Experimental group at the Pre-Test level is accepted.

TABLE.10.4: Significant Difference between the Mean Scores of Control Group and Experimental Group at Post-Test level

Group	N	Mean	SD	t value	Remarks
Control	37	64.19	15.63	4.01	S
Experimental	42	75.89	11.93		

S: Significant

It is evident from the table 10.4 that the obtained mean value of Experimental group is greater than the control group. The calculated 't' value shows that there is significant difference between the Control group and Experimental group. Hence the stated Null hypothesis that there is no significant difference between Student Achievement Scores in Chemistry of Control group and Experimental group at Post-Test level is rejected.

TABLE.10.5: Influence of various Category over the performance of the Control Group and Experimental Group at Pre- Test level

Category	Group	N	Mean	SD	t value	Remarks
Boys	Control	18	20.83	9.09	1.59	NS
	Experimental	21	25.6	9.66		
Girls	Control	19	15.53	12.05	0.54	NS
	Experimental	21	13.81	7.82		
OC/BC	Control	23	22.07	11.48	0.14	NS
	Experimental	26	21.63	10.56		
MBC/SC/ST	Control	14	11.61	6.09	1.68	NS
	Experimental	16	16.56	9.84		
Above 70%	Control	21	21.55	10.73	0.78	NS
	Experimental	18	18.89	10.28		
Below 70%	Control	16	13.59	9.72	1.88	NS
	Experimental	24	19.9	11.24		

The above table 10.5 shows that the calculated 't' values of Control group and Experimental group at the Pre-Test level at various Categories has no significant difference at 5 % level. Hence it is concluded that Gender, Caste, SMSX has no influence over the performance of Control group and Experimental group at the Pre-Test level. Therefore the stated Null hypothesis is that, there is no influence of Gender, Caste, SMSX over the performance of Student Achievement Scores in Chemistry of the Control group and Experimental group at the Pre-Test is accepted.

TABLE.10.6: Significant Difference between the Mean Scores of Pre-Test and Post -Test for Control Group

Test	N	Mean	SD	t value	Remarks
Pre	37	18.11	11.03	**14.62**	**S**
Post	37	64.19	15.63		

It is evident from the table 10.6 that the obtained mean value of Post-Test is greater than the Pre-Test. The calculated't' value shows that there is significant difference between the Pre-Test and Post-Test conducted for the Control group. Hence the stated Null hypothesis that there is no significant difference between Student Achievement Scores in Chemistry for the Pre-Test and Post-Test of Control group is rejected.

TABLE.10.7: Significant Difference between the Mean Scores of Pre-Test and Post-Test for Experimental Group

Test	N	Mean	SD	t value	Remarks
Pre	42	19.70	10.58	22.61	S
Post	42	75.89	11.93		

The above table 10.7 reveals that the obtained mean Student Achievement Scores in Chemistry of the Post-Test is greater than Pre-Test of Experimental group. The calculated 't' value also indicates there is significant difference at 5% level between Pre-Test and Post-Test of Experimental group. Hence the stated Null Hypothesis is that, there is no significant difference between the mean Student Achievement Scores in Chemistry for the Pre-Test and Post – Test of Experimental group is rejected.

TABLE10.8: Influence of Gender over the Performance of the Control Group and Experimental Group at Post – Test level

Gender	Group	N	Mean	SD	t value	Remarks
Boys	Control	18	65.97	13.31	4.02	S
	Experimental	21	81.67	10.24		
Girls	Control	19	62.5	17.37	1.52	NS
	Experimental	21	70.12	10.62		

The above table 10.8 shows that the calculated 't' values of Control group and Experimental group at the Post-Test level of the Boys has significant difference between the mean scores at 5 % level. The above table also reveals that the calculated 't' values of Control group and Experimental group at the Post-Test level of the Girls has no significant difference between the mean scores at 5 % level. Therefore the stated Null hypothesis is that, except Boys the Girls has no influence over the performance of Student Achievement Scores in Chemistry of the Control group and Experimental group at the Post-Test is accepted.

TABLE.10.9: Influence of Caste over the Performance of the Control Group and Experimental Group at Post-Test level

Caste	Group	N	Mean	SD	't' value	Remarks
OC/BC	Control	23	65.43	16.57	**2.63**	S
	Experimental	26	76.44	11.99		
MBC/SC/ST	Control	14	62.14	13.69	**2.62**	S
	Experimental	16	74.68	12.58		

The calculated 't' values from the above table 10.9 reveals that Control group and Experimental group at the Post-Test level of the Caste has significant difference between the mean scores at 5 % level. The mean values of the above table shows that there is influence of caste over the performance of Control group and Experimental group at the Post-Test level. Hence the stated Null Hypothesis is that, there is influence of caste over the performance of Student Achievement Scores in Chemistry of the Control group and Experimental group at the Post-Test is rejected.

TABLE.10.10: Influence of Students Secured Science Marks in Standard X over the performance of the Control Group and Experimental Group at Post-Test level

SMSX	Group	N	Mean	SD	't' value	Remarks
Above 70%	Control	21	68.21	11.34	3.43	S
	Experimental	18	78.89	9.33		
Below 70%	Control	16	62.66	16.31	2.45	S
	Experimental	24	73.65	13.11		

It is evident from the table 10.10 that the obtained mean value of Experimental group is greater than the Control group. The calculated 't' value shows that there is significant difference between the Control group and Experimental group at the Post-Test level with respect to SMSX at 5 % level. The mean values of the above table shows that there is influence of SMSX over the performance of Control group and Experimental group at the Post-Test level. Hence the stated Null Hypothesis is that, there is influence of SMSX over the performance of Student Achievement Scores in Chemistry of the Control group and Experimental group at the Post-Test is rejected.

FINDINGS & DISCUSSION

The salient findings of the study are i) the Eureka Educational Software has considerable effect in Teaching Chemistry, ii) there is a significant difference between the mean scores of Pre-Test and Post-Test level for both Control Group and Experimental Group, iii) Gender, Caste and SMSX has no influence over the performance of Student Achievement Scores in Chemistry of the Control group and Experimental group at the Pre-Test level, iv) Caste and SMSX has influence over the performance of Student Achievement Scores in Chemistry of the Control group and Experimental group at the Post-Test level and v) Experimental group Boys show significant higher mean scores in the Achievement Scores than the Control group, but Girls has no influence over the performance of Student Achievement Scores in Chemistry of the Control group and Experimental group.

While conducting the Pre-Test it was observed that both Control and Experimental group's possess similar level of pervious knowledge on the selected contents in Chemistry. The same trend was observed with respect to different variables such as Gender, Caste and SMSX. When the analysis was made between Pre-Test and Post-Test Scores of the Control and Experimental groups it was observed that both methods of teaching such as traditional Lecture

Method and Educational Software method, Educational Software method is found to be effective method. While comparing the Mean Achievement Scores between Control and Experimental group it was observed that students who learnt through Eureka Educational Software score significant higher than the Control group Students. The significant difference of the Experimental group may be due to the reason that the Eureka Educational Software has incorporated with interactive presentation, animated movies, special effects and puzzles, these special features might have attracted the Experimental Students to score more marks.

CONCLUSIONS

Eureka Educational Software is more suitable method for teaching Chemistry at XI Standard level. Eureka Educational Software is the one of the best method in the Teaching Learning process of Chemistry for XI Standard Students without considering the individual variables such as Gender, Caste and SMSX this is due to the subject contents are taught through more animations and interactions. Due to this Educational Software Students concentrations increased and they easily understood the subject contents. At the Post-Test level the Girls shows no significant difference in the Achievement Scores in Chemistry of the Control group and Experimental group.

❒

11

Edu-Digital Skill

The end of the 20th Century and beginning of the 21st Century witnessed very exciting changes, one of them being in the field of Information and Communication Technology. Educators have begun to realize that in the fast changing world of today, the students have to be prepared to cope intelligently with the social, economic and technological changes. The educational environment is changing rapidly as a consequence of ICT and will continue to change. Information and Communication Technologies (ICT) are electronic and/or computerized devices and associated human interactive materials that enable the user to employ them for a wide range of teaching and learning processes in addition to personal use. Around the world, educational systems are under increasing pressure to use the new information and communication technologies to teach students the knowledge and skills they need in the 21st Century. With the emerging new technologies, the teaching profession is evolving from an emphasis on teacher-centered, lecture-based instruction to student-centered, interactive learning environments. The present study aims to find out the effectiveness of edu-digital skill among higher secondary students in Coimbatore District.

Education, the foremost weapon for social reform, is now under the forces of change. Newly formed branches of knowledge and techniques of education facilitate the physical, mental and emotional development of the learners. Schools have an unavoidable role in acquainting the students with the nature of changing field of education and in making necessary changes in the instructional techniques. In the modern world of technological innovations, all educational institutions are trying to improve their quality in terms of facilities and academic outputs. Scientific knowledge is exploding every day. Knowledge available to mankind today is emerging in the form of science and technology. There is no limit or end to the accumulation of scientific knowledge. It also satisfies the intellectual thirst of human beings. Science education is a bridge between science and education, using psychology. It links the most powerful concepts of science to the growing minds of children through active experimental pedagogy. Science education plays a prominent role in Indian educational system. It has, as its objective, the aim of providing individual learners a firm grasp of the concepts and processes of science as also to impart the ability to use scientific method of problem-solving. As a result of it, every aspect of human civilization has been influenced to a very great extent.

OBJECTIVES

1. To know the edu-digital skill among higher secondary students in Coimbatore district.
2. To find out the effectiveness of Multimedia Programme in teaching among higher secondary students.

METHODOLOGY

Research may be termed as a systemic inquiry of verified knowledge; it is an organized deliberate effort to collect information, to analyze it, to put it together and finally to evaluate it. This research paper on methodology describes elaborately, the sample that was chosen, research design, objectives of the study, data collection, statistical techniques used for data and analysis.

POPULATION

Population selected for this study was 100 higher secondary students in a selected school at Coimbatore District.

ATTITUDE SCALE TOWARDS MULTIMEDIA PROGRAMME

The attitude scale was used to measure the level of attitude towards Multimedia programme. The scale was constructed and validated by the investigator.

The attitude scale towards multimedia programme, consisting of 40 items, was designed by the investigator and was given to experienced teachers who were handling Computer Science in higher secondary schools, professors of Computer Science and Education and Educational psychologists. On the basis of the suggestions of above experts, some items were restructured and some were eliminated. Finally 25 items were selected for this test. The scale for measuring the higher secondary student's attitude towards multimedia programme in the study is of the Liker type. This scale has as many as 25 statements of which 20 are favourable towards multimedia programme and the remaining are unfavorable towards it.

SCORING

In the Liker type of scale, against each statement, five alternatives namely "Strongly agree", "Agree", "Undecided", "Disagree", and "Strongly disagree" are given. The subjects have to indicate their choice by putting a tick-mark (√) under one of the five columns against each statement.

For favourable statement weight age of 4,3,2,1 and 0 were given from strongly agree to strongly disagree in that order. For unfavourable statements the scoring was reversed. Thus the strongly agree response will get 0 and the strongly disagree response will get 4. Here the weight age of 0,1,2,3 and 4 were given from strongly agree to the strongly disagree in that order.

Thus the score value lies between 0-100. The content validity of the tool was established based on the opinion given by the experts. The reliability of the tool was established by Split-Half method. It was found to be 0.83 which was significant.

DATA COLLECTION

Primary data, required for the present research work were collected by conducting direct interviews using questionnaire. All the respondents were given sufficient information about the Project work. These respondents were provided with the same questionnaires. They were also informed that they have to answer in the same fashion.

HYPOTHESIS

There is no significant difference between the pre and post-test mean scores of experimental group students in their attitude towards multimedia programme.

ADMINISTRATION OF RETENTION TEST

The Attitude Scale towards Multimedia Programme was constructed and validated by the investigator and was administered to the subjects of the experimental group. The pre test scores on attitude towards multimedia programme were collected. Thus pre-test and post test scores on attitude towards multimedia programme were computed for analysis.

ANALYSIS AND INTERPRETATION

To find out the significance of the difference between the pre and post-test mean scores of experimental group students in their attitude towards multimedia programme the 't' test was used.

TABLE.11.1: Distribution of 't' value between the pre and post-test mean scores of experimental group students in their attitude towards multimedia programme

Group	N	Mean	S.D	't' value	Level of Significant
Pre- test	50	42.08	10.42	24.47	p<0.05
Post-test	50	93.58	2.57		

There is no significant difference between the pre and post-test mean scores of experimental group students in their attitude towards multimedia programme.

The obtained 't' value is statistically significant since it is greater than the table 't' value 1.96 at 0.05 level of significance. Hence the null hypothesis is rejected. It shows that there is significant difference between the pre and post-test mean scores of experimental group students in their attitude towards multimedia programme. It is therefore concluded that the experimental group students show more favourable attitude towards multimedia programme in the post test than the pre-test.

TABLE.11.2: Showing the Stepwise Regression Analysis Predicting Factors Influencing Effectiveness of Edu-Digital Skill among Higher Secondary Students and Demographic Variables

Sl. No	Step/Source	Unstandardized Coefficients Beta	Std. Error	Standardized Coefficients Beta Beta	Step t	P
1.	Gender	1.144	0.156	0.242	7.324	0.01
2.	Father education	1.254	0.359	0.163	3.495	0.01
3.	Mother education	2.615	0.462	0.361	5.661	0.01
4.	Monthly Income	2.175	0.402	0.280	5.410	0.01
5.	Father Occupation	1.022	0.513	0.137	1.992	0.01

* P < 0.01

Five variables viz Gender, Father Education, Mother Education, Monthly income and Father Occupation have significantly contributed for predicting the factors influencing effectiveness of edu-digital skill among higher secondary. The first variable Gender seems to be 7.324, Father Education seems to be 3.495, Mother education seems to be 5.661, Monthly income seems to be 5.410 and Father Occupation seems to be 1.992. The predictive value of these variables separately is 0.01.

TABLE.11.3: Showing the Correlation between the Effectiveness of Edu-Digital Skill among Higher Secondary Students and Demographic Variables

Factors	Effectiveness of Edu-Digital Skill among Higher Secondary Students
Gender	0.920**
Father education	0.849**
Mother education	0.914**
Monthly Income	0.880**
Father Occupation	0.855**

* Significant at 0.01 level

Effectiveness of edu-digital skill among higher secondary students is positively and significantly related to Gender (0.920), Father education (0.849), Mother education (0.914), monthly income (0.880) and Father Occupation (0.855). So, the direct relationship between the effectiveness of edu-digital skill among higher secondary students and selected demographic variables.

CONCLUSION

Computer and multimedia technology for education offers a number of benefits. They allow the teacher to structure and present the information with varying special effects to the students. They can also be used for the storage of audio-visual information of various types. Multimedia programmes provide a lot of benefits. The benefits for learners include flexibility of scheduled instruction at a location convenient to learners, reduced student time, assured progress in skill development, increased achievement and increased retention and continuous report to the learners of progress and accomplishments, specified performance criteria, good response and feedback. The application of multimedia programme would definitely create a good learning environment in classroom, sustaining attention and motivating the students to learn effectively. The application of multimedia may create a congenial learning climate in schools and can bring real life situations.

The present study has found out that the multimedia programme is very effective in higher secondary level. As the present teaching-learning process in higher secondary classes is very rigid, time bound and outmoded, it was proposed to use multimedia programme. As multimedia programme develops a favourable attitude towards multimedia programme, motivates the students to involve in the process of learning, attracts students' attention in learning, accelerates the students' understanding of concepts of subjects, increases the retention power and that it is highly suitable for all categories of students ranging from low to high achievers, it is suggested that this multimedia programme be widely adopted and implemented in educational institutions as computer laboratory facilities are available in all the schools and colleges to enable the learners to learn the subjects of their choice according to their own pace and ability. Learning through multimedia programme is very easy, understandable and comfortable to all categories of students for all types of subjects.

❐

12

Multimedia in Teaching Economics

The computer has revolutionized the whole society overwhelmingly inclusive of all human activities especially those of education. The computer is changing the total educational system namely, content, methodology, learner participation learning process, teacher roles, curricular implication etc. "The computers are very powerful instructional media that enhance quality of instruction". By programming the subject of study in computers, teaching and learning become full of contexts and situations. The student can take his own time to learn the contents because they are individualized instructional situation. The performance of the student in instruction as well as in test will automatically record in the computer. The present study aims to find out the implications of multimedia in teaching economics with special reference to higher secondary education in Chennai. A samples of 155 samples selected randomly were studied. A questionnaire method of survey was used to find out the implications of multimedia in teaching economics. The data were collected by using questionnaire as an instrument. Primary data were collected by conducting direct structured interview using questionnaire. All the respondents were asked the same questions in the same fashion and they were informed the purpose of study. t-test, ANOVA and Correlation analysis were applied to test the hypotheses. The findings and observations are the result and outcome of the interpretations made during the study of analysis.

OBJECTIVES

1. To find the effect on learning competency of the students by using Multi media for teaching economics
2. To find the active participation of the teachers in using multi media for teaching economics.
3. To find how the teaching of economics has been efficiently improved using the multi media.
4. To find the importance of computers and internet in teaching economics.

METHODOLOGY

The investigator, for the present study adopts the survey method of research. It is a procedure in which data is systematically collected from a population through some form of direct solicitation such as face to face interview, questionnaire or schedule. The survey is extensive and cross sectional dealing with the relatively large number of cases of a particular time and yielding statistics that are abstracted from particular cases. It is the method of investigation which attempts to describe and interpret what exists at present in the form of conditions, practices, process, trends, effects, attitudes, and beliefs. Using this method the investigator had gathered information's measure the Effect of Multi Media Aids in teaching economics for Higher Secondary Students in Chennai.

SAMPLE

For the present study 155 Higher Secondary Students in Chennai.

DATA COLLECTION

Primary data, required for the present research work were collected by conducting direct interviews using questionnaire. All the respondents were given sufficient information about the study. These respondents were provided with the same questionnaires. They were also informed that they have to answer in the same fashion.

STATISTICAL TOOLS FOR ANALYSIS

The following tools statistical tools were used for the analysis of data. t-test, one way ANOVA and correlation analysis is used for the present study.

ANALYSIS AND INTERPRETATION

TABLE.12.1: Six Wise Distribution of 't' Value between the Boys and Girls of the Higher Secondary Economics Students using Multimedia Resources in their Schools

Dimensions	Boys N = 55		Girls N = 100		Calculated value of 't'	Level of significance at 5% level
	Mean	S.D	Mean	S.D		
Working knowledge of computers	79.42	8.17	80.42	8.68	0.71	NS
Knowledge about internet	78.15	9.51	76.88	9.80	0.91	NS
Knowledge using A.V. Aids	79.76	7.48	76.26	10.79	2.37	S
Preparation of computer based study materials	76.40	7.97	74.77	11.04	1.06	NS
Assignment and project	81.75	6.31	78.35	10.18	2.56	S
Interaction with others through web	395.47	28.53	386.5	42.77	1.56	NS

(At5% level of significance, the table value of 't' is 1.96)

It is refereed from the above table that there is a significant difference between boys and of Higher Secondary Students of economics group in there, Knowledge in using A.V. Aids and Assignment and project but there is no significant difference between Male and Female Higher Secondary students of economics group in their Working knowledge of computers, knowledge about internet, Preparation of computer based study materials, interaction with others through web.

TABLE.12.2: Area Wise Distribution of 't' Value between the Urban and Rural Higher Secondary Economics Students using Multimedia Resources in their Schools

Dimensions	Urban N = 55		Rural N = 100		Calculated value of 't'	Level of significance at 5% level
	Mean	S.D	Mean	S.D		
Working knowledge of computers	79.42	8.17	80.42	8.68	0.71	NS
Knowledge about internet	78.15	9.51	76.88	9.80	0.91	NS
Knowledge using A.V. Aids	79.76	7.48	76.26	10.79	2.37	S
Preparation of computer based study materials	76.40	7.97	74.77	11.04	1.06	NS

Assignment and project	81.75	6.31	78.35	10.18	2.56	S
Interaction with others through web	395.47	28.53	386.5	42.77	1.56	NS

(At 5% level of significance, the table value of 't' is 1.96)

It is referred from the above table that there is no significant difference between urban and rural Higher Secondary Students of economics group in there, Knowledge in using A.V. Aids, Assignment and project, Working knowledge of computers, Knowledge about internet, Preparation of computer based study materials, Interaction with other through web.

TABLE.12.3: 'f' Value among the Boys and Girls of Higher Secondary Economics Group Students in Using Multimedia Resources

Dimensions	df = 2,152			Calculated 'f' Value	Remarks at 5% Level
	Source of variation	Sum of squares	M.S.V		
Working knowledge of computers	Between With in	118.75 11110.63	59.38 73.10	0.81	NS
Knowledge about internet	Between With in	7.94 14650.81	3.97 96.39	0.04	NS
Knowledge in using A.V. Aids	Between With in	23.44 15123.38	11.72 99.50	0.12	NS
Preparation of computer study materials	Between With in	155.56 15619.63	77.78 102.76	0.76	NS
Assignment and project	Between With in	164.39 12793.88	82.19 84.17	0.98	NS
Interaction with others through web	Between With in	216.00 23034.00	108.00 1515.39	0.07	NS

(For 2,152 df. At 5% level of Significance, the Table Value of 'f' is 3.06)

It is inferred from the above table that there is no significance difference among the boys and girls of Higher Secondary economics group students in using Multimedia resources in the Higher Secondary schools of Chennai.

TABLE.12.4: 'f' value among the Rural and Urban Higher Secondary Students of Economics Group in Using Multimedia source in Chennai

Dimensions	df= 2,152			Calculated 'f' Value	Remarks at 5% Level
	Source of variation	Sum of squares	M.S.V		
Working knowledge of computers	Between With in	39.50 11189.88	19.75 73.62	0.27	NS
Knowledge about internet	Between With in	394.39 14264.50	197.16 93.85	2.10	NS

Knowledge in using A.V. Aids	Between With in	130.31 15016.50	65.16 98.79	0.66	NS
Preparation of computer study materials	Between With in	444.44 153330.75	222.22 100.86	2.20	NS
Assignment and project	Between With in	364.69 12593.56	182.32 82.85	2.20	NS
Interaction with others through web	Between With in	5628.00 224924.00	2814.00 11479.76	1.90	NS

(for 2,152 df.at 5% level of significance, the table value of 'f' is 3.06)

It is inferred from the above table that there is no significance difference among the Rural and Urban Higher Secondary students of economics group in using Multimedia resource in the Higher Secondary Schools of Chennai.

TABLE.12.5: 'f' value among the Higher Secondary Students of economics Group in Using Multimedia source in Government and Private Higher Secondary Schools in Chennai

Dimensions	df= 2,152			Calculated 'f' Value	Remarks at 5% Level
	Source of variation	Sum of squares	M.S.V		
Working knowledge of computers	Between With in	39.50 11189.88	19.75 73.62	0.27	NS
Knowledge about internet	Between With in	394.39 14264.50	197.16 93.85	2.10	NS
Knowledge in using A.V. Aids	Between With in	130.31 15016.50	65.16 98.79	0.66	NS
Preparation of computer study materials	Between With in	444.44 153330.75	222.22 100.86	2.20	NS
Assignment and project	Between With in	364.69 12593.56	182.32 82.85	2.20	NS
Interaction with others through web	Between With in	5628.00 224924.00	2814.00 11479.76	1.90	NS

(For 2,152 df. at 5% level of significance, the table value of '' is 3.06)

It is inferred from the above table that there is no significance difference among the Government and Private Higher Secondary students of economics group in using Multimedia resource in the Higher Secondary School of Chennai

TABLE.12.6: The Correlation Value between the Male and Female Higher Secondary Students in using Multimedia Resources in the Higher Secondary Schools of Chennai

Category	?X	?X²	?Y	?Y²	?XY	Calculated	Remarks
Boys	683	8595	545	5495	6775	.68	NS
Girls	1199	14757	970	9584	11740	.425	S
Total	1882	23354	1515	15079	18515	.325	S

(Table value of Correlation Co-efficient at 5% level of Significance is 0.161)

It is inferred from the above table that there is no significant relationship between the rural and high secondary economics group boys in using multimedia resources and there is a significant relationship between rural and urban high secondary economics group girls in using multimedia resources.

FINDINGS

There a significant difference among the higher secondary commence group students of boys and girls, higher secondary commence students of government and private schools, higher secondary commence group students of rural and urban schools, in their interest towards learning commence through multimedia resources in Chennai.

There is significant difference among the higher secondary economics group students in their levels of using multimedia shows moderate knowledge except interaction with others through web and no significant difference in low of using multimedia except interaction with other through web and no significant difference in higher level knowledge of using multimedia.

There is no significant difference among the higher secondary economics group boys in their level of using multimedia shows moderate knowledge and higher level of using multimedia and there is a significant difference low of using multimedia at the area of assignment and project, interaction with others though web.

There is no significant difference among the secondary economics group girls in all the levels of using multimedia resources. There is no significant difference among the higher secondary economics group students of government school in their level of using multimedia shows moderate knowledge and there is a significant difference in low level of interaction with others though web and shows significant difference in higher level of in knowledge about internet, knowledge in using A.V.aids and in the preparation of computer based study materials.

CONCLUSION

The present study aims to find out the implications of multimedia in teaching economics with special reference to higher secondary. The researcher framed objectives and hypotheses on the basis of the above context. The research was carried out in 155 samples based randomly. A questionnaire constructed by R was used to collect the relevant data. After collecting the data they were analyzed using statistical tools such as t-test, ANOVA and Correlation analysis. The result concluded that students have average implications of multimedia in teaching at Higher Secondary level.

❐

13

Multimedia in Teaching Human Anatomy

In view of growing importance of science education, old concepts of science teaching have therefore, rather become completely outmoded and an entirely new ethos and approach to science curriculum have come into existence. Moreover, unprecedented development of scientific research, new discoveries, and new methods of investigation, in the early twentieth century, has created a need and urge to examine and reorganize science teaching programmes at all levels in schools. Institutions are functioning in an era of rapidly emerging new technologies. Some of them, like information and communications technology, have fuelled a veritable explosion of rising expectations everywhere. When such is the pace of developmental processes, it becomes fairly imperative on the part of the students not only to possess sound knowledge and understanding of fundamental concepts, but also to understand and appreciate the ramifications of various developments in the field of science and technology, especially in the context of their future career. The situation underscores the significance of research in science education and it is time for the educationists to evolve a proper and appropriate strategy for teaching science.

Research work is being continuously done in the field of science and also in the related teaching methods and materials. In order to keep pace with the development of science, the need for new instructional strategies was greatly felt. One such innovative teaching strategy, called multimedia programme, has been chosen and studied by the investigator in this research work. Upgrading Biology curriculum by introducing Human anatomy demands a change in the instructional strategy. The need for developing an instructional strategy for teaching Human anatomy and physiology is very important to make the teachers and students aware of the scientific principles that govern the advances being made in medicine. The functions of the internal organs of human body can be easily explained through a multimedia programme. This also saves the use of expensive chemicals and sophisticated instruments which are beyond the reach of higher secondary schools. In schools, the required equipment to explain the human anatomy is not available. In this situation, the working mechanism of internal organs can be explained by a multimedia programme, which when used as an instructional strategy will make the task of learning human anatomy easier, effective and less expensive. The present study aims to find out the effectiveness of multimedia programme in perceiving human anatomy among higher secondary students in Tindivanam.

A samples of 100 higher secondary students selected randomly were studied. A questionnaire method of survey was used to find out the effectiveness of multimedia programme in perceiving human anatomy. The data were collected by using questionnaire as an instrument. Primary data were collected by conducting direct structured interview using questionnaire. All the respondents were asked the same questions in the same fashion and they were informed the purpose of study. Mean, SD, and t-test analysis was applied to test the hypotheses. The findings and observations are the result and outcome of the interpretations made during the study of analysis. The result found that majority of the higher secondary students satisfied about multimedia programme.

At the Higher Secondary level, the science subject is divided into Physics, Chemistry, Botany, and Zoology according to Tamil Nadu State Board syllabus. Zoology deals with the life history, distribution, structure, reproduction, and importance of animals including Homosapiens, the human beings. 'Human anatomy' is one of the units of the Zoology subject. Human anatomy is the branch of anatomy devoted to the structure of the human body. In general the study of human anatomy helps the students to do their higher studies in Medicine, Physiotherapy, Nursing, Degree courses like B.Sc., Zoology, and Microbiology etc. Apart from acquiring the technical knowledge, it is necessary for human beings to know and control their own systems of their body for healthy life. Hence the investigator has selected the unit "human anatomy" to teach through multimedia programme for the higher secondary students in the present investigation.

OBJECTIVES

1. To develop a Multimedia Programme for the unit of Human anatomy from XI standard Zoology subject in order to teach the higher secondary students.
2. To find out the effectiveness of Multimedia Programme in teaching Human anatomy among higher secondary students.

METHODOLOGY

The methodology adopted for the study is explained in detail. The sampling technique, size of the sample, variables of the study, description of the tool used and administration of tool are elaborated.

SAMPLE

A samples of 100 higher secondary students in selected randomly were studied in Tindivanam Town.

DATA COLLECTION

The present study aims at developing and using Multimedia programme for perceiving human anatomy for higher secondary students to enable them to understand the concepts very easily through individualized instructional technique. It is maintained that the Multimedia programme may reduce monotony in the classroom by bringing out real life situations and motivate them for self-study and provides opportunities for individual pace and ability.

The study intends to develop a multimedia programme for human anatomy for XI standard Zoology subject prescribed by Tamil Nadu State Board Syllabus and find out the effectiveness of the Multimedia programme through experimentation in perceiving human anatomy among the higher secondary students. The study provides scope for the development and use of many Multimedia programmes in the concerned discipline as well as other disciplines for the benefit of learners of different categories. Hence the multimedia programme can be used as an individualized instructional technique for the students of different categories in the science subjects as well as other subjects.

ANALYSIS AND INTERPRETATION

Performance of control group students between the pre-test and post-test in human anatomy.

The Mean, Standard Deviation and Co-efficient of Variation were computed for the control group students in their performance in human anatomy between the pre-test and post-test.

TABLE.13.1: Distribution of Mean, Standard Deviation and Co-Efficient of Variation on the Performance of Control Group Students between the Pre-Test and Post-Test in Human Anatomy

Group	N	Mean	S.D	CV
Pre-test	100	42.69	13.60	31.86
Post-test	100	52.46	13.28	25.31

The Co-efficient of Variation of the pre-test and post-test for the control group students was found to be 31.86 and 25.31, which reveals that the control group students are more consistent in their performance in human anatomy in the post-test than the pre-test. It reveals that the control group students have improved in their performance in human anatomy in the post-test than the pre-test.

To find out the significance of the difference between the control and experimental group students in their performance in human anatomy in the pre-test, the 't' test was used.

TABLE.13.2: Distribution of 't' Value between the Control and Experimental Group Students in their Performance in Human Anatomy in the Pre-Test

Group	N	Mean	S.D	't' value	Level of Significant
Control	100	42.69	13.60	0.17	p>0.05
Experimental	100	43.31	12.59		

There is no significant difference between the control and experimental group students in their performance in human anatomy in the pre-test.

The obtained 't' value 0.17 is not statistically significant since it is less than the table 't' value 1.96 for 50 df at 0.05 level of significance. Hence the null hypothesis is accepted. It shows that there is no significant difference between the control and experimental group students in their performance in human anatomy in the pre-test. It is therefore concluded that both control and experimental group students have the same level of performance in human anatomy in the pre-test.

To find out the significance of the difference between the control and experimental group students in their performance in human anatomy in the post-test, the 't' test was used.

TABLE.13:3: Distribution of 't' Value between the Control and Experimental Group Students in their Performance in Human Anatomy in the Post-Test

Group	N	Mean	S.D	't' value	Level of Significant
Control	100	52.46	13.28	14.38	p<0.05
Experimental	100	92.81	5.31		

There is no significant difference between the control and experimental group students in their performance in human anatomy in the post-test.

The obtained 't' value 14.38 is statistically significant since it is greater than the table 't' value 1.96 for 50 df at 0.05 level of significance. Hence the null hypothesis is rejected. It shows that there is significant difference between the control and experimental group students in their performance in human anatomy in the post-test. It is therefore concluded that the experimental group students performed significantly better in human anatomy than that of control group students in the post-test.

To find out the significance of the difference between the pre and post-test mean scores of control group students in the performance in human anatomy, the 't' was used.

TABLE.13.4: Distribution of 't' Value for the Pre and Post-Test mean Scores of Control Group Students in the Performance in Human Anatomy

Group	N	Mean	S.D	't' value	Level of Significant
Pre-test	100	42.69	13.60	2.62	p<0.05
Post-test	100	52.46	13.28		

There is no significant difference between the pre and post-test mean scores of control group students in the performance in human anatomy.

The obtained 't' value 2.62 is statistically significant since it is greater than the table 't' value 1.96 for 50 df at 0.05 level of significance. Hence the null hypothesis is rejected. It shows that there is significant difference between the pre and post-test mean scores of control group students in the performance in human anatomy. It is therefore concluded that the control group students have improved in their performance in human anatomy in the post-test.

SUGGESTIONS

The present study aims at developing and using Multimedia programme for perceiving human anatomy for higher secondary students to enable them to understand the concepts very easily through individualized instructional technique. It is maintained that the Multimedia programme may reduce monotony in the classroom by bringing out real life situations and motivate them for self-study and provides opportunities for individual pace and ability.

CONCLUSION

The study intends to develop a multimedia programme for human anatomy for XI standard Zoology subject prescribed by Tamil Nadu State Board Syllabus and find out the effectiveness of the Multimedia programme through experimentation in perceiving human anatomy among the higher secondary students. The study provides scope for the development and use of many Multimedia programmes in the concerned discipline as well as other disciplines for the benefit of learners of different categories. Hence the multimedia programme can be used as an individualized instructional technique for the students of different categories in the science subjects as well as other subjects.

The present study reveals that the experiment group students who used multimedia programme performed significantly better than that of the control group students who did not use, which implies that the multimedia programme has tremendous impact upon the performance in human anatomy than the students learning through traditional method. This proves the effectiveness of the multimedia programme in human anatomy developed by the investigator. The present study reveals that the performance of the control and experimental group students in the post-test is significantly higher than the pre-test. But the performance of the experimental group students in the post-test is more significantly higher than the post-test performance of control group students. Thus, it proves the supremacy of the multimedia programme over traditional method.

❐

14

Task Oriented Language Teaching of English

Language is one of the most important forms of human behavior. The purpose of language is communication which means that language helps a person to formulate his thoughts and encode it for the benefit of others to decode it. Language is the words, their pronunciation, and the methods of combining them used and understood by a community. It is a form or manner of verbal expression. It is audible, articulate, meaningful sound as produced by the action of the vocal organs. It is a systematic means of communicating ideas or feelings by the use of conventionalized signs, sounds, gestures, or marks having understood meanings. It is language than anything else that distinguishes man from the rest of other creatures in world. Language is any formal system of gestures, signs, sounds, and symbols used or conceived as a means of communicating thought. Language is ultimately important because it is the primary means through which humans have the ability to communicate and interact with one another.

Language is the human ability to acquire and use complex systems of communication, and a language is any specific example of such a system. The scientific study of language is called linguistics. Another definition sees language as a formal system of signs governed by grammatical rules of combination to communicate meaning. This definition stresses that human languages can be described as closed structural systems consisting of rules that relate particular signs to particular meanings. Chomsky considers these rules to be an innate feature of the human mind and to constitute the rudiments of what language is. This learning process is referred to as first-language acquisition, since unlike many other kinds of learning, it requires no direct teaching or specialized study.

Language is obviously a vital tool. Not only is it a means of communicating thoughts and ideas, but it forges friendships, cultural ties, and economic relationships. Throughout history, many have reflected on the importance of language. For instance, the scholar Benjamin Whorf has noted that language shapes thoughts and emotions, determining one's perception of reality. John Stuart Mill said that "Language is the light of the mind."

NEED AND SIGNIFICANCE OF THE STUDY

Like speech, writing has been considered a powerful mode of communication. After all, one writes with the purpose of being understood. Unlike speech, writing is not always for the audience present and hence it demands clear and comprehensive message. While one speaks, he uses a variety of prosodic features such as pitch, loudness, speed, rhythm, pauses and so on that help us to get the feedback from listeners but this does not happen in case of writing where the context is created through the words alone and without the direct interaction between the writer and the reader.

The study, "Effectiveness of task based language teaching of English in enhancing the writing skill among VII standard students" is important. It helps to understand the effectiveness of task based language teaching of English in writing skill. It also helps to give solutions to enhancing the writing skill among VII standard students.

STATEMENT OF THE PROBLEM

Effectiveness of Task Oriented Language Teaching of English in Enhancing the Writing Skill among VII Standard Students

SCOPE OF THE STUDY

This study plays the role of model for further research. This study mainly focuses on VII standard students' effectiveness of task oriented language teaching of English in enhancing the writing skill. It also paves way for further research such as. It helps others to write a dissertation on effectiveness of task oriented language teaching of English in enhancing the writing skill of secondary students.

1. It helps others to write a dissertation on effectiveness of task oriented language teaching of English in enhancing the writing skill of higher level students.

2. It helps others to write a dissertation on effectiveness of task oriented language teaching of English in enhancing the writing skill of college level students.
3. It is a scope to write a dissertation on Effectiveness of task oriented language teaching of English in enhancing the speaking skill among VII standard students .
4. It is a scope to write a dissertation on Effectiveness of task oriented language teaching of English in enhancing the reading skill among VII standard students.
5. It is a scope to write a dissertation on Effectiveness of task oriented language teaching of English in enhancing the listening skill among VII standard students.

OBJECTIVES OF THE STUDY

1. To find out whether there is any significant difference between the pre-test mean scores of Control and Experimental groups students in writing.
2. To find out whether there is any significant difference between the pre-test and post-test mean scores of Control groups students in writing.
3. To find out whether there is any significant difference between the pre-test and post-test mean scores of Experimental groups students in writing
4. To find out whether there is any significant difference between the post-test mean scores of Control group and Experimental groups students in writing.
5. To find out whether there is any significant difference between the post-test mean scores of experimental groups students in writing between Male and Female.
6. To find out whether there is any significant difference between the post-test mean scores of experimental groups students in writing between Rural area and Urban area students.
7. To find out whether there is any significant difference between the post-test mean scores of experimental groups students in writing between Joint Family and Nuclear Family.
8. To find out whether there is any significant difference between the post-test mean scores of experimental groups students in writing between the students of Parent's Qualification Educated and Uneducated.
9. To find out whether there is any significant difference between the post-test mean scores of Experimental groups students in writing with regard to the parent's Occupation Government job and Private job.

HYPOTHESIS OF THE STUDY

1. There is no significant difference between the pre-test mean scores of Control and Experimental groups students in writing.
2. There is no significant difference between the pre-test and post-test mean scores of Control groups students in writing.
3. There is no significant difference between the pre-test and post-test mean scores of Experimental groups students in writing
4. There is no significant difference between the post-test mean scores of Control group and Experimental groups students in writing.
5. There is no significant difference between the post-test mean scores of Experimental groups students in writing with regard to the Male and Female.
6. There is no significant difference between the post-test mean scores of experimental group's students in writing with regard to the Rural area and Urban area students.
7. There is no significant difference between the post-test mean scores of experimental group's students in writing with regard to the Joint Family and Nuclear Family.
8. There is no significant difference between the post-test mean scores of experimental groups students in writing with regard to the Educated Qualification Educated and Uneducated.
9. To find out whether there is any significant difference between the post-test mean scores of Experimental groups students in writing with regard to the parent's Occupation Government job and private job.

LIMITATION OF THE STUDY

The limitations of the study are as follows,

1. This study confined to the high school students in Erode district.
2. The sample consist of forty students (20 control group and 20 experimental group)
3. The task based language teachings are designed to develop the writing skill of the student.
4. The experiment was conducted for a period of twenty working days (1 hour a day)
5. The achievement tests used in this study are to writing skill of the students.
6. The study confined to the task oriented language teaching of English only. It is not able to extend any other approaches.
7. The study restricted to seek enhancing writing skill only; it is not able to extent to other three skills like Reading, Speaking and Listening.

8. The study restricted to examine VII standard students only

RESEARCH DESIGN

Research design is the "blue print" of the study. The first chapter discusses the need and significance, scope of the study, objectives of the study, hypothesis of the study and limitation of the study.

STATEMENT OF THE PROBLEM

"Effectiveness of Task Oriented Language Teaching of English in Enhancing the Writing Skill among VII Standard Students".

LIMITATION OF THE STUDY

The limitations of the study are as follows,

1. This study confined to the high school students in the Erode district.
2. The sample consist of forty students (20 control group and 20 experimental group)
3. The task based language teachings are designed to develop the writing skill of the student.
4. The experiment was conducted for a period of twenty working days (1 hour a day)
5. The achievement tests used in this study are to writing skill of the students.
6. The study confined to the task based language teaching of English only. It is not able to extend any other approaches.
7. The study restricted to seek enhancing writing skill only; it is not able to extent to other three skills like Reading, Speaking and Listening.
8. The study restricted to examine VII standard students only

RESEARCH METHOD

Experimental method is the research method that used in this study. The Experimental design is the blue print of the procedures that enables the researcher to the hypothesis by reading valid conclusions about relationship between the independent and dependant variables. The researcher comes to an inference with the help of feedback of the students. The most common research methods are: literature searches, talking with people, focus groups, personal interviews, telephone surveys, mail surveys, email surveys, and internet surveys.

RESEARCH TOOL

A questionnaire is a research instrument consisting of a series of questions other prompts for the purpose of gathering information from respondents. Questions which enhance the writing skill are choosing as a research tool in this study. Questionnaires typically contain multiple choice questions, attitude scales, closed questions and open-ended questions. Researchers may even decide to administer the questionnaire in person which has the advantage of including people who have difficulties reading and writing. In this case, the participant may feel that he is taking part in an interview rather than completing a questionnaire as the researcher will be noting down the responses on his behalf.

SAMPLES OF THE STUDY

The sample was drawn from the VII standard of selected schools as follows, Alagappa Model School in Erode district, were assigned to two groups based on the marks scored by them in the achievement test in English conducted prior to the pre-test of the study. Then they were assigned to the experimental group 20 students and control group 20 students. Thus the sample of 20 VII standard students in a single group has been formed.

PILOT STUDY

Select the population of VII standard students in sample schools. The researcher select 40 students for experimentation from each schools and to construct the criterion referenced test and t evaluate of the criterion reference test and to conduct pre-test and to select the strategies for understanding Differential methods and to verify the applicability of the strategies by connecting experts and teachers and to implement the strategies among the select students and to conduct a post-test and analyzing the result.

VALIDITY OF THE TOOL

As the teaching methods, reading methods and the syllabus designing changes the validity of the tool. Hence, this tool valid up to one academic year.

RELIABILITY OF THE TOOL

This study has the tool of list of questionnaire which needs the answer from the student. As this study method originally conducted in selected schools, it has the reliability of its own. Experimental method is one of the highly reliable methods in the research study.

COLLECTING THE DATA

After the administration of try out and finalization of the research tool they were administration to both the groups of the sample population. The tools were administered the tools personally. It took few minutes to answer all the items in the inventory. Since the investigator administered the tool personally all the subjects had responded properly.

STATISTICAL TECHNIQUES USED

Statistical techniques used for analyzing the data are:

1. 't' test to find out the significance of difference between the attitude towards reading research journal among B.Ed students in the means of sex, college, area and so on
2. Graphical representation to show the comparison of variables with one another.

ANALYSING AND INTERPRETATION OF DATA

Hypothesis-1

S. No.	Type of Group	No. of Students	Mean	Standard Deviation	"t" Value	df	Level of Significant at 0.05
1	Control Group (pre test)	20	5.45	3.18	1.84	38	Not Significant
2	Experimental Group (pre test)	20	28.5	6.68			

There is no significant difference between the pre-test mean scores of control and experimental groups' students in writing.

Since the calculated t-value (1.84) in less than table value (2.02), it is that there is no significant difference between pre-test mean scores of control group and experimental group students in writing. Hence the Hypothesis formed by the investigator is accepted.

Hypothesis-2

There is no significant difference between the pre-test mean scores of Control and Experimental group's students in writing.

S. No.	Control group	No. of students	Mean	Standard Deviation	" t" Value	df	Level of Significance At 0.05
1	Pre - test	20	25.45	3.18	1.84	38	Not Significant
2	Post test	20	28.50	6.68			

Since the calculated t-value (1.84) in less than table value (2.02), it is that there is no Significant difference between pre-test and post test mean scores of control group students in writing. Hence the Hypothesis formed by the investigator is accepted.

Hypothesis-3

There is no significant difference between the pre-test and post test mean scores of experimental group students in writing.

S. No.	Experimental Group	No. of students	Mean	Standard Deviation	" t " Value	df	Level of Significance At 0.05
1	Pre – test	20	28.5	6.68	5.09	38	Significant
2	Post test	20	38.5	5.67			

Since the calculated t-value (5.09) in greater than table value (2.02), it is that there is significant difference between pre-test and post test mean scores of experimental group students in writing. Hence the Hypothesis formed by the investigator is rejected.

Hypothesis-4

There is no significant difference between the post-test mean scores of control and experimental group students in writing.

S. No.	Type of Group	No. of Students	Mean	Standard Deviation	"t" Value	df	Level of Significant at 0.05
1	Control Group	20	28.50	6.68	5.09	38	Significant
2	Experimental Group	20	38.5	5.67			

Since the calculated t-value (5.0965) in greater than table value (2.02), it is that there is significant difference between post- test mean scores of control group and experimental group students in writing. Hence the Hypothesis formed by the investigator is rejected.

Hypothesis-5

There is no significant difference between the post-test mean scores of experimental group students in writing between Male and Female.

S. No.	Gender	No. of Students	Mean	Standard Deviation	"t" Value	df	Level of Significant at 0.05
1	Male	6	40.5	3.81	1.26	18	Not Significant
2	Female	14	37.64	6.11			

Since the calculated t-value (1.26) in less than table value (2.10), it is inferred that there is no significant difference between post- tests mean scores of experimental group students in writing between Male and Female. Hence the Hypothesis formed by the investigator is accepted.

Hypothesis-6

There is no significant difference between the post-test mean scores of experimental group students in writing with regard to the rural area and urban area students.

S. No.	Type of Locality	No. of Students	Mean	Standard Deviation	"t" Value	df	Level of Significant at 0.05
1	Rural Area	17	38.29	6.84	0.42	18	Not Significant
2	Urban Area	3	40	4.02			

Since the calculated t-value (0.42) in less than table value (2.10), it is inferred that there is no Significant difference between post- test mean scores of experimental group students in writing with regard to the Rural area and Urban area students . . Hence the Hypothesis formed by the investigator is accepted.

Hypothesis-7

There is no significant difference between the post-test mean scores of experimental group students in writing with regard to Joint Family and Nuclear Family.

S. No.	Type of Family	No. of Students	Mean	Standard Deviation	"t" Value	df	Level of Significant
1	Nuclear Family	8	39.12	4.72	.03	18	Not Significance
2	Joint Family	12	38.41	5.43			

Since the calculated t-value (0.03) in smaller than table value (2.10), it is inferred that there is no Significant difference between post- test mean scores of experimental group students in writing with regard to Joint Family and Nuclear Family. Hence the Hypothesis formed by the investigator is accepted.

Hypothesis-8

There is no sigTask Oriented Language Teaching of English nificant difference between the post-test mean scores of experimental group students in writing with regard to their parent's Qualification Educated and Uneducated.

S. No	Parent's Qualification	No. of Students	Mean	Standard Deviation	"t" Value	df	Level of Significant at 0.05
1	Educated	18	8.55	5.74	0.01	18	Not Significant
2	Un Educated	2	38.50	3.50			

Since the calculated t-value (0.01) in less than table value (2.10),it is inferred that there is no Significant difference between post- test mean scores of experimental group students in writing with regard to parent's Qualification Educated and Uneducated. Hence the Hypothesis formed by the investigator is accepted.

Hypothesis-9

There is no significant difference between the post-test mean scores of experimental group students in writing with regard to their parent's Occupation Govt. job and Private job.

S. No.	Parent's Occupation	No. of Students	Mean	Standard Deviation	"t" Value	df	Level of Significant at 0.05
1	Government job	4	41	4.18	1.17	18	Not Significant
2	Private job	16	38	5.86			

Since the calculated t-value (1.17) in less than table value (2.10), it is inferred that there is no significant difference between post- tests mean scores of experimental group students in writing with regard to their parent's Govt. job and Private Job. Hence the Hypothesis formed by the investigator is accepted.

FINDINGS OF THE STUDY

In this study VII standard students are involved as a sample of students' Effectiveness of the Task Oriented Language Teaching of English in Enhancing the Writing Skill. After analyzing the achievement scores of the pre-test and post-test of the control group and experimental group, one could arrive at the following findings:

1. There is no significant difference between the pre-test mean scores of Control and Experimental groups students in writing.
2. There is no significant difference between the pre-test and post-test mean scores of Control groups students in writing.
3. There is significant difference between the pre-test and post-test mean scores of Experimental groups students in writing
4. There is significant difference between the post-test mean scores of Control group and Experimental groups students in writing.
5. There is no significant difference between the post-test mean scores of Experimental groups students in writing with regard to the Male and Female.
6. There is no significant difference between the post-test mean scores of experimental groups students in writing with regard to the Rural area and Urban area students.
7. There is no significant difference between the post-test mean scores of experimental groups students in writing with regard to the Joint family and nuclear family
8. There is no significant difference between the post-test mean scores of experimental groups students in writing with regard to the Educated Qualification Educated and Uneducated.
9. There is no significant difference between the post-test mean scores of Experimental groups students in writing with regard to the parent's Occupation Govt job and Private job.

SUGGESTION FOR THE STUDY

The study was limited to a sample of VII standard students in Erode District. Similar studies may be undertaken for the samples selected from different districts.

The same study may be conducted on a wide range of higher secondary schools in the district and also in different districts of Tamil Nadu.

The effectiveness of task based language may be studied through experiments with other language such as listening, speaking and reading.

A parallel study can be conducted to find out the effectiveness of task oriented language teaching of the VII students in learning the mother tongue.

A separate study can be undertaken to assess the effectiveness of task Oriented language teaching by using computer assisted instruction in learning the language skill in English language education. Attempt can be made to develop task based language teaching of English and other language at school level and there by the effectiveness of task based language teaching can be assessed.

A study can be made to assess the attitude of the VII standard students in the use of task based language teaching in developing the various skills in English.

RECOMMENDATION OF THE STUDY

1. This study plays the role of model for further research. This study mainly focuses on VII standard students' effectiveness of task oriented language teaching of English in enhancing the writing skill.
2. It also paves way for further research such as:"Effectiveness of task oriented language teaching of English in enhancing the writing skill among VII standard students" is a model for other thesis writing.
3. It helps others to write a dissertation on effectiveness of task oriented language teaching of English in enhancing the writing skill of secondary students.
4. It helps others to write a dissertation on effectiveness of task oriented language teaching of English in enhancing the writing skill of higher level students.
5. It helps others to write a dissertation on effectiveness of task oriented language teaching of English in enhancing the writing skill of college level students.
6. It is a scope to write a dissertation on Effectiveness of task oriented language teaching of English in enhancing the speaking skill among VII standard students

CONCLUSION

There are various ways of teaching and learning writing skill in English. Different linguists have advocated different methods and techniques to enhance the learning the writing skill at the VII standard students. Yet, the task based language teaching of English which is the recent method, is more effective than all other method of teaching writing skill at VII standard students level.

❐

15

English Grammar through Computer

Practical command of English means that Indian children should be able to read speak write and understand English. It is imperative for us to try to identify the challenges and seek their solutions in the field of English language teaching, particularly in respect of the rural area students English as a second language (ESL) as an optional. The objectives of the test have been determined on the basis of inter sine needs analysis. The text covers five English language skills namely Listening, Reading, writing, along with grammar and literary Appreciation. Teachers teach and help the learners to learn. The learning that takes place is assessed or evaluated not only for the learner's benefit but also for the teacher to evaluate his/her own work.

Education is the life long process of acquiring new knowledge and skin through formal and informal exposure of information ideas and experience technologies to adopt in teaching the concepts of the subjects in the school. There are many means by which effective instruction can be imparted in the classroom. The use of computer Assisted instruction in the schools is having computers. So use of technology enhances effect of a learning experience.

AIMS OF TEACHING ENGLISH IN INDIA

English is an important international language according to Thompson and Wyatt; there are four aims of teaching English to Indian Children. They are:

1. To understand simple, spoken English
2. To understand simple written English
3. To speak simple, correct and idiomatic English
4. To write simple, correct and idiomatic English.

Grammar resembles a vitamin in that ill effects may spring from a deficiency and an excessive close must be wasteful and may even be harmful. It is like a medicine not a form of diet". Whatever grammar is taught must be functional and help the students in improving their use of English. It launching grammar example is more important them the rules.

METHODS OF TEACHING GRAMMAR

1. The Traditional method
2. The informal method
3. The inductive - deductive method
4. Inductive process
5. Deductive process

TEACHING OF ENGLISH

The objectives of the test have been determined on the basis of inter sine needs analysis. The text covers five English language skills namely, Listening, Reading, writing, along with grammar and literary Appreciation. Speaking skill was deliberately excluded from the text due to the constraints against individual testing and recording. The tug of war between the "mentalistic" and "mechanistic" language theories like monitor, model, accuracy and fluency theory, semantic approach, structural approach, situational approach, communicative approach, interactive approach, error analysis, and contrastive analysis along with the age old grammar–translation method and direct method came into existence.

NEED FOR TEACHING ENGLISH GRAMMAR

The grammar is the means through which linguistic creativity is ultimately achieved and an inadequate knowledge of the grammar would lead to serious limitations on the creativity for communication. The Indian contexts in which English is used are taken into account. Thus the teaching of grammar means the effective presentation of language items in a systematic way in meaningful contexts.

STATEMENT OF THE PROBLEM

Statement of the problem is "Effect of teaching grammar through computer among XII standard students".

BACKGROUND OF THE PROBLEM

Learning through computer is more effective as compared to class room teaching. At present time, the teachers have a lack of basic computer knowledge so that the investigator decided to investigate to the English grammar teaching through computer under the topic "Effect of Teaching grammar through computer among XII std students".

OBJECTIVES

To find out the level of effect of teaching grammar through computer among XII standard students.

1. To find out the level of significant difference among boys and girls in Post-Test.
2. To find out the level of significant difference among rural and urban in Post-Test.
3. To find out the level of significant difference among hosteller and day scholar in Post-Test.

HYPOTHESIS

The following null hypothesis was formulated on the basis of the objectives framed.

1. There is no significant difference between boys and girls in Pre-Test.
2. There is no significant difference between rural and urban in Pre-Test.
3. There is no significant difference between hosteller and day scholar in Pre-Test.
4. There is no significant difference between hosteller and day scholar in Post-Test.

SCOPE OF THE STUDY

The topic is an effect of Teaching Grammar through computer among XII Std students. Since this is the Experimental Study. This study will be of great help for the educationists particularly for the teachers since the concept of education has been changing from time to time.

DELIMITATIONS

Broadly speaking, any study is impossible without delimitation. Research Studies in general will have delimitation due to many factors. This study too has some delimitation. It is the responsibility of the researcher to see that the study is conducted with maximum care in order to be reliable. The following delimitations were unavoidable in the present study. The present investigation is confined to the XII std student studying at Erode District in Tamil Nadu.

The study is confined only to a sample of 123students from Government schools located in rural area.

In this present study the investigator analyzed about the variables such as gender, Locality, Hosteller and day scholar students.

METHODOLOGY

The present study is an experimental research. Tool used for the study, Samples of the study, procedure, Pilot study, scoring methods, statistical measures used in the study etc., have been reported in detailed manner in this present study and ends with the Delimitations of the study.

DESIGN

Research design is a plan, a structure and a strategy of investigation conceived to obtain answers to various issues in research. The object of research design is to test the research hypotheses. The research design, therefore, is built in the principle of maximization of the results of study; minimization of variance. The present study belongs to Experimental Research. The Demographic variables used are Gender, Locality and stay at. The tool "ETGTC" was used in the study for 8th standard students in Government schools at Erode District for sample selection. Stratified Random sampling technique was followed in this study. Data were collected from 123 students and the statistical techniques Mean, S.D and 't' test were used.

SELECTION OF THE SUBJECT

The researcher selected Computer Assisted Instruction (CAI) as the technique for his study and the area selected was teaching English grammar.

SELECTION OF THE TOPIC

The grammar units were taken after consultation with language exports, educational scholars, programmers and senior teacher of English with rich experience at the secondary level. The topic selected is introduced as 'Idioms and Phrases'.

PILOT STUDY

Before administering the questionnaire to the actual sample, pilot study was conducted. The aim of pilot study not only to test and refine the tools of research but also to force the nature of analysis and processing that may be needed at a later stage, after a questionnaire was prepared. It was given a trial on small sample. This is necessary to know XII standard students whether they are meaningful and whether there is any ambiguity in thought or in the wording of questions.

BLUE PRINT OF THE ACHIEVEMENT TEST

The test paper, thus prepared, consisted of 40 items. The items found in the paper were of multiple choice types. The blue print of the question paper marks given below.

TABLE.15.1: Blue Print

Unit	Knowledge	Understanding	Application	Skill	Total
Idioms & phrases	15	13	12	0	40
	15	13	12	0	40

TABLE.15.2: Weight age of Objectives

Objectives	Marks	Percentage
Knowledge	15	37.5%
Understanding	13	32.5%
Application	12	30%
Skill	0	0
Total	**40**	**100%**

RESEARCH METHODS

The investigator followed Experimental method as this study aims of eliciting the opinions of the XII standard students on the effective learning by them in using computer.

TOOL USED FOR THE STUDY

1. Achievement test with multiple choice questions.
2. A questionnaire was prepared to get the information about grammar in XII std students.
3. Test method Pre-Test and Post-Test of 40 marks was conducted.

SAMPLE

A sample of 123 students studying in XII Std students for collecting the data–Experimental design was followed and purposive sampling technique was used to select the sample. The sample consisted of 123 students of 8th standard in Government School of Erode District. (71 Boys, 52 Girls and Rural 87, Urban 36, Students)

PROCEDURE

The questionnaire was prepared which included questions in XII std English Grammar given to the students during extra periods. The students wrote the truthful answers. Further the classification and analysis of the results was carried out.

PRE-TEST AND POST-TEST

The pre-test was carried out after regular teaching. After the conduct of the achievement test a Post-test was also conducted after an interval of one week. The same achievement test prepared for conducting the post-test was used as the post-test.

PERSONAL DATA SHEET

To know the background of the students, the investigator used separate personal data sheets along with the Developed Questionnaires. It asked for details of Gender, Locality and stay at students.

SCORING KEY

Achievement test had 40 questions. Correct answer cues one mark and wrong answer cues zero marks. So maximum score of the achievement test is 40 and minimum score the achievement test is zero of achievement in English grammar among XII standard students.

STATISTICAL MEASURES USED

After valued the achievement test, a master table was prepared by plotting the scores in different statistical measures such as Mean, Standard deviation and't'- test for analyze the significant Difference in the present study.

STATISTICAL ANALYSIS OF DATA AND INTERPRETATION

Statistical analysis of data enables a researcher to arrive at empirical findings about the problem taken for research. The purpose of present investigation is to study the Effect of Teaching Grammar through computer. The data of for the study were collected from the students by means of a questionnaire.

TABLE.15.3: Mean and Standard Deviation of Gain Score on English Grammar through Computer in Pre-Test and Post-Test

Test	N	Mean	SD
Pre Test	123	41.46	10.71
Post Test	123	53.81	40.27

The table 15.3 shows that, the mean and standard Deviation of the single group in Pre-Test are 41.46 and 10.71 respectively and the mean and standard deviation of the single group in post test are 53.81 and 40.27 respectively.

TABLE.15.4: Significant Difference between Boys and Girls in Pre-Test

Gender	N	Mean	SD	't' value	0.05 level
Boys	71	36.17	8.93	7.89 *	1.98
Girls	52	48.67	8.49		

* Significant

The above table 15.4 shows, the calculated 't' value (7.89) is greater than the table value of (1.98) at 0.05 level of significance. Hence the null hypothesis is rejected. Thus there is significant difference on the Boys and Girls in Pre-Test.

TABLE.15.5: Significant Difference between Boys and Girls in Post-Test

Gender	N	Mean	SD	't' value	0.05 level
Boys	71	51.45	13.28	2.167*	1.98
Girls	52	57.04	14.75		

* Significance

The above table 15.5 shows the calculated 't' value (2.167) is greater than the table value of 1.98 at 0.05 level of significance. Hence the null hypothesis is rejected. Thus there is significant difference on the Boys and Girls in Post-Test.

TABLE.15.6: Significant Difference between Rural and Urban in Post-Test

Locality	N	Mean	SD	't' value	0.05 level
Rural	87	55.82	14.95	2.86*	1.98
Urban	36	48.97	10.66		

* Significance

The above table 15.6 shows the calculated 't' value (2.86) is greater than the table value of 1.98 at 0.05 level of significance. Hence the null hypothesis is rejected. Thus there is no significant difference on the Rural and Urban students in Post-Test.

TABLE.15.7: Significant Difference between Hosteller and Day Scholar in Post- Test

Stay at	N	Mean	SD	't' value	0.05 level
Hosteller	31	46.39	7.66	4.77*	1.98
Day scholar	92	56.32	14.98		

* Significance

The above table 15.7 shows the calculated 't' value (4.77) is greater than the table value of 1.98 at significance. Hence the null hypothesis is rejected. Thus there is significant difference on the Hosteller and day scholar students in Post-Test.

MAJOR FINDINGS

There is significant difference between Boys and Girls in Pre-Test and Post-Test.

1. There is no significant difference between Rural and Urban in Pre-Test and Post-Test.
2. There is no significant difference between Hosteller and Day scholar in Pre-Test and Post-Test.

EDUCATIONAL IMPLICATION

1. Learning through computer is extended to all level of school.
2. The government must give in-service training to the teachers for teaching through computer.
3. Various educational CD's can be implemented in schools to improve the quality of education with audio visual effect. Computer based tutorials (CBT) and web based tutorials (WBT) can also be used to get more ideas on subject and to refer websites regarding latest technologies. Online education test can also be implemented to check student's objective type talents with immediate valuation and answers for student's references.

RECOMMENDATIONS FOR FURTHER STUDY

The findings of the study the investigator observed the following areas recommended for the further research.

1. The same research study may be carried out in different Areas in Tamil Nadu.
2. CAI may be used for those with poor study habits as the study has shown a favourable result.
3. CAI may be used for underachievers to benefit more by this technique of teaching.
4. CAI may be incorporated into the regular curriculum to enable learners benefit more.
5. CAI soft-wares on other topics in Grammar can be developed and experimented for their effective.

CONCLUSION

The present investigation showed that the CAI technique was a versatile tool for a grammar teacher in importing competency in foreign language even to the rural area pupils. The study also revealed interesting quantitative improvement in learning. The 't' test used to analysis the hypothesis led to the conclusion that there is no significant difference between XII standard students in rural and urban Locality in their Post-test.

❐

16

ICT Competency and Performance

The main focus of the present study is to assess the ICT Competency and performance competency of distance mode B.Ed. students of Madurai Kamaraj University. The distance mode B.Ed. students are the population of the study. 200 distance mode B.Ed. students of Madurai Kamaraj University is the sample for the study, of which 24 % were male and 76 % were females. To measure the level of ICT Competency and Performance Competency, ICT Com **TABLE.15.1:** petency scale and Teaching Competency Scale were used respectively. Computer technology has become a fundamental part of education in India and will likely be more so in the future. Unfortunately, Information Technology innovation initiatives in Tamilnadu are still characterized by a lack of research into possible options for policies and strategies. A key concern of this study was to assess the ICT competency and performance competency of distance mode B.Ed. students.

For longer than a decade, one of the key challenges to the professional development of teachers has been to help the integration of ICT into education. Rationales for an increase in ICT use are based on the assumption that the future will be dominated by knowledge-intensive professions, and employees need, therefore, sophisticated information processing skills and versatile ICT tools. Therefore, ICT in teaching is considered important in the facilitation of equal opportunities for citizens to study and develop their own knowledge to ensure the success and welfare of the nation. However, the implementation of ICT innovations into school practice is difficult. Thus, it is important to initiate research and development in this field in order to discover what contributes to successful adoption of these innovations.

Teachers feel a lack of up-to-date computer equipment and software. One interpretation could be that computers tend to be located in computer labs, not in ordinary classrooms or labs. The second interpretation could be that teachers have had insufficient time to learn about the use of ICT and its applications in classrooms consequently, they have no confidence in ICT use. Research suggests that in any topic, including the benefits of ICT in education, it has been difficult to change teachers' beliefs about teaching and learning. Teachers' beliefs have remained stable, and their resistance to change is one of the main explanations behind the diminutive adoption of ICT in education found evidence that teachers' beliefs regarding the usefulness of ICT in education appear to be surprisingly consistent across nations and cultures.

OBJECTIVES OF THE STUDY

1. To find out the level of ICT competency of distance mode B.Ed. students with reference to certain background variables.
2. To find out the level of performance competency of distance mode B.Ed. students with reference to certain background variables.
3. To find out the significant difference in ICT competency of distance mode B.Ed. students with reference to certain background variables.
4. To find out the significant difference in performance competency of distance mode B.Ed. students with reference to certain background variables.
5. To find out the significant correlation between performance competency and ICT competency of distance mode B.Ed. students with reference to certain background variables.

HYPOTHESES OF THE STUDY

1. The ICT competency level of distance mode B.Ed. students with reference to certain background variable is average.
2. The performance competency level of distance mode B.Ed. students with reference to certain background variable is average.
3. There is no significant difference in ICT competency of distance mode B.Ed. students with reference to certain background variables.
4. There is no significant difference in performance competency of distance mode B.Ed. students with reference to certain background variables.

5. There is no significant correlation between performance competency and ICT competency of distance mode B.Ed. students with reference to certain background variables.

SAMPLE

A total sample of 200 teachers was taken up for the present study. It consists of teachers who are studying B.Ed. degree in distance mode of Directorate of Distance Education, Madurai Kamaraj University, Madurai. Stratified random sampling technique is used for the selection of sample. The stratification has been done on the basis of gender, marital status and locality of the school.

TOOLS

The investigators developed and validated the tools to measure ICT Competency and Performance Competency.

1. **ICT Competency Scale:** This scale consists of 5 dimensions namely basic computer operation skill, word processing, spreadsheet, power point presentation and internet knowledge. The items have five responses namely not aware, little experience, occasional usage, regular user, confident and can explain. After the pilot study, 6 items had to be deleted from the draft and 40 items were selected for the final tool.
2. **Performance Competency Scale:** This scale consists of six major dimensions namely preparation, presentation, teacher behaviour, generalization, student-teacher interaction and classroom management with a 5 point rating scale as Unsatisfactory, Satisfactory, Good, Very Good, Excellent. The scoring was done by adding the ratings on the Teaching Competency Scale against all the items given by the investigator after observation of the teaching process by the teacher educators.

DATA COLLECTION

For the data collection, the investigators visited Nagercoil and Madurai B.Ed. study centre of DDE, Madurai Kamaraj University and collected the data from the respondents. The data were collected with the help of the developed tools. The questionnaire was distributed to the students and the investigators assured that their responses would be kept confidential and used for research purpose only. Clear instruction was given to enable them to give their response meaningfully. The gathered responses were scored.

STATISTICAL ANALYSIS

The data collected were analyzed by using descriptive and inferential analysis. The statistical techniques Percentage Analysis, 't' Test, and Pearson's Product-Moment Correlation were employed for the analysis and interpretation of the data.

ANALYSIS OF THE DATA

TABLE.16.1: The ICT Competency level of Distance Mode B.Ed. Students with Reference to Certain Background Variables

Background Variables	Category	Low		Average		High	
		No.	%	No.	%	No.	%
Gender	Male	11	23.9	26	56.5	9	19.6
	Female	30	19.5	101	65.6	23	14.9
Marital Status	Married	30	20.5	92	63.0	24	16.4
	Unmarried	10	18.5	36	66.7	8	14.8
Locality of School	Rural	20	21.1	60	63.2	15	15.8
	Urban	20	19.0	70	66.7	15	14.3

As far as ICT competency is concerned the average level of distance mode B.Ed. students is more than 50 percentages. So we can say that most of distance mode B.Ed. students are having average level of ICT competency. This may be due to the fact that the teachers are being provided with in-service trainings on educational technology and its innovations.

TABLE.16.2: The Performance Competency level of Distance Mode B.Ed. Students with Reference to Certain Background Variables.

Background Variables	Category	Low		Average		High	
		No.	%	No.	%	No.	%
Gender	Male	7	15.2	30	65.2	9	19.6
	Female	24	15.6	106	68.8	24	15.6
Marital Status	Married	23	15.8	101	69.2	22	15.1
	Unmarried	7	13.0	39	72.2	8	14.8
Locality of School	Rural	19	20.0	61	64.2	15	15.8
	Urban	15	14.3	73	69.5	17	16.2

As far as performance competency is concerned the average level of distance mode B.Ed. students is more than 50 percentages. So we can say that most of the distance mode B.Ed. students are having average level of performance competency. This may be the impact of B.Ed. training programme of Madurai Kamaraj University.

HYPOTHESIS TESTING

Hypothesis-1

There is no significant difference in the ICT Competency of distance mode B.Ed. students with reference to certain background variables.

TABLE.16.3: Difference in the ICT Competency of the Distance mode B.Ed. Students with Reference to Certain Background Variables

Background variables	Category	Count	Mean	SD	t-value	Remark
Gender	Male	46	51.5	10.4	1.54	NS
	Female	154	48.8	9.7		
Marital Status	Married	146	50.2	10.4	1.90	NS
	Unmarried	54	47.5	8.3		
Locality of School	Rural	95	50.2	10.3	1.05	NS
	Urban	105	48.7	9.6		

Hypothesis-2

There is no significant difference in the performance competency of distance mode B.Ed. students with reference to certain background variables.

TABLE.16.4: Difference in the Performance Competency of the Distance Mode B.Ed. Students with Reference to Certain Background Variables

Background variables	Category	Count	Mean	SD	t-value	Remark
Gender	Male	46	53.4	8.5	2.24	S
	Female	154	50.1	9.7		
Marital Status	Married	146	50.9	9.4	0.06	NS
	Unmarried	54	50.8	10.2		
Locality of School	Rural	95	52.9	9.6	2.83	S
	Urban	105	49.1	9.2		

Hypothesis-3

There is no significant relationship between Performance competency and ICT competency of distance mode B.Ed. students with reference to certain background variables.

TABLE.16.5: Relationship between Performance Competency and ICT Competency of Distance Mode B.Ed. Students with Reference to Certain Background Variables

Background Variables	Category	N	Table Value	γ	Remark
Gender	Male	46	0.28	0.124	NS
	Female	154	0.16	0.076	NS
Marital Status	Married	146	0.16	0.152	NS
	Unmarried	54	0.27	0.053	NS
Locality of the school	Rural	95	0.21	0.135	NS
	Urban	105	0.20	0.042	NS

FINDINGS OF THE STUDY

1. ICT Competency and Performance Competency of distance mode B.Ed. students are found to be average.
2. There is no significant difference in the ICT Competency of the distance mode B.Ed. students with reference to their gender, marital status and locality of the school.
3. There is no significant difference in the Performance Competency of the distance mode B.Ed. students with reference to their marital status, whereas there is significant difference with reference to their gender and locality of the school.
4. There is no significant relationship between ICT competency and performance competency of distance mode B.Ed. students with reference to their gender, marital status and locality of the school.

CONCLUSION

Rapid changes in technology will ensure that ICT will proliferate in the classroom. It is predicted that there will be many benefits for both the learner and the teacher, including the promotion of shared working space and resources, better access to information, the promotion of collaborative learning and radical new ways of teaching and learning. ICT will also require a modification of the role of the teacher, who in addition to classroom teaching will have other skills and responsibilities. Many will become specialists in the use of distributed learning techniques, the design and development of shared working spaces and resources, and virtual guides for students who use electronic media. Ultimately, the use of ICT will enhance the learning experiences for children, helping them to think and communicate creatively. ICT will also prepare our children for successful lives and careers in an increasingly technological world.

❐

17

E-Learning in Class-Romm

The modern Information and Communication technologies are technological tools and resources used to communicate, and to create, disseminate, store and manage information. ICT enables self-paced learning to help all students to achieve high academic standards. It also helps to provide immediate feedback, enhancing active participation in the learning process, sharing ideas and information. Hence investigator sorted out the utilization of e-learning which is one of the resources of ICT's in Classroom Instruction which has become more result-oriented in improving the teaching learning process. Educational Technology is the communication process resulting from the application of scientific methods to the behavioural science of teaching and learning. E-Learning is an environment in which the lessons, and lecture notes are deployed on CD's or Web servers. A complete Learning Management System (LMS) helps the learners in the process. E-Learning is considered a more effective way of teaching to a large group of students, thereby providing consistency in educational quality. e -Learning is considered a more effective way of teaching to a large group of students, thereby providing consistency in educational quality.

The root meaning of education is given as bringing up or leading out or making manifest the inherent potentialities in a pupil. Education refers to any act or experience that has a formative effect on the personality of an individual.

Education in broad terms means, "The life-long process of acquiring new knowledge and skills through both formal and informal exposure to information, ideas and experiences". Education in narrow terms means, "Systematic planned instruction that takes place in school". Education has a very important role to play in the present set up of world.

ELECTRONIC LEARNING -E- LEARNING CONCEPTS

One of the main resources of Educational Technology is e-learning. The concepts of e-learning features are discussed elaborately below. E-Learning is defined as a learning environment supported by continuously evolving, collaborative processes focused on individual and organizational performance. The "e" in e-learning stands for Evolving or everywhere or enhanced or extended.

TYPES OF E-LEARNING

The following are few of the most common types of e – Learning,

1. Technology -Based Learning (TBL)
2. Web- Based Training (WBT)
3. Computer- Based Training (CBT)
4. Synchronous e-learning
5. Asynchronous e-learning
6. Role of teachers in e-Learning

A shift form teacher-centered instruction to learner-centered instruction is needed to enable students to acquire the new dimension knowledge and skills. This new environment also involves a change in the roles of both teachers and students. Therefore Teacher should be made aware of various tools and advantages of on-line teaching in order to bring about great changes in the field of education in the country at large. The creation of virtual classrooms- i.e. classrooms in the cyber space.

1. Provision of Web-based learning materials.
2. Communication through e-mail and electronic discussion groups such as mailing lists and news groups.

Need for the study

One of the main tasks of education in a modern society is to keep pace with the advancement of Technology in acquiring the related information from the reliable e-Resources. The rapid development of information and communication technologies during the past two decades has had many points of contact with education and training. The development of technology is placing new demands on expertise and it is also leading to the increasing use of information technology in teaching and learning.

The Attitude on e-Learning in Classroom Instruction is important factor among B.Ed. Students in order to implement the usage of it in a productive way. Therefore the present study attempts to assess the Attitude on e-Learning in Classroom Instruction among the B.Ed. Students at the colleges of Education.

Statement of the Problem

Technology in education is an unavoidable element in present age. In this developing state, the preparation and presentation of the content by the Teachers should have an expertise's skills towards the reach ability of students especially in the Classroom situation. The Investigator identified most common utilization of e-learning resources in the Classroom Instruction by the Teacher-Educators at colleges of education.

This experience will help them to integrate e-Learning in Classroom Instruction when they are becoming Teachers in the schools. In this backdrop, the present study attempts to find out the "Attitude on e-learning in Classroom Instruction among B.Ed. Trainees in Karur District, Tamil Nadu".

Objectives of the Study

The Major objective of the study is to find out the Attitude on e-Learning in Classroom Instruction among the B.Ed. Students at Colleges of Education. The Specific objectives of the study are

1. To measure the level of different component of e-Learning such as Multimedia, WEB, Video Conferencing and CCTV towards the Attitude by the B.Ed. Students in Classroom Instruction at Colleges of Education.
2. o measure the priority pattern of e-Learning Attitude for the Classroom Instruction in the Colleges of Education.
3. To measure the influence of Demographic variables such as gender, age, parent's qualification and occupation with respect to the Attitude on e-Learning in Classroom Instruction.
4. (o measure the level of Attitude by the B.Ed. Students with respect to the different types of Management Institutions.

HYPOTHESIS OF THE STUDY

1. There is no significant difference in mean values of level of Attitude with respect to the e-learning in Classroom Instruction.
2. There is no significant difference in mean values on the influence of Demographic variables such as gender, age, parent's qualification and occupation with respect to the Attitude on e-Learning in Class-room Instruction
3. There is no significant difference in mean values of Attitude on e-Learning in Classroom Instruction with respect to the B.Ed. Students in their subject.

METHODOLOGY OF THE STUDY

As the present study is descriptive by nature, a Normative Survey technique was adopted. As many as 203 B.Ed. Students from 3 colleges were chosen as sample using simple random sampling technique. A questionnaire, aimed at assessing the B.Ed. Student's Attitude on e-Learning in Classroom Instruction was developed by the investigator himself for the purpose of collecting and interpreting data. The collected data were subjected to "t" and percentage analysis.

SCOPE OF THE STUDY

The investigator attempted to know the attitude of B.Ed. Students towards e-Learning in Classroom Instruction. This study will be of great help for the educationists to adopt to integrate e-Learning features which is one of the main resources of Information and Communication Technologies (ICT) in Classroom Instruction.

LIMITATION OF THE STUDY

Though e-Learning is a vast subject the investigator restricted himself only to limited area of his study. The investigation is only on Attitude on e-Learning in Classroom Instruction among B.Ed. Students which is restricted to 3 Colleges which includes 3 Self-Aided colleges only. Also other various resources of Information Communication Technology which can be utilized in the Classroom Instruction cannot be accessed due to time constraints and cost-factors.

ANALOGY OF THE STUDIES

All the reviewed studies were related to E-learning awareness and attitude towards the teaching-learning Process. Mean, Standard Deviation, 't' test and Percentage analysis were the Statistical Technique followed in the majority of the studies. Other Statistical Techniques used in some of the studies were ANOVA, ANCOVA, Correlation Co-efficient, Chi-square.

The findings of the various studies conducted in India revealed that Educational Technology such as the Effect of E-learning, Multimedia Approach and Computer Aided Instruction showed positive effect. From the analysis of studies conducted Abroad, the results of all the studies were in support of learning through Computer Assisted Instruction, Computer Mediated Instruction and Multimedia Instruction and so on.

METHODOLOGY OF THE STUDY

After selecting the problem, framing the objectives and reviewing the related literature, the next important step in research is to explain the details of the various steps followed in the research design. Studyss I and II were devoted to presenting the significance of the problem under investigation and for reviewing the related literature. In this studys, the research procedure adopted for the study undertaken is described in detail.

Methodology of the Present Study

The method of research adopted for this study is Survey method, and the present study which aims to assess the Attitude on e-learning in Classroom Instruction among B.Ed. Students.

Statement of the Problem

As a first step towards widespread popularization and practice of e-Learning, it becomes essential to find out the level of the B.Ed. Students Attitude on e-Learning in Classroom Instruction. Hence, the problem of the present study is stated as "Attitude on e-Learning in Classroom Instruction among the B.Ed. Students at Colleges of Education".

SELECTION OF THE POPULATION AND SAMPLE FOR THE STUDY

The population was entirely covered with regard to all the colleges in the karur district. From that 3 Colleges from Self-Aided were selected as Sample for the present study.

The present descriptive part of the research adopts the survey techniques for data collection. Questionnaire was the tool used to collect the data for this descriptive study.

STAGES IN THE CONSTRUCTION OF TOOL

Establishing Reliability and Validity

"Reliability and Validity are tools of an essentially positivist epistemology" Walting as cited in Winter (2000).

Reliability is a concept used for testing or evaluating quantitative research. This idea is most often used in all kinds of research.

The face validity of the present tool was established by the fact that the test was constructed by methods suggested and endorsed by eminent people and experienced teachers in the field. The content validity was also established since an analysis was the first make of the skill itself and decisions were made on what dimensions of the skills need to be tested, and in what proportions. As the analysis and the resultant tests accord with the views of recognized authorities in the skills area, the tests can be said to have content validity.

Collection of Data

The e-Learning Attitude Questionnaire developed for the purpose of collecting data for the present study was administered to as many as 203 B.Ed. Students randomly selected from 3 Self-Aided colleges.

STATISTICAL TECHNIQUES USED IN THE STUDY

As the present study is descriptive in nature, the data collected through the questionnaire were subjected to descriptive statistical analysis. To find out solutions to the problems Mean, Standard Deviation and "t" test were used to analyze the Significant Difference between the Mean scores of the Attitude on e-Learning in Classroom Instruction with respect to the B.Ed. students in the Colleges of Education. The Percentage Analysis was used to find out the priority pattern of the various components of e-Learning perspectives towards the attitude among the B.Ed. students.

ANALYSIS AND INTERPRETATION OF DATA

Processing and analysis of information are the major operations of this studys. The information from different colleges obtained from the survey is presented. The data gathered through the Questionnaire was subjected to quantitative analysis, i.e. ., percentage analysis and "t" test.

STATISTICAL ANALYSIS USED FOR THE PRESENT STUDY

The data obtained from the sample through the administration of the developed tool have been subjected to descriptive analysis.

DESCRIPTIVE ANALYSIS

It involves the measures of central tendency and measures of variability. These two are useful to study the nature of distribution of any variable.

Differential Analysis

In the present investigation't' values were calculated to test the significant difference between the mean scores of sub variables.

Responses of the B.Ed. Students were converted into scores. The following statistical techniques were followed,

1. Percentage
2. Mean
3. Standard Deviation
4. "t" Test

The analysis of data is presented in the form of tables below along with the discussions.

HYPOTHESIS TESTING

Hypothesis formulated in this study were tested on the basis of results obtained through analysis of the data using the statistical procedure and the level of significance.

The following is the hypothesis framed for this study

1. There is no significant difference in mean values of level of Attitude with respect to the e-learning in Classroom Instruction.
2. There is no significant difference in mean values on the influence of Demographic variables such as gender, age, parent's qualification and occupation with respect to the Attitude on e-Learning in Class-room Instruction
3. There is no significant difference in mean values of Attitude on e-Learning in Classroom Instruction with respect to the B.Ed. Students in their subject.

ANALYSIS OF DATA AND INTERPRETATION

Measuring the Level of B.Ed. Students attitude towards e-learning in Class-room Instruction.

TABLE.17.1: B.Ed. Students' Attitude Towards E-learning in Class-Room Instruction

N	Minimum %	Maximum %	Mean	SD
203	50	200	157.89	13.48

Table 17.1 shows the mean and standard deviation towards Attitude on e-Learning in Classroom Instruction among the B.Ed. Students at Colleges of Education. The mean attitude towards e-Learning in Classroom Instruction is 157.89. The attitude towards e-Learning in Classroom Instruction score varies from 50 to 200. The percentage of attitude on e-Learning in Classroom Instruction among the B.Ed. Students is 78.94%. Since the percentage score is greater than 50%, the hypothesis "Attitude on e-Learning in Classroom Instruction among the B.Ed. Students at Colleges of Education" is accepted.

To Measure the influence of Demographic variables such as gender, age, parent's qualification and occupation with respect to the Attitude on e-Learning in Class-room Instruction.

TABLE.17.2: Mean, Standard Deviation and 't' Value of B.Ed. Students Attitude towards E-learning in Class-room Instruction with Respect to their Age.

Age	N	Mean	S.D.	't'	Level of Significance at 0.01 Level
Below 25	176	158.28	13.314	1.0076	Significant
25-35	27	155.29	14.51		

From the Table 17.2 indicates that the calculated 't' value 1.0076 is less than the table value 1.96 for df = 201 at 0.01 level of significance. Hence the null hypothesis, "There is no significant difference between the mean attitude of B.Ed. students towards e-learning in class-room instruction with respect to Age" is accepted. It is concluded that the B.Ed. students below 25 years and 25-35 years have equal attitude towards e-learning in class-room instruction. It is good to note that B.Ed. Students of all ages have attitude towards e-Learning.

To measure significance of mean scores of B.Ed. students attitude towards e-learning in Class-room Instruction with respect to their Gender.

TABLE.17.3: Gender wise M, S.D. and "t" value of B.Ed. Students Attitude towards E-learning in Classroom Instruction

Gender	N	Mean	S.D.	't'	Level of Significance at 0.01 Level
Male	57	157.77	14.3	0.0777	Significant
Female	146	157.94	13.196		

The above table indicates that the calculated 't' value 0.0777 is less than the table value 1.96 for df = 201 at 0.01 level of significance. Hence the null hypothesis namely "There is no significant difference between the mean scores of the attitude of B.Ed. students towards e-learning in class-room instruction with respect to Gender" hence the hypothesis is accepted. It is concluded that the B.Ed. students of male and the B.Ed. students of female have equal attitude towards e-learning in class-room instruction.

To measure significance of mean scores of B.Ed. students attitude towards e-learning in Class-room Instruction with respect to their Locality of Residence

TABLE.17.4: Locality of Residence -wise M, S.D. and "t" value of B.Ed. Students Attitude Towards E-learning in Classroom Instruction

Residence	N	Mean	S.D.	't'	Level of Significance at 0.01 Level
Rural	159	157.949	13.226	0.1108	Significant
Urban	44	157.68	14.518		

Table 17.4 indicates that the calculated 't' value 0.1108 is more than the table value 1.96 for df = 201 at 0.01 level of significance. Hence mean scores of the B.Ed. students attitude towards e-learning with respect to the locality of residence is significant and hence the null hypothesis is accepted. It is inferred that B.Ed. students belonging to Urban area and B.Ed students of Rural area have equal attitude towards e-learning in class-room instruction.

To measure the level of significance of the mean scores B.Ed. students attitude towards e-learning in Class-room Instruction with respect to their Academic Qualification.

TABLE.17.5: The mean, Standard Deviation and 't' Value of B.Ed. Students Attitude towards E-learning in Class-room Instruction with Respect to their Academic Qualification

Academic Qualification	N	Mean	S.D.	't'	Level of Significance at 0.01 Level
U.G.	164	157.689	13.565	0.4443	Significant
P.G.	39	158.743	13.254		

Table 17.5 indicates that the calculated 't' value 0.4443 is more than the table value 1.96 for df = 201 at 0.01 level of significance. Hence mean scores of the B.Ed. students attitude towards e-learning with respect to Academic qualification is significant and hence the null hypothesis is accepted. It is inferred that the Academic qualification of P.G. students and U.G. students have same attitude towards e-learning in Classroom Instruction.

SUMMARY OF FINDINGS, CONCLUSIONS, SUGGESTIONS AND RECOMMENDATIONS

This study's recalls the statement of the problem, need for the study, objectives, methodology of the study and sums up the findings and conclusions from the survey and also suggestions and recommendations.

MAJOR FINDINGS OF THE STUDY

The major findings which have emerged from the study are as follows:

1. The percentage level of attitude on e-Learning in Classroom Instruction among the B.Ed. Students is 78.94%. The study reveals that the B.Ed. Students have attitude on e-learning in Classroom Instruction with higher percentage factor.
2. In measuring the influence of Demographic variables such as gender, age, Parent's qualification and occupation, the study reveals that there was no significant difference between the mean scores of the B.Ed. students attitude on e-learning in classroom instruction of the ages below and 25-35 years.
3. It was found out there is no significant difference between the mean scores of the attitude of B.Ed. students towards e-learning in classroom instruction with respect to Gender.

EDUCATIONAL IMPLICATIONS OF THE STUDY

The study revealed that the attitude on e-Learning in Classroom Instruction among the B.Ed. students having 78.94%. It is a higher factor, which implies that the B.Ed. students have higher attitude towards e-Learning in their classroom instruction. On another aspect, it is good to note that the B.Ed. students of all ages having the attitude on e-learning in classroom instruction as there was not much difference between the students of ages below25 and 25-35 years. In measuring the influence of Demographic variables such as locality of Residence, it implies that the B.Ed. students belonging to Urban area and Rural area were same. In the case of discipline of their subject both had same attitude. There is no significant difference between the mean scores of attitude on e-learning towards Parent's Qualification and their occupation. It is clear to note that the students are not dependent towards their Parent's factor. In the case of Academic Qualification P.G. students and U.G. students have same attitude.

RECOMMENDATIONS OF THE PRESENT STUDY

1. The attitude on e-Learning can be used to enhance both the theoretical knowledge and practical knowledge.
2. The attitude on e-Learning is found to be more effective in Classroom Instruction since simulation, 3D images, experiments, dissections, phenomena etc can be presented effectively.
3. Teachers and Professors should be trained to produce e-Learning material at various levels. In-service training and orientation courses can be provided.
4. Since e-Learning is a self instructional method it encourages active participation and able to cater all needs of the students with full satisfaction. It is a motivating factor in their learning process.
5. The attitude on e-Learning perspectives among B.Ed. students is needed to improve. As they are future teachers they should be well-versed with concepts of e-Learning and have the ability to utilize them in their teaching.

SUGGESTIONS FOR FURTHER RESEARCH STUDY

1. As the study is limited to study the attitude on e-Learning in Classroom Instruction among the B.Ed. students, it can be enhanced to find out the effectiveness of e-learning material and other e-Resources.
2. The study can be also conducted for the students of other Professional colleges such as Engineering, Medical, Management and Agriculture.
3. Since e-Learning is the emerging field of Instructional technology, there is a wide horizon of possibilities for further researchers in this area of study.
4. The study also suggests carrying out research in terms of level of utilization of e-Learning components in the Classroom Instruction among the B.Ed., M.Ed., M.Phil. Students in the colleges of education.

CONCLUSION

A notable feature is that in the extensive literature reviewed in the present study, there has been no recorded evidence of any research work having been carried out on Attitude on e-Learning in Classroom Instruction among the B.Ed. Students at Colleges of Education. It is in this context that the present study becomes important and essential as endorsed by the specific concerns of earlier researchers both in its aims of the study and its procedures. The research design of the present study included the selection of problem, selection of sample, construction of appropriate tool, administration of the tool for collection of data and analysis and interpretation of data. The collected data were subjected to appropriate statistical analysis as shown in this study. It is inferred that the B.Ed. Students have attitude on e-learning in Classroom Instruction with the lesser percentage. The present study is the first of its kind with its specific reference to Attitude on E-learning in Classroom Instruction towards B.Ed. Students. The findings of the study would be of immense use to the Teacher-Educators. Only on ethical teacher can create an efficient student. In the training period of the B.Ed. Students itself, it is important to impart the need and value of Attitude on e-learning and its various applications. They have to possess awareness, knowledge and skills with regard to e-Learning.

❐

18

Need and Significance of Multimedia

Educational Technology consists of all Materials. Media and Methodology which are used for optimization of learning. It comprises teaching aids like projected aids and non projected aids, media and micro teaching, programmed learning, Team teaching etc., as modern methods of technology and learning processes. In the modern age, Education is regarded as an essential expenditure and productive investment. Modernization is generally regarded as a process of change, change of traditional society into a society based on science and technology. Education is learning and learning is life. Learning, living and working go together. Education is not only lifelong but also life wide. Modern technologies have great potential to enhance the learning of students and increase their productivity. With the advancement of technologies such as web-based learning, on-line instruction, e-learning, etc, it is the right time for the teachers to get techno-pedagogical skills. The use of information and communication technologies in education has brought tremendous changes. The conventional chalk and talk method is out of date. Technology Enabled Learning (TEL) is not unlike any other form of education - and it is widely accepted that Technology Enabled Learning (TEL) can be as rich and as valuable as the classroom experience or even more so.

Science and technology have always been instrumental in bringing efficiency and improvement in the process and products of the human works. It has provided valuable help in improving the task of the teacher, smoothening the process of teaching-learning and enriching the goals of education. Educational Technology consists of all Materials. Media and Methodology which are used for optimization of learning. It comprises teaching aids like projected aids and non projected aids, media and micro teaching, programmed learning, Team teaching etc., as modern methods of technology and learning processes. It is essentially intended to help improving the quality of education.

CONCEPT OF TECHNOLOGY ENABLED LEARNING (TEL)

Technology Enabled Learning (TEL) is an umbrella term that describes learning done on a computer, usually connected to a network, giving us the opportunity to learn almost anytime, anywhere. With its unique features Technology Enabled Learning (TEL) is an experience that leads to comprehension and mastery of new skills and knowledge, just like its traditional counterpart.

EDUCATIONAL RADIOS

Gyan Vani

Gyan Vani is not only for the conventional educational system but also a main tool in making available the dream of education for all come true. Gyan Vani's main intention is to take education to the doorsteps of the people.

Community Radio

India's first community based radio Anna Community Radio launched by Anna University in 2004. The primary social objective of Anna Community Radio is to create awareness about health care, education, female literacy, self-employment and environment preservation in the minds of the local communities residing within a radius of approximately 15 Kms.

EDUCATIONAL TELEVISION

Television as the most powerful medium of communication has revolutionized lifestyles of many people in the world. It has remarkable versatility in treatment of themes and outstanding impact on the various aspects of modern life. It can reach an enormous cross-section of population with simultaneous presentations. It combines all kinds of audio-visual aids and equipment.

TELEVISION AND HIGHER EDUCATION

The Verghese Committee (1978) strongly recommended granting broadcast franchises to educational intuitions. This would empower national institutions of higher learning to use low-power radio or television transmission solely for the propagation of quality education to large masses of students and others.

The UGC Higher Education Project launched in August 1984, serves this purpose. Known as Countrywide Classroom. And co-ordinate by the Consortium for Educational Communication (CEC), New Delhi, its ETV programmes is beamed across the country every weekday-morning and afternoon. According to a 1993ADMAR study, the UGC Programmes have a viewer ship of over 19 million. Of these, 12 million watch the programmes at least once a week, and around seven million are regular viewers, watching two-to-five transmissions per week, though only 45% of the regular viewers are students.

STATEMENT OF THE PROBLEM

Only through the teachers, that the students and parents become aware of Technology Enabled Learning (TEL) and develop a favorable attitude towards the same. The present study has been taken up to find out the level of the Salem district Higher Education Teacher's attitude towards Technology Enabled Learning (TEL).

OBJECTIVES OF THE STUDY

The objectives of the study are

1. To find out the level of the Salem District Higher Education Teachers Attitude towards Technology Enabled Learning (TEL).
2. To compare the Male and Female teachers of Salem District in terms of their attitude towards Technology Enabled Learning (TEL).
3. To compare the Higher Education Teachers of Government and Self –Finance Colleges in Salem District in terms of their attitude towards Technology Enabled Learning
4. To compare the M.Phil., and PhD., holding Higher Education Teachers of Salem District in terms of their Technology Enabled Learning (TEL).

HYPOTHESES OF THE STUDY

The hypotheses of the study are as follows:

1. There is no significant difference between the attitudes of Male and Female Higher Education Teachers towards Technology Enabled Learning.
2. There is no significant difference between attitudes of Government College Teachers and Self - Finance College Teachers towards Technology Enabled Learning.

3. There is no significant difference between attitudes of M.Phil., holders and Ph.D., holders towards Technology Enabled Learning (TEL).

METHODOLOGY

As the present study is descriptive by nature, the normative survey technique was adopted. As many as 110 teachers of five colleges in Salem district were chosen as sample using simple random sampling technique. An Attitude Scale, aimed at assessing the Higher Education teachers attitude towards Technology Enabled Learning was developed by the investigator for the purpose of collecting data. The collected data were subjected to differential and descriptive statistical analysis.

METHODOLOGY

Research is a systematic and scientific investigation of a branch of knowledge to gain new and higher levels of knowledge to bring to the understanding of the ways to handle existing systems and problems. The different meanings attached to educational research can be inferred from different methods, and processes employed in research. Thus, educational research by its very nature can be classified and described in many ways.

1. **Qualitative Approach:**
   The qualitative approach involves the collection of extensive narrative data in order to gain insights into phenomena of interest. Data analysis includes the coding of the data and production of a verbal synthesis (Inductive Process). It includes Historical Research and Qualitative Research.
2. **Quantitative Approach:**
   The quantitative approach involves the collection of numerical data in order to explain, predict and/or control phenomena of interest. Data analysis is mainly statistical (Deductive Process). It includes Descriptive Research, Correlation Research, Causal–comparative Research and Experimental Research.

RESEARCH DESIGN

Research design constitutes a blue print for the collection, measurement and analysis of the data pertaining to the research problem investigated.

SAMPLE FOR THE STUDY

The present study aims to find out the Higher Education Teacher's Attitude towards Technology Enabled Learning.

SELECTION OF TOOL

As the present study is descriptive and survey research, the investigator chose "Attitude Scale" as a tool for collection of data. Data regarding General Information of the respondents Attitude towards Technology Enabled Learning were collected from Higher Education Teachers of Salem District who formed the sample through the Attitude Scale.

CONSTRUCTION OF THE TOOL

The investigator developed Technology Enabled Learning Attitude Scale (TELAS) in two parts viz., Part- A for collecting general information regarding teachers (Name, Sex, Age, Details of Academic Qualifications, Name of the Department, Designation, Type of Institution, Type of Management, Locality of the Institution, etc) and Part – B for finding out the Higher Education Teachers attitude towards Technology Enabled Learning. TELAS consists of 36 items, i.e., 28 positive items and 8 negative items. The positive items are 1, 2, 3, 5, 7, 8, 9, 11, 13, 14, 15,17,18,19,22,23,24,25,26,28,29,30,31,32,33,34,35,36 and negative items are 4, 6, 10, 12, 16, 20, 21, 27. Each item can be marked on a five point scale. For each positive item, a score of 5 was assigned to the response 'Strongly agree', 4 was assigned to the response 'agree', 3 was assigned to the response 'undecided', 2 was assigned to the response 'disagree' and 1 was assigned to the response 'strongly disagree' respectively. For the negative items the scoring procedure was vice-versa.

VALIDATION OF THE TOOL

The preliminary scale was developed after a careful analysis of a few similar tools. The developed tool was given to experts in the field of education, ICT and educational research. The finalized questionnaire was subjected to another review by the same experts. Thus, the face validity and content validity of the attitude scale were established. The attitude scale is given as Appendix.

COLLECTION OF DATA

The investigator himself visited the colleges located in Salem District, met the Principals of the colleges and got permission to administer the questionnaire. The investigator explained the aim and the purpose of the study before administering the tool to teachers. The teachers freely responded to each and every item of the statement that is given the attitude scale.

ANALYSIS OF DATA

The collected data were analyzed by using appropriate statistical techniques such as Mean, Standard Deviation and t-test.

TABLE. 18.1: Analysis of the Sample in Terms of Sex, Age, Research Qualification and Type of Management of Institutions

Sex	No of Teachers	Percentage %
Male	50	45.45
Female	60	54.55
Age	**No. of Teachers**	**Percentage**
21 – 30	53	48.18
31 – 40	36	32.72
41 – 50	17	15.5
51 and above	4	3.6
Research Qualification	**No. of Teachers**	**Percentage**
M. Phil	93	84.5
PhD	17	15.5
Type of Management	**No. of Teachers**	**Percentage**
Government	53	48.18
Private	57	51.82

The above table presents the distribution of the sample in terms of sex, age, research qualification and type of management of the institution. From the table it can be understood that out of the sample of 110, 45.45% percent of the Higher Education teachers are male and the remaining 54.55% percent are female.

From the table it can be understood that out of the total sample of 110, 48.18 percent of the teachers are aged between 21- 30, 32.72 percent of the teachers between 31- 40, 15.5 percent of the teachers between 41- 50 and 3.6 percent of the teachers belong to 51 and above age group. The table further reveals that 84.5 percent of teachers hold M.Phil., and 15.5 percent of them teachers hold Ph.D., in their respective disciplines that formed the sample. As seen in the above table, 48.18 percent of teachers belong to Government Institutions and 51.82 percent of them belong to Self–Financing distributions.

TABLE. 18.2: Significance of Difference between the Mean Technology Enabled Learning Attitude Scores of Male and Female Teachers

Sex	N	Mean	S.D.	't' Value	Level of Significance
Male	50	132.7	14.7	0.11	Not Significant at 0.05 level.
Female	60	132.98	11.44		

The about table 18.2 presents an analysis of the Technology Enabled Learning Attitude Scores of the Male and Female teachers who formed the sample. 50 male teachers and 60 Female teachers formed the sample. The mean of the TEL Attitude Scores of Meal Teachers is 132.7 and that of the Female

Teachers is 132.98. The calculated 't'- value (0.11) is less than the table value of 1.98 at 0.05 level of significance. Hence, there is no significant difference between the mean Technology Enabled Learning Attitude Score of the male and female teachers of Higher Education Institution. It implies that the male and female teachers of Higher Education Institutions in Salem District do not, significantly differ in their Technology Enabled Learning Attitude.

TABLE. 18.3: Significance of Difference between the Mean Technology Enabled Learning Attitude Scores of Teachers with Different Research Qualifications

Research Qualification	N	Mean	SD	't' value	Level of Significance
M.Phil	93	131.88	12.1	1.52	Not Significant at 0.05 level
PhD	17	138.18	16.3		

The above table 18.3 presents an analysis of the Technology Enabled Learning Attitude Scores of Higher Education teachers with different Research Qualifications who formed the sample. Out of the total 110 Higher Education Teachers who formed the sample 93 hold M. Phil and the remaining 17 hold PhD in their Respective Departments. The calculated 't' value i.e., 1. 52 is less than the table value of 1.98 at 0.05 level of significance. Hence, there is no significant difference between mean Technology Enabled Learning Attitudes scores of Higher Education teachers with respect to the difference in their research degrees M.Phil., and Ph.D., It implies that the M.Phil., and Ph.D., holding teachers of Higher Education Institutions of Salem District do not differ in their Technology Enabled Learning Attitude.

FINDINGS AND CONCLUSIONS OF THE STUDY

The major findings and conclusions of the study are:

1. More than 46.5% of the Higher Education Teachers have 6 years and above experience in using computer and only a very few of them 14.5% have less than one year experience in computer.
2. Only 48 Higher Education Teachers out of 110 (43.64%) make use of the computer Daily and 4 Higher Education Teachers out of 110 (3.64%) do not use computers at all.
3. Only 40 Higher Education Teachers out of 110 (36.4%) make use of the Internet Daily and 4 Higher Education Teachers out of 110 (3.64%) do not use Internet at all.
4. The Higher Education Teachers of Salem District have favorable attitude towards Technology Enabled Learning.
5. The male and female teachers of Higher Education Institution do not differ in their attitude towards Technology Enabled Learning Attitude however, the female teachers have more favorable attitude towards Technology Enabled Learning than the Male teachers.

SUGGESTIONS AND RECOMMENDATIONS

Based on the above given findings and conclusions, the present study offers suggestions and recommendations.

1. Steps must be taken to sustain the Higher Education Teachers favorable Attitude towards Technology Enabled Learning.
2. Workshops and capacity development programmes are to be organized as in service training programmes to the Higher Education Teachers so as to convert their favorable attitude to action in practices Technology Enabled Learning.
3. Facilities for the viewing ETV and listening to Educational Radio, Accessing web resources must be made available in all colleges.
4. Steps must be taken to incorporate a practical component in the UGC's Orientation and Refreshers Courses, viz., watching and listening to Educational Radio Programmes, ETV Programmes and critical evaluation of them.

SUGGESTIONS FOR FURTHER RESEARCH

Findings of the present study open up a few areas for further investigation. They are as follows.

1. As the study has been taken up with only Higher Education teachers of Salem District as sample, studies with Higher Education teachers of other areas as sample may be taken up.
2. Comparative studies can also be taken up to compare Salem District Higher Education Teachers Attitude towards TEL with that of the Higher Education teachers of other areas.
3. Studies on the relationship between Technology Enabled Learning Attitude and other aspects like teachers effectiveness may be undertaken.
4. A similar study may be undertaken to find out Technology Enabled Learning Attitude of Teacher Educators with different backgrounds.

CONCLUSION

The present study has investigated the attitude of Higher Education Teachers of Salem District towards Technology Enabled Learning. The study has shown that there is wide scope for improving the attitude of Higher Education Teachers towards Technology Enabled Learning. Against this backdrop, it becomes essential that the National Council for Teacher Education, Ministry of Human Resource Development and other National level agencies take stock of the situation and evolve strategies to create a positive attitude in the minds of the Higher Education Teacher towards Technology Enabled Learning.

❐

19

Teachers Attitude of New Technology

There is a tremendous revolution in science and technology. Information in communication technologies has a deep Cultural Revolution changing. There is a need to make a realistic assessment of what technology cannot do to reach a plateau of productivity when the technology consistently delivers to realistic goals. Digital skill is a vast technique used by all people. Educational technology and mobile learning, multi- media learning are all digital skill. Science is a boon. Man has discovered many wonderful things from the treasure of developing every day. It has made our life easier, happier and more secure. Science and technology has conquered time and space. It has made very good communication and made the transport easier. With the help of science and technology, modern medicine and medical treatments, the doctors save the life of sick people from the jaws of death. Many organs are now transplanted. It is used in the field of agriculture. The impact of science and technology among students in the field is both good and bad. Science laboratory, space centre ISRO are taken in the highest form. Television, telecommunication, type- recorder, films, LCD projectors, digital and white board, e- learning, e-teaching, teleconferencing, teaching machine cell phones such as all types of multimedia are boons to us. But the students are affected by this because of misusing.

By the wrong use of face book, web site, web-camera, especially cell phones, net connection, lab top etc. Science and technology become down. But once for all where we use science and technology in proper, correct and perfect way it is a boon to us otherwise it is curse and demon to us. A secondary Information and Communication Technology curriculum should contribute to the building up of teams of professionals with these new competencies. The use of Information and Communication Technology cuts across all aspects of economic and social life. Technological developments in Information and Communication Technology are very rapid. Technology quickly becomes obsolete requiring new skills and knowledge to be mastered frequently. Adaptation is only possible when based on a sound understanding of the principles and concepts of Information and Communication Technology.

OBJECTIVES

1. To study the level of teachers attitude towards using new technology in teaching
2. To find out whether there is any significant relationship between teachers attitude towards the use of new technology and their interest in teaching.

METHODOLOGY

The methodology adopted for the study is explained in detail. The sampling technique, size of the sample, variables of the study, description of the tool used and administration of tool are elaborated.

SAMPLE

The study was conducted on 100 school teachers, Coimbatore district, Tamil Nadu.

DATA COLLECTION

Primary data, required for the present research work were collected by conducting direct interviews using questionnaire. All the respondents were given sufficient information about the study. These respondents were provided with the same questionnaires. They were also informed that they have to answer in the same fashion.

ANALYSIS AND INTERPRETATION

Gender and attitude towards the use of new technology

Hypothesis-1

There is no significant difference between male and female teachers attitude towards the use of new technology.

TABLE.19.1: The Significance of the Difference ('t' value) between mean Scores of Male and Female Teacher's Attitude Towards the use of New Technology

Gender	N	Mean	SD	't' value	Level of Significance (0.05)
Male	50	100.30	11.81	4.89	Significant
Female	50	107.30	12.57		

It is evident from the table the calculated 't' value is 4.89 is significant at 0.05 level. Hence, the framed null hypothesis is rejected and research hypothesis is accepted. It is inferred that there is significant difference found between male and female teachers attitude towards the use of new technology.

Qualification and Attitude Towards the use of New Technology

Hypothesis-2

There is no significant difference between undergraduate and post graduate teachers with respect to their attitude towards the use of new technology.

TABLE.19.2: The Significance of the Difference ('t' value) between Undergraduate and Post Graduate Teachers with Respect to their Attitude towards the use of New Technology.

Qualification	N	Mean	SD	't' value	Level of Significance (0.05)
Under graduate	35	103.64	11.44	0.28	Not Significant
Post graduate	65	103.23	13.53		

It is evident from the table the calculated 't' value is 0.28 which is not significant at 0.05 level. Hence, the framed null hypothesis is accepted. It shows that there is no significant difference between undergraduate and post graduate teachers with respect to their attitude towards the use of new technology.

Locality of the School and Attitude Towards the use of New Technology

Hypothesis-3

There is no significant difference between rural and urban school teachers attitude towards the use of new technology.

TABLE. 19.3: The Significance of the Difference ('t' value) between Rural and Urban School Teachers Tttitude Towards the use of New Technology

Locality of the school	N	Mean	SD	't' value	Level of Significance (0.05)
Rural	65	103.42	11.23	0.06	Not Significant
Urban	35	103.33	14.15		

It is evident from the table the calculated 't' value is 0.06 which is not significant at 0.05 level. Hence, the framed null hypothesis is accepted. It shows that there is no significant difference between rural and urban school teachers attitude towards the use of new technology.

Type of School and Attitude Towards the use of New Technology

Hypothesis-4

There is no significant difference between private and government school teachers attitude towards the use of new technology.

TABLE. 19.4: The Significance of the Difference ('t' value) between Private and Government School Teachers Attitude Towards the use of New Technology

Type of School	N	Mean	SD	't' value	Level of Significance (0.05)
Private	65	104.79	11.54	1.26	Not Significant
Government	35	102.78	13.01		

It is evident from the table the calculated 't' value is 1.26 which is not significant at 0.05 level. Hence, the framed null hypothesis is accepted. It shows that there is no significant difference between private and government school teachers attitude towards the use of new technology.

Level of Teaching and Attitude Towards the use of New Technology

Hypothesis-5

There is no significant difference between secondary and higher secondary school teachers attitude towards the use of new technology.

TABLE. 19.5: The Significance of the Difference ('t' test) between Secondary and Higher Secondary School Teachers Attitude Rowards the use of New Rechnology

Level of teaching	N	Mean	SD	't' value	Level of Significance (0.05)
Secondary School	60	102.12	12.12	1.85	Not Significant
Higher secondary School	40	104.82	13.03		

It is evident from the table the calculated 't' value is 1.85 which is not significant at 0.05 level. Hence, the framed null hypothesis is accepted. It is inferred that there is no significant difference between secondary and higher secondary school teachers attitude towards the use of new technology.

Teaching Experience and Attitude Towards the use of Bew Technology

Hypothesis-6

There is no significant difference among teachers who have different years of teaching experience with respect to their attitude towards the use of new technology.

TABLE.19.6: The Significance of the Difference ('F' test) among School Teachers with Respect to their Attitude Towards the use of New Technology

Teaching Experience	Sum of Squares	Mean Squares	df	'F' Value	Level of Significance (0.05)
Between Groups	2281.690	1140.845	2	7.48	Significant
Within Groups	45273.227	152.435	97		
Total	**47554.917**	--	**99**		

It is evident from the table the calculated 'F' value is 7.48 which is significant at 0.05 level. Hence, the framed null hypothesis is rejected and research hypothesis is accepted. It is inferred that there is significant difference among teachers who have different years of teaching experience with respect to their attitude towards the use of new technology.

CORRELATION ANALYSIS

Correlation Analysis between teacher's attitude towards the use of new technology and interest in teaching

One of the important objectives of the present investigation is to study the significant relationship between teacher's attitude towards the use of new technology and interest in teaching. For this purpose, the investigator applied the co-efficient of correlation ('r'). The computed values are given in the table. The investigator also framed a null hypothesis for testing the relationship between teacher's attitude towards the use of new technology and interest in teaching.

Hypothesis-7

There is no significant relationship between teacher's attitude towards the use of new technology and interest in teaching.

TABLE. 19.7: Co-Efficient of Correlation between Teacher's Attitude towards the use of New Technology and Interest in Teaching

Correlation	N	'r' value	Level of Significance at 0.05 level
Teacher's attitude towards the use of new technology and interest in teaching	100	0.56	Significant

It is evident from the table the computed correlation coefficient 'r' for entire sample is 0.56, which is significant at 0.05 level. Hence, the framed null hypothesis is rejected. It is inferred that there is significant relationship found between teacher's attitude towards the use of new technology and their interest in teaching.

SUGGESTIONS

The present study gives a clear-cut view about the present position of teachers attitude towards the use of new technology and their interest in teaching. Based on the important findings stated earlier the following recommendations are suggested.

1. Teachers must be provided with adequate opportunities to enhance their knowledge in new technologies and equipments. The government should provide more effective environment through schools for them to improve their skills in application of new technologies in teaching.
2. Periodical in-service training programmes should be organized to keep their interest and quest in teaching.
3. The finding of the present study reveals that the teachers have neutral attitude towards the use of new technology in teaching and low interest in teaching. This indicates that the Heads of the institutions must look into the varied problems that influence the interest of teachers and find amicable solutions to their difficulties.
4. More activities should be planned in the curriculum to bring forth different modes of creative expressions which will provide competition and generate interest of teachers in teaching.
5. Sincere work and involved performances of teachers must be recognized and honoured by the authorities. And application of innovative methods and technologies in instruction must be encouraged.
6. In addition with the above recommendation the government and all the other concerned authorities should realize the problems of experienced teachers and provide conductive environment of growth and mutual help of teachers should be ensured.

CONCLUSION

The present study is conducted on teacher's attitude towards the use of new technologies in teaching and their interest in teaching. The findings of the present study revealed that the teachers have neutral attitude towards the use of new technology and low interest in teaching. Therefore, the authorities and government should find suitable measures to improve the interest of teachers in teaching and the application of innovative technologies in Teaching Learning Process.

❐

20

Computer Based Learning

Multimedia refers to any computer-mediated software or interactive application that integrates text, color, graphical images, animation, audio sound, and full motion video in a single application. Multimedia learning systems consist of animation and narration, which offer a potential venue for improving student understanding. Multimedia programme is an integral part of the educational technology. As a technique, it offers a high potential in application at different stages of education for the purpose of enhancing the teaching and learning processes, as is evident from the experience of developed countries.The integration of multimedia technology into the communication environment has the potential to transform the students from passive recipients of information to active participants in a media-rich learning process. The introduction of multimedia or any other computer-based information technology is not intended to substitute a presenter. This new technology is intended to provide the presenter with a powerful tool that can greatly enhance communication by delivering a multisensory experience. With interactive multimedia technology, a teacher can communicate with the students by means of a presentation that becomes more than message-it becomes an active, exciting experience in a multisensory environment to create a multisensory experience. Multimedia reaches users in many different ways, enabling them to retain more knowledge and increase their understanding.

Multimedia consists of the combination of video and movie clips and sound, text and graphic files all controlled by a piece of software and a computer which is equipped with a sound card, a video card, a CD-ROM drive and speakers or headphone. Sometimes, there is also a videodisk player, which is controlled by the software.

OBJECTIVES

1. To measure behaviour and performance of high school student.
2. To assess effectiveness in performance of high school student.
3. To assess effective in behaviuoral outcome of the high school student.
4. To assess effectiveness in traditional and multimedia method of teaching.
5. To find out relevant effectiveness of computer based multimedia learning material on performance and behaviour outcome.

HYPOTHESIS OF THE STUDY

1. High school students do not differ in their average level of relevant effectiveness of computer based on multimedia learning material on performance and behaviour outcome in traditional method and multimedia teaching of entire samples.
2. Respondents do not differ in their relevant effectiveness of computer based multimedia learning material on performance and behaviour outcome in pre-test on the basis of groups.
3. Respondents do not differ in their relevant effectiveness of computer based multimedia learning material on performance and behaviour outcome in pre-test on the basis of type of school.
4. Respondents do not differ in their relevant effectiveness of computer based multimedia learning material on performance and behaviour outcome in pre-test on the basis of parents education.
5. Respondents do not differ in their relevant effectiveness of computer based multimedia learning material on performance and behaviour outcome in pre-test on the basis of parents income.
6. Respondents do not differ in their relevant effectiveness of computer based multimedia learning material on performance and behaviour outcome in post-test on the basis of type of school.
7. Respondents do not differ in their relevant effectiveness of computer based multimedia learning material on performance and behaviour outcome in post-test on the basis of parents education.
8. Respondents do not differ in their relevant effectiveness of computer based multimedia learning material on performance and behaviour outcome in post-test on the basis of parents income.

METHODOLOGY

The methodology adopted for the study is explained in detail. The sampling technique, size of the sample, variables of the study, description of the tool used and administration of tool are elaborated.

SAMPLING TECHNIQUE

The random sampling techniques used in the present study. The survey should cover all the aspects of the subject selected of the study others are inferred from a study of a sample group carefully selected to be representative of the total population. At time, the survey describes a limited population which is the only group under consideration. It involves a clearly defined problem and defined objectives. It requires expert and imaginative planning. Careful analysis and interpretation of the data gathered and logical and skillful reporting of the findings. There are different findings such as social surveys, market surveys. The survey method is applied to the analysis of existing social conditions including educational conditions and to the analysis of public opinion. So in this present study, the investigator has used stratified disposition random sampling method.

SAMPLE

Samples of 100 high school students selected randomly were studied in Tindivanam Town. Out of these high schools as many as 5 higher secondary schools have been chosen by appropriate method. All the available high school students studying in each of this selected high school were chosen as sample. Stratified disposition random sampling technique has been used in the selection of the sample.

DATA COLLECTION

Primary data, required for the present research work were collected by conducting direct interviews using questionnaire. All the respondents were given sufficient information about the study. These respondents were provided with the same questionnaires. They were also informed that they have to answer in the same fashion.

TOOLS USED FOR THE STUDY

Development of effectiveness of multimedia programme and Scale by the investigator. The scale for measuring the high school student's effectiveness of multimedia towards science in the study. This scale has as many as 25 statements of which 3 point scale method.

ANALYSIS AND INTERPRETATION

TABLE.20.1: Showing the Mean, Standard Deviation of Relevant Effectiveness of Computer based Multimedia Learning Material on Performance and Behaviour Outcome in Pre and Post-Test of entire samples

Groups	N	Mean	SD	r value
Pre-test	100	14.79	2.69	0.346**
Post-test	100	19.30	2.86	

Hypothesis

High school students do not differ in their average level of relevant effectiveness of computer based on multimedia learning material on performance and behaviour outcome in traditional method and multimedia teaching of entire samples.

The mean and standard deviation of relevant effectiveness of computer based multimedia learning material on performance and behaviour outcome scores of entire samples are 14.79 and 2.69 in pre-test and 19.30 and 2.86 in post-test. The mean score of all categories are lay in between ($M \pm 1\sigma$) value. So it is concluded that average level of relevant effectiveness of computer based multimedia learning material on performance and behaviour outcome of entire samples.

TABLE. 20.2: Showing the Mean, Standard Deviation and T-Test for Relevant Effectiveness of Computer based Multimedia Learning Material on Performance and Behaviour Outcome on the basis of Groups

Groups	Sample size	Mean	Standard Deviation	t-value	Level of Significance
Pre-test	100	14.79	2.69	12.86	0.01 (Significant)
Post-test	100	19.30	2.86		

Hypothesis

Respondents do not differ in their relevant effectiveness of computer based multimedia learning material on performance and behaviour outcome in pre-test on the basis of groups.

The calculated t-value (12.86), which is significant at 0.01 level, confirms that there is a significant difference between relevant effectiveness of computer based multimedia learning material on performance and behaviour outcome on the basis of groups. So the null hypothesis is rejected and alternate hypothesis is accepted. Therefore it is concluded that pre-test and post-test groups differ in their effectiveness of computer based multimedia learning material on performance and behaviour outcome.

TABLE.20.3: Showing Mean, Standard Deviation and T-Value for Traditional Method among the High School Student on the basis of Type of School

Sl.No	Type of school	Sample size	Mean	Standard Deviation	t-value	Level of Significance
1	Government	75	14.73	2.71	0.37	0.716 (Not Significant)
2	Aided	25	14.96	2.67		

Hypothesis

Respondents do not differ in their relevant effectiveness of computer based multimedia learning material on performance and behaviour outcome in pre-test on the basis of type of school.

The calculated t-value (0.37), which is not significant, confirms that there is a no significant difference between relevant effectiveness of computer based multimedia learning material on performance and behaviour outcome in pre-test on the basis of type of school. So the null hypothesis is accepted and alternate hypothesis is rejected. Therefore it is concluded that government and aided school groups do not differ in their pre-test score.

TABLE.20.4: Showing Mean, Standard Deviation and T-Value for Traditional Method among the High School Student on the basis of Parents Education

Sl. No	Parents education	Sample size	Mean	Standard Deviation	F-value	Level of Significance
1	School	86	14.82	2.75	0.58	0.560 (Not Significant)
2	Under graduate	8	14.13	2.03		
3	Post graduate	6	14.21	2.44		
	Total	**100**	**14.79**	**2.69**		

Hypothesis

Respondents do not differ in their relevant effectiveness of computer based multimedia learning material on performance and behaviour outcome in pre-test on the basis of parents education.

The calculated F-value (0.58), which is not significant, confirms that there is a no significant difference between relevant effectiveness of computer based multimedia learning material on performance and behaviour outcome in pre-test on the basis of parents education. So the null hypothesis is accepted and alternate hypothesis is rejected. Therefore it is concluded that different parents education students groups do not differ in their pre-test score.

TABLE.20.5: Showing Mean, Standard Deviation and T-Value for Traditional Method among the High School Student on the basis of Parents Income

Sl. No	Parents income	Sample size	Mean	Standard Deviation	F-value	Level of Significance
1	Below Rs.50,000	70	14.51	2.53	1.56	0.215 (Not Significant)
2	Rs.50,000 – 2,00,000	24	15.50	3.09		
3	Above Rs.2,00,000	6	16.00	2.65		
	Total	**100**	**14.79**	**2.69**		

Hypothesis

Respondents do not differ in their relevant effectiveness of computer based multimedia learning material on performance and behaviour outcome in pre-test on the basis of parents income.

The calculated F-value (1.56), which is not significant, confirms that there is a no significant difference between relevant effectiveness of computer based multimedia learning material on performance and behaviour outcome in pre-test on the basis of parents income. So the null hypothesis is accepted and alternate hypothesis is rejected. Therefore it is concluded that different parents income students groups do not differ in their pre-test score.

TABLE. 20.6: Showing Mean, Standard Deviation and T-Value for Multimedia Method among the High School Student on the basis of Type of School

Sl. No	Type of school	Sample size	Mean	Standard Deviation	t-value	Level of Significance
1	Government	75	18.75	2.91	4.33	0.01 (Significant)
2	Aided	25	20.96	1.93		

Hypothesis

Respondents do not differ in their relevant effectiveness of computer based multimedia learning material on performance and behaviour outcome in post-test on the basis of type of school.

The calculated t-value (4.33), which is significant at 0.01 level, confirms that there is a significant difference between relevant effectiveness of computer based multimedia learning material on performance and behaviour outcome in post-test on the basis of type of school. So the null hypothesis is rejected and alternate hypothesis is accepted. Therefore it is concluded that aided school students (20.96) scored higher mean value than government school students (18.75).

TABLE. 20.7: Showing Mean, Standard Deviation and T-Value for Multimedia Method among the High School Student on the basis of Parents Education

Sl.No	Parents education	Sample size	Mean	Standard Deviation	F-value	Level of Significance
1	School	86	19.34	2.87	3.19	0.01 (Significant)
2	Under graduate	8	16.75	3.01		
3	Post graduate	6	20.12	2.63		
	Total	**100**	**19.30**	**2.86**		

Hypothesis

Respondents do not differ in their relevant effectiveness of computer based multimedia learning material on performance and behaviour outcome in post-test on the basis of parents education.

The calculated F-value (3.19), which is significant at 0.01 level, confirms that there is a significant difference between relevant effectiveness of computer based multimedia learning material on performance and behaviour outcome in post-test on the basis of parents education. So the null hypothesis is rejected and alternate hypothesis is accepted. Therefore it is concluded that different parents education students groups differ in their post-test score.

TABLE.20.8: Showing Mean, Standard Deviation and T-Value for Multimedia Method among the High School Student on the basis of Parents Income

Sl. No	Parents income	Sample size	Mean	Standard Deviation	F-value	Level of Significance
1	Below Rs.50,000	70	19.11	2.64	3.29	0.01 (Significant)
2	Rs.50,000 – 2,00,000	24	20.04	3.24		
3	Above Rs.2,00,000	6	16.00	4.58		
	Total	**100**	**19.30**	**2.86**		

Hypothesis

Respondents do not differ in their relevant effectiveness of computer based multimedia learning material on performance and behaviour outcome in post-test on the basis of parents income.

The calculated F-value (3.29), which is significant at 0.01 level, confirms that there is a significant difference between relevant effectiveness of computer based multimedia learning material on performance and behaviour outcome in post-test on the basis of parents income. So the null hypothesis is rejected and alternate hypothesis is accepted. Therefore it is concluded that different parents income students groups differ in their post-test score.

Findings

1. High school students differ in their average level of relevant effectiveness of computer based on multimedia learning material on performance and behaviour outcome in traditional method and multimedia teaching of entire samples.
2. Respondents differ in their relevant effectiveness of computer based multimedia learning material on performance and behaviour outcome in pre-test on the basis of groups.
3. Respondents do not differ in their relevant effectiveness of computer based multimedia learning material on performance and behaviour outcome in pre-test on the basis of type of school.
4. Respondents do not differ in their relevant effectiveness of computer based multimedia learning material on performance and behaviour outcome in pre-test on the basis of parents education.
5. Respondents do not differ in their relevant effectiveness of computer based multimedia learning material on performance and behaviour outcome in pre-test on the basis of parents income.
6. Respondents differ in their relevant effectiveness of computer based multimedia learning material on performance and behaviour outcome in post-test on the basis of type of school.
7. Respondents differ in their relevant effectiveness of computer based multimedia learning material on performance and behaviour outcome in post-test on the basis of parents education.
8. Respondents differ in their relevant effectiveness of computer based multimedia learning material on performance and behaviour outcome in post-test on the basis of parents income.

CONCLUSION

In the present study, the researcher arrive the following conclusion based on the findings. In the present study, science students have relevant effectiveness of computer based multimedia learning material on performance and behaviour outcome of high school students in Tindivanam Town when compared with other students. The researcher framed objectives and hypotheses on the basis of the above context. 100 samples were selected randomly. A standard questionnaire was used to collect the relevant data. After collecting the data they were analyzed using statistical tools such as t-test and ANOVA in the both groups (pre and post-test). The result concluded that the all the science students of average level of relevant effectiveness of computer based multimedia learning material on performance and behaviour outcome.

❐

21

Importance of Teaching English Language

Education is the life long process of acquiring new knowledge and skin through formal and informal exposure of information ideas and experience technologies to adopt in teaching the concepts of the subjects in the school. There are many means by which effective instruction can be imparted in the classroom. The use of computer Assisted instruction in the schools is having computers. So use of technology enhances effect of a learning experience.

Aims of Teaching English in India

English is an important international language according to Thompson and Wyatt, there are four aims of teaching English to Indian Children. They are:

1. To understand simple, spoken English
2. To understand simple written English
3. To speak simple, correct and idiomatic English
4. To write simple, correct and idiomatic English.
5. Teaching Grammar

Grammar resembles a vitamin in that ill effects may spring from a deficiency and an excessive close must be wasteful and may even be harmful. It is like a medicine not a form of diet". Whatever grammar is taught must be functional and help the students in improving their use of English. It launching grammar example is more important them the rules.

Methods of Teaching Grammar

1. The Traditional method
2. The informal method
3. The inductive – deductive method
    - Inductive process
    - Deductive process

Teaching of English

English as a second language (ESL) as an optional. The objectives of the test have been determined on the basis of inter sine needs analysis. The text covers five English language skills namely, Listening, Reading, writing, along with grammar and literary Appreciation. Speaking skill was deliberately excluded from the text due to the constraints against individual testing and recording.

English Language Teaching

The tug of war between the "mentalistic" and "mechanistic" language theories like monitor, model, accuracy and fluency theory, semantic approach, structural approach, situational approach, communicative approach, interactive approach, error analysis, and contrastive analysis along with the age old grammar–translation method and direct method came into existence.

Need for Teaching English Grammar

The grammar is the means through which linguistic creativity is ultimately achieved and an inadequate knowledge of the grammar would lead to serious limitations on the creativity for communication. The Indian contexts in which English is used are taken into account. Thus the teaching of grammar means the effective presentation of language items in a systematic way in meaningful contexts.

Statement of the Problem

Statement of the problem is ***"Effect of teaching grammar through computer among XII standard students".***

Background of the Problem

Learning through computer is more effective as compared to class room teaching. At present time, the teachers have a lack of basic computer knowledge so that the investigator decided to investigate to the English grammar teaching through computer under the topic "Effect of Teaching grammar through computer among XII std students".

Objectives of the Study

1. To find out the level of effect of teaching grammar through computer among XII standard students.
2. To find out the level of significant difference among boys and girls in Post-Test.
3. To find out the level of significant difference among rural and urban in Post-Test.
4. To find out the level of significant difference among hosteller and day scholar in Post-Test.

Hypothesis of the Study

The following null hypothesis was formulated on the basis of the objectives framed.

1. There is no significant difference between boys and girls in Pre-Test.
2. There is no significant difference between rural and urban in Pre-Test.
3. There is no significant difference between hosteller and day scholar in Pre-Test.
4. There is no significant difference between hosteller and day scholar in Post-Test.

Scope of the Study

The topic is an effect of Teaching Grammar through computer among XII Std students. Since this is the Experimental Study. The investigator attempt to know the Effect of Teaching Grammar through computer among XII Std students. This study will be of great help for the educationists particularly for the teachers since the concept of education has been changing from time to time.

Delimitations of the Study

Broadly speaking, any study is impossible without delimitation. Research Studies in general will have delimitation due to many factors. This study too has some delimitation. It is the responsibility of the researcher to see that the study is conducted with maximum care in order to be reliable. The following delimitations were unavoidable in the present study.

1. The present investigation is confined to the XII std student studying at Erode District in Tamil Nadu.
2. The study is confined only to a sample of 123 students from Government schools located in rural area.
3. In this present study the investigator analyzed about the variables such as gender, Locality, Hosteller and day scholar students.

Methodology of the Study

The present study is an experimental research. Tool used for the study, Samples of the study, procedure, Pilot study, scoring methods, statistical measures used in the study etc., have been reported in detailed manner in this present study and ends with the Delimitations of the study.

Design of the Study

Research design is a plan, a structure and a strategy of investigation conceived to obtain answers to various issues in research. The object of research design is to test the research hypotheses. The research design, therefore, is built in the principle of maximization of the results of study; minimization of variance. The present study belongs to Experimental Research. The Demographic variables used are Gender, Locality and stay at. The tool "ETGTC" was used in the study for 8th standard students in Government schools at Erode District for sample selection. Stratified Random sampling technique was followed in this study. Data were collected from 123 students and the statistical techniques Mean, S.D and 't' test were used.

Selection of the Subject

The researcher selected Computer Assisted Instruction (CAI) as the technique for his study and the area selected was teaching English grammar.

Selection of the Topic

The grammar units were taken after consultation with language exports, educational scholars, programmers and senior teacher of English with rich experience at the secondary level. The topic selected is introduced as 'Idioms and Phrases'.

Pilot Study

Before administering the questionnaire to the actual sample, pilot study was conducted. The aim of pilot study not only to test and refine the tools of research but also to force the nature of analysis and processing that may be needed at a later stage, after a questionnaire was prepared. It was given a trial on small sample. This is necessary to know XII standard students whether they are meaningful and whether there is any ambiguity in thought or in the wording of questions.

Blue Print of the Achievement Test

The test paper, thus prepared, consisted of 40 items. The items found in the paper were of multiple choice types. The blue print of the question paper marks given below.

TABLE.21.1: Blue Print

Unit	Knowledge	Understanding	Application	Skill	Total
Idioms & phrases	15	13	12	0	40
	15	13	12	0	40

TABLE.21.2: Weight age of Objectives

Objectives	Marks	Percentage
Knowledge	15	37.5%
Understanding	13	32.5%
Application	12	30%
Skill	0	0
Total	**40**	**100%**

Research Methods

The investigator followed Experimental method as this study aims of eliciting the opinions of the XII standard students on the effective learning by them in using computer.

Tool Used for the Study

1. Achievement test with multiple choice questions.
2. A questionnaire was prepared to get the information about grammar in XII std students.
3. Test method Pre-Test and Post-Test of 40 marks was conducted.

Samples of the Study

A sample of 123 students studying in XII Std students for collecting the data–Experimental design was followed and purposive sampling technique was used to select the sample. The sample consisted of 123 students of 8th standard in Government School of Erode District. (71 Boys, 52 Girls and Rural 87, Urban 36, Students)

Procedure

The questionnaire was prepared which included questions in XII std English Grammar given to the students during extra periods. The students wrote the truthful answers. Further the classification and analysis of the results was carried out.

Pre-Test and Post-Test

The pre-test was carried out after regular teaching. After the conduct of the achievement test a Post-test was also conducted after an interval of one week. The same achievement test prepared for conducting the post-test was used as the post-test.

Personal Data Sheet

To know the background of the students, the investigator used separate personal data sheets along with the Developed Questionnaires. It asked for details of Gender, Locality and stay at students.

Scoring Key

Achievement test had 40 questions. Correct answer cues one mark and wrong answer cues zero marks. So maximum score of the achievement test is 40 and minimum score the achievement test is zero of achievement in English grammar among XII standard students.

Statistical Measures Used in the Study

After valued the achievement test, a master table was prepared by plotting the scores in different statistical measures such as Mean, Standard deviation and't'- test for analyze the significant Difference in the present study.

Statistical Analysis of Data and Interpretation

Statistical analysis of data enables a researcher to arrive at empirical findings about the problem taken for research. The purpose of present investigation is to study the Effect of Teaching Grammar through computer. The data of for the study were collected from the students by means of a questionnaire.

TABLE. 21.3: Mean and Standard Deviation of Gain Score on English Grammar through Computer in Pre-Test and Post-Test

Test	N	Mean	SD
Pre Test	123	41.46	10.71
Post Test	123	53.81	40.27

The table 21.3 shows that, the mean and standard Deviation of the single group in Pre-Test are 41.46 and 10.71 respectively and the mean and standard deviation of the single group in post test are 53.81 and 40.27 respectively.

TABLE. 21.4: Significant Difference between Boys and Girls in Pre-test

Gender	N	Mean	SD	't' value	0.05 level
Boys	71	36.17	8.93	7.89 *	1.98
Girls	52	48.67	8.49		

* Significant

The above table 21.4 shows, the calculated 't' value (7.89) is greater than the table value of (1.98) at 0.05 level of significance. Hence the null hypothesis is rejected. Thus there is significant difference on the Boys and Girls in Pre-Test.

TABLE. 21.5: Significant Difference between Boys and Girls in Post-Test

Gender	N	Mean	SD	't' value	0.05 level
Boys	71	51.45	13.28	2.167*	1.98
Girls	52	57.04	14.75		

* Significance

The above table 21.5 shows the calculated 't' value (2.167) is greater than the table value of 1.98 at 0.05 level of significance. Hence the null hypothesis is rejected. Thus there is significant difference on the Boys and Girls in Post-Test.

TABLE. 21.6: Significant Difference between Rural and Urban in Post-Test

Locality	N	Mean	SD	't' value	0.05 level
Rural	87	55.82	14.95	2.86*	1.98
Urban	36	48.97	10.66		

* Significance

The above table 21.6 shows the calculated 't' value (2.86) is greater than the table value of 1.98 at 0.05 level of significance. Hence the null hypothesis is rejected. Thus there is no significant difference on the Rural and Urban students in Post-Test.

Table. 21.7: Significant Difference between Hosteller and Day Scholar in Post- Test

Stay at	N	Mean	SD	't' value	0.05 level
Hosteller	31	46.39	7.66	4.77*	1.98
Day scholar	92	56.32	14.98		

* Significance

The above table 21.7 shows the calculated 't' value (4.77) is greater than the table value of 1.98 at significance. Hence the null hypothesis is rejected. Thus there is significant difference on the Hosteller and day scholar students in Post-Test.

Major Findings of the Study

1. There is significant difference between Boys and Girls in Pre-Test and Post-Test.
2. There is no significant difference between Rural and Urban in Pre-Test and Post-Test.
3. There is no significant difference between Hosteller and Day scholar in Pre-Test and Post-Test.

Educational Implication

1. Learning through computer is extended to all level of school.
2. The government must give in-service training to the teachers for teaching through computer.
3. Various educational CD's can be implemented in schools to improve the quality of education with audio visual effect. Computer based tutorials (CBT) and web based tutorials (WBT) can also be used to get more ideas on subject and to refer websites regarding latest technologies. Online education test can also be implemented to check students objective type talents with immediate valuation and answers for students references.

Recommendations for Further Study

The findings of the study the investigator observed the following areas recommended for the further research.

1. The same research study may be carried out in different Areas in Tamil Nadu.
2. CAI may be used for those with poor study habits as the study has shown a favourable result.
3. CAI may be used for underachievers to benefit more by this technique of teaching.
4. CAI may be incorporated into the regular curriculum to enable learners benefit more.
5. CAI soft-wares on other topics in Grammar can be developed and experimented for their effective.

CONCLUSION

The present investigation showed that the CAI technique was a versatile tool for a grammar teacher in importing competency in foreign language even to the rural area pupils. The study also revealed interesting quantitative improvement in learning. The 't' test used to analysis the hypothesis led to the conclusion that there is no significant difference between XII standard students in rural and urban Locality in their Post-test.

❒

22

Economics Influence in Education

Economics is one of the important subjects at school level. The life of human being is well associated with economics at every moment. Today's children are tomorrows' citizens. The development of any nation depends mainly on the standards of its' educational institutions. Globalization, industrialization, privatization and liberalization have been causing a lot of changes in the system of school education not only in the developing country like India; but also in the developed countries. A lot of innovations and development are taking place in the teaching methods & tools, infrastructure and appointments of faculties. Working hours of schools are also increased. The new curriculum for economics framed by NCERT at national level and SCERT at state level are excellent. But, it is necessary to know what is going on in schools. What is the attitude of students towards economics? What types of teaching methods are using in schools to teach economics? Whether teachers are providing activities to learn economics in the class room? Students are participating in the field works to learn economics? Students really want to learn economics effectively? Are students learning economics from the society? Are students using economics in the day to day life? To answer all the above questions, a case study has been conducted for ninth class students. By using

Random Sampling Technique, data has been collected through five point scale questionnaire from 120 students of ninth class including boys and girls both in rural and urban areas of Erode District in Tamil Nadu. In the present paper an attempt has been made to analyze the real situation of learning and teaching economics at school level.

We are living in the highly modernized society. With the help of science and technology we are enjoying each and every moment with great pleasure. We are seeing day and night one after another. In the same manner problems and solutions are always move towards side by side. But to find a solution we want some exercise. Nothing will happen if any one sits like a stone. The development of any nation depends mainly on its human resources and education including technology. The standards of any nation depends mainly on its' educational institutions. It is more important to give priority for Economics influence in Education at school level. Economic stability is important for national development. Another, slightly different, definition of economics, favored by many economists, is this: Economics is the study of how our scarce productive resources are used to satisfy human wants. This definition emphasizes two central points. First, productive resources are scarce, in the sense that we are not able to produce all of everything that everyone wants free; thus, we must "economize" our resources, or use them as efficiently as possible. Second, human wants, if not infinite, go so far beyond the ability of our productive resources to satisfy them all that we face a major problem in "economizing" those productive resources so as to satisfy the largest possible number of our wants. Indeed, most major economic problems arise from this fact of scarcity, and the need to make effective use of our resources to satisfy our wants. If there were plenty of everything for everyone to have without working or paying for it, there would be no economic problem. In the recent years we are facing problem of economic crisis by some of the unethical officials.

NEED OF THE STUDY

Understanding economics is essential to becoming an involved and productive citizen that makes wise financial choices. Getting informed about supply, demand and real cost makes us all better consumers. Economics is the social science that studies the methods by which individuals and societies organize production activities and allocate scarce resources to meet material wants and needs. The study of Economics helps to prepare students to make rational economic choices both in their own lives and in their participation in policy decisions as citizens of a city, state, nation, and the world. The study of Economics provides students with analytical tools for interpreting economic events and making personal economic choices, even under changed conditions.

Economics is the study of how the goods and services we want get produced, and how they are distributed among us. This part we call economic analysis. Economics is also the study of how we can make the system of production and distribution work better. This part we call economic policy. Economic analysis is the necessary foundation for sound economic policy.

OBJECTIVES

The study is designed with the following specific objectives:

1. To study the attitude of IX class students towards economics.
2. To know the methods of teaching in economics.
3. To know the status of learning through activities.
4. To know the importance of field work in economics.
5. To study the status of usage of economics in daily life.
6. To find how many students are encouraged by their parents to study economics.
7. To find the rate of students to study economics at higher level.

METHODOLOGY

Tools

The investigator searched for the tools for economics of education. The investigator has not found suitable tool for economics of education. Hence, the investigator planned to develop a tool for economics of education. On the basis of review of literature, a list of 33 items on Economics influence in Education was prepared. These items were given to some experts. The experts had checked the suitability and vocabulary used in the items. 8 items were deleted on the advice of the experts and 25 items retained were suitable to measure the attitude of IX class students towards economics of education. Each item of the inventory was arranged on a 5 point scale with responses: Strongly Agree (SA), Agree (A), Doubtful (D), Disagree (DA) and Strongly Disagree (SDA). A personal data sheet was prepared to collect personal information of the IX class students.

Locale, Sample, Data Collection and Analysis

The data was collected from IX class students in both rural and urban areas of Erode District. The total number of sample was 120. The data thus collected was pooled and analyzed keeping in view of the objectives of the study.

FINDINGS OF THE STUDY

1. Characteristics of the Sample

To understand the characteristics of the sample, the sample were classified into different groups based on their characteristics and percentage were calculated for each group. The classified information is presented in the table-1.

The characteristics of the sample reveal that the data were collected from 50 per cent of boys and girls in both rural and urban areas of Erode District. The total number of the sample was 120. 82.5 per cent of students are belongs to the age 14 years; 12.5 and 3.33 per cent of students are belongs to < 13 years and > 15 years age group respectively. Among the sample 20 per cent are belongs to OC community; 52.41 per cent are BC community students and remaining 25.83 per cent are SC/ST students. In the case of religion 80.00 per cent students belongs to Hindu; 5.83 per cent are belongs to Muslim and 14.16 per cent are belongs to Christian. The occupation of father and mother; educational qualifications of father, mother and teacher and annual income of the family were given in the table-1.

TABLE. 22.1: Characteristics of the Sample

S. No.	Variable	Group	N	%
1	Sex	Boys	60	50.00
		Girls	60	50.00
2	Age	<13 years	17	12.50
		14 years	99	82.50
		> 15 years	4	03.33
3	Locality	Rural	60	50.00
		Urban	60	50.00
4	Caste	OC	24	20.00
		BC	65	52.41
		SC/ST	31	25.83
5	Religion	Hindu	96	80.00
		Muslim	7	05.83
		Christian	17	14.16
6	Occupation of father	Govt. employee	21	17.5
		Private employee	32	26.66
		Agriculture	50	41.66
		Business	10	08.33
		Part time/Others	7	05.83

7	Occupation of mother	Govt. employee	12	10.00
		Private employee	23	19.16
		Agriculture	37	30.83
		Business	14	11.66
		Part time/Others	10	08.33
		House wife	24	20.00
8	Educational Qualification of father	Illiterate	9	07.50
		I-X	38	31.66
		XI- Degree	40	33.33
		P.G. and above	33	27.50
9	Educational Qualification of mother	Illiterate	15	12.50
		I-X	69	57.50
		XI- Degree	23	19.16
		P.G. and above	13	10.83
10	Educational Qualification of economics teacher	B.A. with B.Ed.	71	59.16
		M.A.	37	30.83
		M.Phil/Ph.D	12	10.00
11	Annual Income of the family	Up to Rs. 50,000/-	4	03.33
		Rs. 50,001/- to 1,00,000/-	32	26.66
		Rs. 1,00,001/-to 2,00,000/-	69	57.50
		Above Rs. 2,00,000/-	15	12.50

2. Attitude of IX Class Students towards Economics of Education

Table. 22.2: Attitude of IX Class Students towards Economics of Education

S. No.	Statement	Strongly Agree (SA) % (N)	Agree (A) % (N)	Disagree (DA) % (N)	Strongly Disagree (SDA) % (N)
1	I like economics very much.	3.33 **(4)**	56.66 **(68)**	38.33 **(46)**	1.66 **(2)**
2	The way of economics teaching of my teacher is excellent.	3.33 **(4)**	55.83 **(67)**	35.00 **(42)**	05.83 **(7)**

3	Activity based learning of economics is available in our school.	10.00 **(12)**	23.33 **(28)**	58.33 **(70)**	08.33 **(10)**
4	I am learning Economics through society.	20.83 **(25)**	31.66 **(38)**	37.50 **(45)**	10.00 **(12)**
5	I like to read economic matters in the news paper.	18.33 **(22)**	05.83 **(7)**	55.83 **(67)**	20.00 **(24)**
6	It is important to know about Indian economy and economists.	20.83 **(25)**	60.00 **(72)**	09.16 **(11)**	10.00 **(12)**
7	Economics is important for everybody in the society.	90.83 **(109)**	01.66 **(2)**	01.66 **(2)**	05.83 **(7)**
8	Economics is useless subject.				100 **(120)**
9	I learned saving method through economics.	46.66 **(56)**	07.50 **(9)**	26.66 **(32)**	19.16 **(23)**
10	It is important to give more value for economics than any other subjects.	03.33 **(4)**	01.66 **(2)**	85.00 **(102)**	10.00 **(12)**
11	I feel some times economics is difficult.	19.16 **(23)**	05.83 **(7)**	56.66 **(68)**	18.33 **(22)**
12	I like to study economics at higher level.	03.33 **(4)**	05.00 **(6)**	35.00 **(42)**	56.66 **(68)**
13	I don't watch TV programmes related to economics.	35.00 **(42)**	30.00 **(36)**	13.33 **(16)**	21.66 **(26)**
14	The impact of economics is much on national development.	68.33 **(82)**	24.16 **(29)**	01.66 **(2)**	05.83 **(7)**

15	Our parent encourages studying economics well.	30.83 **(37)**	35 **(42)**	11.66 **(14)**	22.50 **(27)**
16	I don't like field works in economics.	01.66 **(2)**	05.83 **(7)**	23.33 **(28)**	69.16 **(83)**
17	I like lecture cum demonstration method in economics teaching.	85.00 **(102)**	11.66 **(14)**	0.83 **(1)**	02.5 **(3)**
18	I read economics well.	60.00 **(72)**	06.66 **(8)**	10.83 **(13)**	22.50 **(27)**
19	Economics is an important subject for all students.	60.00 **(72)**	10.83 **(13)**	10.00 **(12)**	19.16 **(23)**
20	I am frequently discussing economics with my friends.	18.33 **(22**	25.83 **(31**	25.00 **(30**	30.83 **(37)**
21	I have much interest to learn economics effectively.	05.00 **(6)**	01.66 **(2)**	45.00 **(54)**	48.33 **(58)**
22	The economics syllabus was not good.	17.50 **(21)**	05.00 **(7)**	37.50 **(45)**	39.16 **(47)**
23	I use economics in my daily life.	89.16 **(107)**	04.16 **(5)**	04.16 **(5)**	02.50 **(3)**
24	I give priority for marks than subject knowledge of economics.	44.16 **(53)**	14.16 **(17)**	12.50 **(15)**	29.16 **(35)**
25	The encouragement of teacher is not good in the process of learning economics.	27.50 **(33)**	10.00 **(12)**	32.50 **(39)**	30.00 **(36)**

MAJOR FINDINGS OF THE STUDY

The following results were found in the present study:

1. Attitude of IX Class Students Towards Economics of Education

Overall 60 per cent of IX class students were liked economics very much. Among the 60 per cent, 3.33 per cent of students were strongly agreed and 56.66 per cent of students were agreed the statement-1. 40 per cent of students were disliked economics. Among the 40 per cent 1.66 per cent were strongly disagreed the statement-1 and 38.33 per cent were disagreed the statement-1.

2. Method of Teaching in Economics

59.16 per cent of IX class students were liked their teachers' way of economics teaching. Among 59.16 per cent only 3.33 per cent of students were strongly agreed the statement-2 and remaining 55.83 per cent were agreed the statement-2. 40.83 (35.00 per cent- DA, 5.83 per cent-SDA) per cent of students were not liked their teachers' way of economics teaching.

96.66 per cent of students were liked 'Lecturer cum demonstration method' (85.00 per cent and 11.66 per cent of IX class students are strongly agree and agree the statement-17).

3. Learning Economics Effectively

Only 6.66 per cent of IX class students were ready to learn economics effectively. Among this 5.00 per cent students were strongly agreed and 1.66 per cent students were agreed the statement-21. 93.33 (45.00 per cent of students –DA, 48.33 per cent of students-SDA) per cent of students were just learning the economics.

76.66 per cent of IX class students were believed that the economics syllabus was good and only 23.33 per cent of students were didn't liked the economics syllabus.

3. Practice of Economics in Daily Life

93.32 per cent of students are practicing economics in their daily life. 89.16 per cent and 4.16 per cent of IX class students are strongly agree and agree the statement-23 respectively. 92.49 per cent of students are feeling that economics is important for everybody in the society and only 7.51 are not agreeing the statement-7 (1.66 per cent of students-DA, 5.83 per cent of students-SDA).

4. Encouragement of Students to Study Economics

65.83 per cent of students are getting encouragement of parents to study economics. Among 65.83 per cent of students 30.83 per cent and 35 per cent of students are strongly agree and agree the statement-15. 34.16 per cent of IX class students were not agreed the statement-15 (11.66 per cent of students were disagreed and 22.50 per cent of students were strongly disagreed the statement-15).

37.50 per cent of IX class students were believed that the teacher encouragement was not good in the process of learning economics. 62.50 per cent of students were believed that the teacher encouragement was good in the process of learning economics.

5. Learning of Economics through Society

52.49 per cent of IX class students are learning economics through society and the remaining 47.51 per cent of IX students are not agreed the statement-4. It shows that 47.51 per cent of IX class students are unable to learn economics through society.

6. Watching and Reading of Economic Matters

24.36 per cent of IX class student are reading economics matters in the news paper and the remaining 75.64 per cent of IX class students are not concentrating economics matters in the news papers.

65.00 per cent of IX class students are watching economics programmes on TV. Only 35.00 per of students are unable to view economics programmes on TV.

CONCLUSION

The development of any nation depends mainly on its' standards of educational institutions. The present study was given a lot of information about IX class students towards economics of education. The students like economics much. At the same time they are not willing to study economics at higher level. The attitude of parents of students is also different. They are encouraging their students to study engineering and medicine. Majority of schools are giving coaching for EAMCET, IIT and other competitive exams from VIII class onwards. They are giving much priority for science and mathematics. The students are also attracted towards science subject compared to arts, especially economics. The students are studying economics to get marks only. They don't know about the job opportunities for economics students. It is the duty of parents and teachers to motivate the students towards economics.

❐

23

Students Attitude towards Audio-Visual Aids Used by the Teachers

Audio Visual aids or Graphic aids are the form of visuals that are represented on plane surface. The subject matter areas that are represented in Audio Visual aids or Graphic aids are in an abridged and easily understandable form. They convey meaning mainly through relatively conventionalized symbols that are nearer to reality perceptually than verbal symbols. They secure the attention of the pupils by their attractive format and simplicity of layout. They convey the expected message by combination of visual and pictorial message made meaningful by suitable captions. Pictures and words blended in harmony deliver the required information. The idea conveyed by any graphic aid should be a single concept. The layout and words should not be complicated so as to puzzle the viewer and make him lose interest in the same. The statement "one good visual which can secure and maintain attention and educate the viewer in the desired area is worth a thousand words" is quite correct. Graphics could be truly considered as the shorthand language of the idea presented. The criteria for good graphics are that they should be simple, bold, legible, brief and have adequate margins. Graphics are only two-dimensional and should be carefully planned to offset the limitation. An Audio Visual aids or a graphic aid by eliminating non–

essentials and by using bold symbolic representations with attractive portrayal should be able to create interest and secure the attention of the pupils. Since the message to be conveyed pertains to a single concept and hence brief, the viewer will not get perplexed on being exposed to the visual but will try to read and understand what is implied (visual and words). Audio Visual aids or a graphic aids could easily be prepared by and teacher using simple materials that are easily available and stored for future use. Making graphics should form an integral part of the teacher's preparation for teaching. Almost any material involving illustrations is basically graphic in nature. There can be an infinite variety of graphic materials. It is difficult to give a rigid list of these materials. The present study aims to find out the students attitude towards audio-visual aids used by the teachers in Coimbatore district. A samples of 100 respondents selected randomly were studied. An interview schedule method of survey was used to find out the attitude towards audio-visual aids. Primary data were collected by using a structured interview scheduled. All the respondents were asked the same questions in the same fashion and they were informed the purpose of study. ANOVA, t-test and regression analysis were applied to test the hypotheses. The data collected through questionnaires have been tabulated. The findings and observations are the result and outcome of the interpretations made during the study of analysis.

Graphs, Diagram, Posters, Maps, Comics, Cartoons, Charts, Globes, Display Board, Peg Boards, Hook and loop board, felt board, magnetic board, marker board, chalk board, bulletin board, models, Epidiascope, slight projector, over head projector (OHP), fields trips, excursion, exhibition, museums, radio, Television, Tape recorder, Video Caste Record VCR and Computers. By using audio visual materials in accessible process, materials givens objects changes in time, speed and space could easily be brought to the class. Audio visual aids can helps to imaginative teachers to solve the communication problems. It also helps to extend human experience. Use of audio visual aids results in greater acquisition of knowledge of facts and ensures longer retention of the information gained. It can provide effective substitutes for direct contact of students with environment-social and physical. It also adds an expected change in attitude and behaviour of the students. It can provide integrated experiences varying from abstract to concrete. It helps in to secure and retain to attention as well as develop the communication skills. It could be used to motivate and stimulate interest of students to gain further knowledge. Lastly, In a conventional teaching method teacher is the centre of attention and the primary sources of information.

An attitude is a mental state of readiness exerting directive or dynamic influence upon individual's response to all objects and situations with which it is related. Therefore if we can have some judgement about the attitude of an individual towards a specific thing or activity then we can have a fair idea as to whether the individual can be persuaded to participate in a particular thing or activity and whether he shall adopt it with interest and sincerity or not.

The attitude is the degree of positive or negative effect associated with some psychological objects namely institution, ideal, symbol, phrase, slogan, job or idea towards which people can differ with respect to positive or negative effect (Thurstone, 1946). The attitude is a dispositional readiness to respond to certain situations, persons, objects in a consistent manner which has been learnt and has become one's typical mode of response (Free Mann, 1950). According to Guild (1950) attitude is a tendency of individual to favour or not to favour some type of situation. The attitude may be considered as motivational perceptual states, which direct perceptions and predispose a person to act in accordance with perceptions (Allport, 1955). The attitudes are learnt pre-dispositions to respond positively to certain objects, situations, institutions, concepts or other persons (Aiken, 1979).

Review of Literature

Glee Harrah Cady and Pat Mc Gregor (2005) describe that "Internet is a network of network and the internet mostly connects network of computers".

Barry (2006) studied the relationship between student's perceptions of their science class room learning environment and attitude to four different scores of scientific information experiments, books, promote positive attitude towards experiment as a source of information, while less favorable environment promoted more positive attitude to the more authoritarian sources of information.

Schafer (2007) compared third and fourth grade students using ESS units with students using laid low science serious on classification skills, science achievements and science attitudes. No achievement or classification skill different were noted but ESS students had more favorable attitudes.

Williams (2008), "Attitude of high school pupils towards general science and its relationship with achievement and its subjects". In her study it is found to examine if there are any differences among the different groups of students such as boys and girls. Rural school pupil and Urban school pupils in respect of their achievement in science, attitude towards science and attitude forwards science education.

Martis Anandi (2009) developed the test on scientific attitudes (TOSA), taking the point of view that attitudes must be inferred from the behavior of students. They developed a multiple – choice format test. The developed behavioral definitions of eight attitudes: (1) critical mindedness, (2) suspended judgment (3) Respect for evidence (4) Honesty, (5) Objectivity, (6) Willingness to change opinions, (7) Open – mindedness and (8) Questioning attitude. The behavioral definitions to these eight attitudes were used to develop items.

Mohanty Ajay Kumar (2010) investigated attitudes towards education, critical thinking ability and specific effective behavious of (1) Students who had studied, the BSCS environmental models "Investing your Environment" (IYE), (2) Those students using one of BSCS biological science version and (3) Those studying models of Biology. He found that the ability of students who had experienced BSCS Biological science was significantly increased but no other differences were found among the students on any of the other variables.

Objective

The present study attempts to investigate the attitude towards Audio-visual aids used by the teachers.

Methodology

Methodology is an important aspect of any research work. There are different methods followed at various stages of any investigation. The details of methods followed in this study such as selection of tools, sample frame, collection of data, and analysis of data are involved in this research paper. The study has been designed with the student's attitude towards Audio-visual aids used by the teacher's achievement. The major aim of the present study is to determine the student's Audio-visual aids used by the teacher.

Method of Data Collection

The investigator personally distributed the questionnaires to each member of the randomly selected sample. They were requested to answer the items in the booklet as per the instructions provided at the beginning of each questionnaire. Confidentiality of response was assured. The questionnaires were collected by the investigator from the employees. The responses were scored as per the scoring key of the respective questionnaire. Then the results were tabulated, analysed and discussed.

Sample

A sample is a finite number of observations (or) cases in a particular universe of which it is a pat (Good 1952). The investigator prepared a representative random sample of students studying VIII & IX standard in different schools at Coimbatore District. A sample of 100 students was finally selected.

Hypothesis

Students have favorable attitude towards use of Audio Visual Aids in Coimbatore district school.

Nature of the Tool

The inventory contained general instruction for the students and information about bio data. In addition to that the specific instruction ware given to on the first page of the inventory. Space for collecting personal data like students name type of school, locality of the school, class, gender, community, religion, group, medium of instruction, birth order of the child and parental literacy.

Data Processing

The collected data were analysed using appropriate statistical techniques. The descriptive statistics such as mean and S.D, t-ratio were computed. In order to study the functional dependencies to indicate the likelihood of causal relationships between the variables, inferential statistical techniques of ANOVA and Percentage analysis were computed.

Analysis and Interpretation

TABLE. 23.1: Showing Mean, SD and T-Test for Respondent about Students Attitude towards Audio Visual aids used by the Teachers on the basis of Type of the School.

Types of the school	N	Mean	SD	t-value	LS
Government	62	70.48	6.50	2.78	0.01
Private	38	73.30	10.33		

Hypothesis-1

Students do not differ in their student's attitude towards audio visual aids used by the teachers on the basis of types of the school.

The calculated t-value (2.78), which is significant at 0.01 level, confirms that there is a significant difference in student audio visual aids on the basis of type of the school. Hence the stated hypothesis is rejected. So government students have high level of audio visual aids than private school students.

TABLE. 23.2: Showing Mean, SD and T-Test for Respondent about Students Attitude towards Audio Visual Aids used by the Teachers on the basis of Locality of the School.

Locality of the school	N	Mean	SD	t-value	LS
Urban	74	72.24	8.11	1.07	NS
Rural	26	71.14	9.19		

Hypothesis -2

Students do not differ in their student's attitude towards audio visual aids used by the teachers on the basis of locality of the school.

The calculated t-value (1.07), which is not significant at 0.05 level, confirms that there is no significant difference in their audio visual aids on the basis of locality of the school. Hence the stated hypothesis is accepted.

TABLE.23.3: Showing Mean, SD and T-Test for Respondent about Students Attitude towards Audio Visual aids used by the Teachers on the basis of Gender.

Gender	N	Mean	SD	t-value	LS
Male	74	70.97	7.41	1.85	NS
Female	26	72.90	9.89		

Hypothesis-3

Students do not differ in their student's attitude towards audio visual aids used by the teachers on the basis of gender.

The calculated t-value (1.85), which is not significant at 0.05 level, confirms that there is no significant difference in their audio visual aids on the basis of gender. Hence the stated hypothesis is accepted.

TABLE. 23.4: Showing Mean, SD and T-Test for Respondent about Students Attitude towards Audio Visual aids used by the Teachers on the basis of Group.

Group	N	Mean	SD	t-value	LS
Arts	56	69.19	5.37	5.58	0.01
Science	44	74.58	10.37		

Hypothesis-4

Students do not differ in their attitude towards audio visual aids used by the teachers on the basis of group.

The calculated t-value (5.58), which is significant at 0.01 level, confirms that there is a significant difference in student audio visual aids on the basis of group. Hence the stated hypothesis is rejected. So science students have high level of audio visual aids than art students.

TABLE. 23.5: Showing Mean, SD and F-Ratio for Students Attitude towards Audio Visual Aids used by the Teachers on the basis of Medium of Instruction.

Medium of instruction	N	Mean	SD	F-ratio	LS
Hindi	50	70.20	9.64	6.49	0.01
English	30	71.75	4.19		
Kannada	20	75.00	11.60		
Total	100	71.78	8.58		

Hypothesis-5

Students do not differ in their attitude towards audio visual aids used by the teachers on the basis of medium of instruction.

The calculated F-ratio (6.49), which is not significant at 0.05 level, confirms that there is a significant difference in students attitude of audio visual aids on the basis of medium of instruction. Hence the stated hypothesis is rejected.

TABLE. 23.6: Regression for Student Demographic Dharacters and their Attitude towards Audio Visual Aids used by the Teachers Model Summary

Model	R	R Square	Adjusted R Square	Std. Error of the Estimate
1	.436[a]	.190	.159	7.87

a. Predictors: (Constant)

ANOVAb

Model	Sum of Squares	df	Mean Square	F	Sig.
Regression	.4189.756	11	380.887	6.155	.000[a]
Residual	17821.724	88	61.881		
Total	**22011.480**	**99**			

a. Predictors: (Constant)

b. Dependent variable

Coefficientsa

Model	Unstandardized Coefficients		Standardized Coefficients	t	Sig.
	B	Std. Error	Beta		
Name of the school	58.979	4.376		13.477	.000
Type of the school	2.387	1.116	.139	2.139	.033**
Locality of the school	-1.000	1.005	-.058	-.995	.320
Class	-.500	1.046	-.028	-.478	.633
Gender	1.989	1.052	.115	1.891	.060
Community	-1.365	.422	-.190	-3.233	.001**
Religion	.757	.627	.068	1.208	.228
Groups	5.255	.947	.306	5.548	.000**
Medium of instruction	2.183	.649	.191	3.365	.001**
Birth order of the child	-9.11	1.032	-.001	-.009	.993
Parental literacy (Father)	-.143	1.003	-.008	-.143	.887
Parental literacy (Mother)	-.585	.955	-.033	-.612	.541

a. Dependent Variable: Attitude towards Audi visual aids

** Significant at 0.01 level

According to the regression result it is known that the demographic variables are influenced nearly 19 per cent to measure their attitude towards audio visual aids. This is proved by the obtained r square value (0.19).

Further the calculated F-value (6.15) also significant at 0.01 level. It indicates that there is a significant influence between students demographic characters and their attitude towards audio visual aids.

Also from the obtained t- values the demographic variables such as type of school, community, group studied and medium of instructions the students studied are significant at 0.01 level. So it is concluded that there is a significant difference regarding attitude towards audio visual aids on the basis of these variables.

CONCLUSION

Audio Visual aids or graphic aids are the form of visuals that are represented on plane surface. The subject – matter areas that are represented in Audio Visual aids or graphic aids are in an abridged and easily understandable form. They convey meaning mainly through relatively conventionalized symbols that are nearer to reality perceptually than verbal symbols. They secure the attention of the pupils by their attractive format and simplicity of layout. They convey the expected message by combination of visual and pictorial message made meaningful by suitable captions. Pictures and words blended in harmony deliver the required information. The idea conveyed by any graphic aid should be a single concept. The layout and words should not be complicated so as to puzzle the viewer and make him lose interest in the same. The statement "one good visual which can secure and maintain attention and educate the viewer in the desired area is worth a thousand words" is quite correct. Graphics could be truly considered as the shorthand language of the idea presented. The criteria for good graphics are that they should be simple, bold, legible, brief and have adequate margins.

Findings of the Study

1. Based on the results that students do not differ in their audio visual aids on the basis of types of the school
2. From the calculation that students do not differ in their audio visual aids on the basis of locality of the school
3. Based on the results that students do not differ in their audio visual aids on the basis of gender
4. Based on the results that students do not differ in their audio visual aids on the basis of group
5. From the analysis that students do not differ in their audio visual aids on the basis of medium of instruction

Discussion

Audio visual aids a process of inward journey to unravel the hidden potentialities of a being. It helps an individual to develop ones personality. A systematic approach of Audio visual aids helps an individual to see the all around development at physical, mental, intellectual and emotional level. The practice of use of audio visual aids makes an individual perfect. It removes the unwanted elements in the mind of the learner. It improves concentration and brings mental stability. Audio visual aids are an essential tool for students to achieve higher score in their studies as if improves concentration, memory and skills. The present study clearly indicates and recommends the students to use of audio visual aids as to develop positive attitude towards everything in their life which helps to excel themselves in their studies. The entire study concluded reveals that the use of audio visual aids has high achievement and expressed more favourable attitude.

Educational Implications

Audio-visual aids are very important and useful aids for teaching. As well as it creates high interest among the students to learn the subjects. So, the department of education shall take a steps to implement the latest audio-visual aids to all the school and colleges for teaching purpose.

For self-learning, these type of aids are very helpful to the students. Also students are very much interested in using latest technologies such as computers and internet. In internet lot of facilities are there to learn new information with visual appearance. From that students are also get more interest to use that.
In the case of teaching, in older days teachers follow interactive methods and oral demonstration. But these are not creating much interest. In order to create interest and attention audio-visual aids are highly useful. So, the concerned educational institution tries to provide these facilities. So that teachers and students get benefited.

Suggestions

The following suggestions are arrived from the research findings. Research found that use of audio visual aids will contribute more in students achievement. Also the result reveals that use of audio visual aids increases the memory power, concentration. Further it sharpens the intelligence. Apart from that it reduces misconception in learning. Further due to use of audio visual aids the sensory expression would be more exercised. So, the present research suggested that in all schools and colleges, the students advised to use of audio visual aids compulsory. The education department forms a rule for that and advises the educational institutions make a step to establish separate infrastructure for this one. Also the Government take a step to use audio visual aids effectively students in their academic. This will definitely help the students to be a good learner imbibing the concepts.

CONCLUSION

The present study attempted to identify the students attitude towards audio-visual aids used by the teachers. For that the researcher framed some objectives. On the basis of objectives, a questionnaire is framed. After framing the questionnaire, these are circulated to the selected samples. 100 samples were selected randomly. The responses were collected and coded using computerised. To test the hypotheses and characteristics of the data, some standard statistical tools were used. The statistical tools such as t-test, F-ratio and correlation were used. From the analysis the result concluded that the students have positive attitude towards audio-visual aids used by the teachers.

❐

24

Learning Styles of Higher Secondary Students in Biological Science

Learning sty.le is a hypothetical contract that has been developed to explain the process of mediation between stimuli and response. Learning style as on integral concept that bridges the personality cognitive dimensions of the individuals. The learning styles are synonymous. He defines learning styles as the course of learning. Laycock (1978) describes learning styles as an individual characteristic way of responding to certain variable in the instructional environment. In simplest terms, a students learning style is the peculiar way with which he learns best. The present study aims to find out the learning styles of higher secondary students in biological science in Villupuram District. A samples of 100 respondents selected randomly were studied. A questionnaire method of survey was used to find out the learning styles of higher secondary students in biological science. The data were collected by using questionnaire as an instrument. Primary data were collected by conducting direct structured interview using questionnaire. All the respondents were asked the same questions in the same fashion and they were informed the purpose of study. Regression and correlation analysis were applied to test the hypotheses.

The data collected through questionnaires have been tabulated. The findings and observations are the result and outcome of the interpretations made during the study of analysis. The result found that average learning styles of higher secondary students in biological science in Villupuram District.

The act or experience of one that learns. Knowledge or skill acquired by instruction or study. Modification of a behavioral tendency by experience (as exposure to conditioning). Adapted from How Learning Works by Ambrose et al.: an engagingly written, evidence-based text, well-illustrated by practical examples, and a book well worth your time, as a TA and as a student.

As teachers, our goal is to encourage learning in our classrooms. But what is learning, and what principles or factors affect how our students learn? In this section, we provide you with the very basics of what learning are, how and when it occurs, and how to structure your lessons to maximize student learning. There are three components to the definition of Learning:

1. **"Learning is a process, not a product."** Exam scores and term papers are measures of learning, but they are not the process of learning itself.
2. **"Learning is a change in knowledge, beliefs, behaviors or attitudes."** This change requires time, particularly when one is dealing with changes to core beliefs, behaviors, and attitudes. Don't interpret a lack of sea change in your students' beliefs or attitudes immediately following a lesson as a lack of learning on their part, but instead, consider that such a change will take time – perhaps a few weeks, perhaps until the end of the term, or even longer.
3. **"Learning is not something done to students, but something that students themselves do."** If you have ever carefully planned a lesson, only to find that your students just didn't "get it," consider that your lesson should be designed not just to impart knowledge but also to lead students through the process of their own learning.

Learning is the process by which one acquires, ingests, and stores or accepts information. Our experiences with learned information compose our bodies of knowledge. Learning is a process unique to each individual. Some learn quickly, scanning the information and mastering the concept or skill seemingly effortlessly. Others stumble while processing information, taking longer to grasp the concept or requiring numerous exposures over a sustained period of time. Some individuals store the information they've learned indefinitely, cementing it in their memories. Others find that the information they've learned slips away rapidly. Some learn best through text, others through practice, some through hearing. Learning styles are as unique and varied as our personalities. Learning is a lifelong endeavor. As long as one remains engaged in life, learning does not cease.

Until recently most people took learning styles for granted and left them to instinct. Realization that studying how learning should come before everything else is spreading in the world of education skill in this field can multiply efficiency. The use of higher level work skills can bring improvement in almost all fields. Improvement in athletic field and industrial productivity has been achieved in the way. Everyone is familiar with the difference in output of a self-taught typist who uses one finger of each hand and an expert who was taught the tough system. Other experiments has shown that the level of performance on such tasks as card sorting, pitch discrimination and puzzle solving is affected by the method employed and the limit to performance might be improved of better work was used.

These findings on effects of work methods on levels of performance led to the significant theoretical contribution to theories regarding the causes of individual difference in competence. It was long assumed that these differences were primarily due to two factors. (1) Learning and (2) Amount of training in a task. Dr. Seashare after studying may findings on effects of work method, concluded that method of work was a third variable in instruction. It is found that new levels in achievement are possible by improving the learning styles.

Both in common speech and educational literature the word "Read" is used to designate a wide variety of learned activities from the socially undesirable to the highly ethnical, form bodily skill, such as walking to mental activities such as learning of critical thinking and from specified abilities to generalized attitudes. The meaning of learning includes the ideal of facility in the performance of an act, combined with a persisting inclination towards the repetition of the act.

As Bagley has said "To teach a child to study effectively is to do that most valuable thing that could be done to help him adjust himself to any environment of modern civilized life into which they live. In 1917 strays and Newsworthy declared "Many teachers have taught subjects, but not how to study subjects, the latter is more important". H.R. Bhatia says, "unless opportunities for doing and respecting things are afforded to children it is futile to expect them to form habits". Sevmors and exhortations may help children to acquire normal vocabulary but not normal character. Percepta in the formation of learning unless children are afforded actual practice in those modes behaviour.

Review of Literature

Mary Lou Koran, John J. Koran (2006), conducted a study "Interaction of Learner aptitudes with question packing in learning from prose, he suggested that, in some cases, reduction in certain information Processing requirements may actually be an important prerequisite to affective utilization of other aptitudes (learning).

The over-all means used in the analysis are presented, both low and high aptitude students in "favourable" classrooms had higher achievements scores than the two groups in 'unfavourable' classroom. This contexts effect was present to some extent in both third and fourth grade class room aptitude, third grade students. It appears that being in a classroom with many high-aptitude students is beneficial for low-aptitude students and some high-aptitude students as well".

K.S Kahlon and Vinod Uppalo, (2007) studied on "women's aptitude and achievement in Relation to achievement motivation.

The Result of the present investigation fully support the hypotheses on the basis of which the study had been undertaken.

1. There is significant, but imperfect relationship between aptitude (learning style) and academic achievement.
2. Discrepancy between aptitude (Learning style) and achievement bears no relationship with ability.
3. Discrepancy between aptitude (Learning Style) and achievement bears significant relationship with academic achievement.
4. Discrepancy between aptitude and achievement bears significant relationship with achievement motivation. That is, high achievement motivation goes with positive discrepancy where as low achievement motivation accounts for negative discrepancy"

Robert B. Burnes (2012) conducted a study on "The Relation of Aptitudes of Learning at different Points in the time during Instruction: The result of this study suggested that some aptitude-learning relations are not stable over time and that his instability is exhibited in different aptitudes being required at different points in time during instruction. These findings supported most of the Junior evidence examining aptitude correlates at different stages of learning and did not support the assumption made in ATI Research that aptitudes relate equally to learning for the during of treatment"

Moraddwaj Varma (2013) conducted a study on "Comparative achievement in science of Tharu Tribals and other at high school level. He found, that the achievement of Tharu tribals is lower than that of the non-tharus in all the three science subjects were significant at .01 level."

In Jamur (2013) made a study in Patna in relationship between study habits and achievement. His study showed a correlation of 0.51 between study habits and achievement of students and a correlation of 0.144 between study habits and intelligence.

Objectives

1. To study the higher secondary learning styles in Biological science.
2. To know the higher secondary different methods learning styles in Biological science.
3. To find out the higher secondary factors learning styles in Biological science.

Methodology

The methodology adopted for the study is explained in detail. The sampling technique, size of the sample, variables of the study, description of the tool used and administration of tool are elaborated.

Sample

The sample selected for the present study is 100 higher secondary students in Villupuram district. Random sampling technique was used for the selection of sample.

Data Collection

Primary data, required for the present research work were collected by conducting direct interviews using questionnaire. All the respondents were given sufficient information about the Project work. These respondents were provided with the same questionnaires. They were also informed that they have to answer in the same fashion.

Tools used in the Study

SOLAT Tool of learning style D. Venketraman (1986) consists of 25 items. The learning style comprises 5 categories.

1. Verbal (1 to 5 items)
2. Content preference (6 to 10 items)
3. Class preference (11 to 15 items)
4. Learning preference (16 to 20 items)
5. Interest (20 to 25 items)

Scoring Procedure

The maximum score that a student obtains is 50 the minimum score that a student gain is 25.

Each item has two alternatives. If the student chooses the First alternative one mark is given. If the student chooses Second alternative the student it secures 2 marks. The first alternative of an item indicates the use of Right hemisphere of the brain and the second alternative of an item indicates the use of left hemisphere of the brain.

Tool Validity and Reliability

The main attributes needed to be considered regarding a good tool are validity and reliability.

Validity: A measuring instrument is said to be valid if it measures what it purpose to measure. Validity may be defined as the extent to which an instrument or a test does the job derived of it. The kind of validity and the extent or degrees to which it should be established are the major consideration while establishing validity.

In the present study the researcher found out the content validity.

Content validity gives the logical evidence that the content of the items of a test is suitable for the purpose for which the test is designed and used. Content validity is established is 0.549.

Reliability

The efficiency of measuring the different items are called on aspect of reliability. Reliability determined test-retest method and it is found to be validity of the tool is (0.82).

HYPOTHESIS

1. The level of learning styles among higher secondary students on the basis of their demographic variables.
2. The level of different method learning styles among higher secondary students on the basis of their demographic variables.
3. The level of factors learning styles among higher secondary students on the basis of their demographic variables.

Analysis and Interpretation

TABLE.24.1: Showing the Stepwise Regression Analysis Predicting learning Styles among Higher Secondary Students and Demographic Variables

Sl. No	Step/Source	Unstandardized Coefficients Beta	Std. Error	Standardized Coefficients Beta	Step t	P
1.	Gender	1.342	0.343	1.245	5.432	0.01
2.	Locality	1.224	0.392	0.269	6.641	0.01
3.	Family Income	1.924	0.549	0.149	4.142	0.01
4.	Father Education	2.334	0.667	0.108	5.339	0.01

* $P < 0.01$

Four variables viz Gender, Locality, Family income and Father Education have significantly contributed for predicting the learning styles among higher secondary students. The Gender seems to be 5.432, Locality seems to be 6.641, Family income seems to be 4.142 and Father education seems to be 5.339. The predictive value of these variables separately is 0.01.

TABLE. 24.2: Showing the Stepwise Regression Analysis Predicting Different Method learning Styles and Demographic Variables

SL. NO	Step/Source	Unstandardized Coefficients Beta	Std. Error	Standardized Coefficients Beta	Step t	P
1.	Type of Family	1.133	0.505	0.434	2.246	0.01
2.	Religion	1.248	0.466	0.782	2.677	0.01
3.	Community	1.792	0.683	0.646	2.625	0.01
4.	Birth Place	2.338	0.670	0.954	3.490	0.01

* P < 0.01

Four variables viz Type of family, Religion, Community and Birth place have significantly contributed for predicting the method learning styles. The first variable Type of family seems to be 2.246, Religion seems to be 2.677, Community seems to be 2.625 and Birth place seems to be 3.490. The predictive value of these variables separately is 0.01.

TABLE. 24.3: Showing the Stepwise Regression Analysis Predicting Factors learning Styles among Higher Secondary Students and Demographic Variables

Sl. No	Step/Source	Unstandardized Coefficients Beta	Std. Error	Standardized Coefficients Beta	Step t	P
1.	Gender	5.195	1.030	0.824	5.041	0.01
2.	Family Monthly Income	1.809	0.451	0.443	4.016	0.01

* P < 0.01

Two variables viz Gender and Family Monthly Income have significantly contributed for predicting the factors learning styles among higher secondary. The first variable Gender seems to be 5.195, when paired with the second variable Family monthly income is 1.809. The predictive value of these variables separately is 0.01.

TABLE. 24.4: Showing the Correlation between the Learning Styles of Higher Secondary Students and Demographic Variables

Factors	Learning styles of higher secondary students
Gender	0.579*
Locality	0.782**
Family Income	0.591*
Father Education	0.572*
Type of Family	0.824**

* Significant at 0.01 level Significant at 0.05 level

Learning styles of higher secondary students is positively and significantly related to Gender (0.579), Locality (0.782), Family Income (0.591), Father Education (0.572) and Type of family (0.824). So the direct relationship between the Learning styles of higher secondary students and demographic variables.

CONCLUSION

The present study aims to find out the higher secondary students learning styles. The researcher framed objectives and hypotheses on the basis of the above context. The research was carried out in 100 samples based randomly. A questionnaire constructed by R was used to collect the relevant data. After collecting the data they were analyzed using statistical tools such as Regression and Correlation analysis. The result concluded that students have average level of learning styles at Higher Secondary level in Biological science in Villupuram District.

❐

25

Transitive Cloud Computing for Teaching-Learning Process

This paper is an introduction to the terms, characteristics and services associated with internet-based computing, commonly referred to as cloud computing. The primary business service models being deployed, such as software, platform and infrastructure as a service - and common deployment models employed by service providers and users to use and maintain the cloud services, such as private, public, community, and hybrid clouds are discussed. Cloud computing is not something that suddenly appeared overnight: in some form it may trace back into our time when computer system remotely shared computing resources and applications. Some of the notable challenges associated with Cloud computing is that it not delivers more services in the cloud, it also can provide opportunities, if resolved with due care and attention in the planning. Lack of standard-clouds have documented inter faces; however, no standards are associated with these, and thus it is unlikely that most clouds will be interoperable. The open grid forum is developing an open Cloud computing interface to resolve this issue and the open cloud consortium is working on Cloud computing standards and practices. An important function of the Cloud is that it automatically saves content, making it impossible to lose or delete any valuable material. This means that even if a computer crashes, all documents and content will remain safe and accessible in the cloud. Any data stored in the Cloud can easily be accessed from almost any device including mobile devices such as phones or tablets. With the availability of content online, it is no longer necessary for teachers to spend time and resources printing or copying lengthy documents or lesson plans. Now, students are able to access homework assignments, lesson notes, and other materials through online.

The term "cloud" as used in this white paper, appears to have its origin in network diagrams that represented the internet, or various part of it, as schematic clouds. "Cloud computing" was coined when applications and services were moved into the internet "Cloud". Cloud computing is not something that suddenly that appeared overnight: in some form it may be traced back into our time when computer system remotely shared computing resources and applications. Cloud computing refers to many different types of services and applications being delivered in the internet cloud and the fact that in many cases the device used to access these services and applications do not require any special applications.

How Cloud Computing is Used in Education?

Cloud computing take education to the next level. There is no surprise that cloud computing education is a necessary tool for many companies and even schools. In this type of calculation, this should not be confused with others such as grid computing, utility computing or autonomic computing. Even if you are not completely familiar with cloud computing, you are certainly in touch with it on a regular basis, such as in use in computer applications like Skype. The interesting part about cloud computing is that entire systems can be set on a rental basis. Rather than more commonly owned tools to be engaged, it is true that cloud computation is another form of resource where teaching can take place. Most people use it to teach through social networking sites such as Face book and MySpace, email systems like Hotmail, gmail etc....

Cloud Computing is an umbrella term used to describe Cloud Computing services that are hosted on a network (typically the internet) and used by the PCs (or other devices) without mentioning specific servers or systems for teaching.

Characteristics of Cloud Computing

- **Shared Infrastructure** – uses a virtualized software model which enables the sharing of physical services, storage and networking capabilities. The cloud infrastructure regardless of deployment model seeks to make the most of the available infrastructure across a number of users.
- **Dynamic Provisioning** – It allows for the provision of service based on current demand requirements. This is done automatically using software automations enabling the expansions and contraction of service capabil-

ity as needed. This dynamic needs to be done while maintaining the high level of reliability and security.

- **Network Access** – needs to be accessed across the internet from a broad range of devices such as PCs, laptops and mobile devices, using standard based APIs (For e.g., ones is based on http). Deployments of services in the cloud include everything from business applications to the latest applications on the newest smart phones.
- **Managed Metering** – uses metering for managing and optimizing the services and to provide reporting and billing information. In this way consumers are billed for services according to how much they actually use during the billing period.

Service Models

- **Software as a Service (SaaS)** - consumers purchase the ability to access and use an application or service that is posted in the cloud.
- **Platform as a Service (PaaS)** - consumers purchase access to the platforms, enabling them to deploy their own software and applications in the cloud.
- **Infrastructure as a Services(IaaS)** - consumers control and manage their systems in terms of the operating system, applications, storage, and network connectivity, but do not themselves control the cloud infrastructure.

Deployment Models

Deploying Cloud computing can differ depending on requirements, and the following four development models have been identified:

- **Private cloud**-the cloud infrastructure has been deployed, and is maintained and operated for a specific organization. The operation may be in-house or with the third party on the premises.
- **Community cloud**- the cloud infrastructure is shared among the number of organizations with similar interest and requirements.
- **Public cloud**- the cloud infrastructure is available to the public on the commercial basis by a cloud service provider.
- **Hybrid cloud**- the cloud infrastructure consists of a number of clouds of any type, but the clouds have the ability through their interfaces to allow their data and/or applications to be moved from one cloud to another.

Advantages

- **Back Up:** An important function of the Cloud is that it automatically saves content, making it impossible to lose or delete any valuable material. This means that even if a computer crashes, all documents and content will remain safe, saved, and accessible in the cloud.
- **Storage:** The Cloud allows its users to store almost all types of content and data including music, documents, eBooks, applications, photos, and much more.
- **Accessibility:** Any data stored in the Cloud can easily be accessed from almost any device including mobile devices such as phones or tablets.
- **Collaboration:** Because the Cloud allows multiple users to work on and edit documents at the same time, it enables effortless sharing and transmission of ideas. With this feature, group projects and or collaborative lesson plans can be optimized for both teachers and students.

  Resource and Time Conscious: With the availability of content online, it is no longer necessary for teachers to spend time and resources printing or copying lengthy documents or lesson plans. Now, students are able to access homework assignments, lesson notes, and other study materials online.
- **Assignments:** I love the Cloud to allow teachers to post assignments online. Students are able to access these assignments, complete them, and save them in a folder to be reviewed later.

Challenges

- **Security and Privacy:** perhaps two of the more "hot button" issues surrounding Cloud computing relate to storing and securing data, and monitoring the use of the cloud by the service providers. These issues are generally attributed to slowing the deployment of cloud services.
- **Lack of Standards:** Clouds have documented inter faces; however, no standards are associated with these, and thus it is unlikely that most clouds will be interoperable. The open grid forum is developing an open Cloud computing interface to resolve this issue and the open cloud consortium is working on Cloud computing standards and practices. The findings of these groups will need to mature, but it is not known whether they will address the needs of the people deploying the services and the specific interfaces these services need.
- **Continuously Evolving:** user requirements are continuously evolving, as are the requirements for interfaces, networking and storage. This means that a "cloud," especially a public one, does not remain static and is also continuously evolving.

CONCLUSION

As cloud computing is achieving increased popularity, concerns are being voiced about the security issues introduced through adoption of this new model. The effectiveness and efficiency of traditional protection mechanisms are being reconsidered as the characteristics of this innovative deployment model can differ widely from those of traditional architectures. Any data stored in the Cloud can easily be accessed from almost any device including mobile devices such as phones or tablets. With the availability of content online, it is no longer necessary for teachers to spend time and resources printing or copying lengthy documents or lesson plans. Now, students are able to access homework assignments, lesson notes, and other materials through online.

❒

26

Effectiveness of Edu-Digital Skill among Higher Secondary Students

The end of the 20th Century and beginning of the 21st Century witnessed very exciting changes, one of them being in the field of Information and Communication Technology. Educators have begin to realize that in the fast changing world of today, the students have to be prepared to cope intelligently with the social, economic and technological changes. The educational environment is changing rapidly as a consequence of ICT and will continue to change. Information and Communication Technologies (ICT) are electronic and/or computerized devices and associated human interactive materials that enable the user to employ them for a wide range of teaching and learning processes in addition to personal use. Around the world, educational systems are under increasing pressure to use the new information and communication technologies to teach students the knowledge and skills they need in the 21st Century. With the emerging new technologies, the teaching profession is evolving from an emphasis on teacher-centered, lecture-based instruction to student-centered, interactive learning environments. The present study aims to find out the effectiveness of edu-digital skill among higher secondary students in Coimbatore District. A samples of 100 higher secondary students selected randomly were studied. A questionnaire method of survey was used to find out the effectiveness of edu-digital skill higher secondary students. The data were collected by using questionnaire as an instrument. Primary data were collected by conducting direct structured interview using questionnaire. All the respondents were asked the same questions in the same fashion and they were informed the purpose of study. t-test, Regression and correlation analysis were applied to test the hypotheses. The findings and observations are the result and outcome of the interpretations made during the study of analysis. The result found that edu-digital skill is positively correlated with higher secondary students.

Education, the foremost weapon for social reform, is now under the forces of change. Newly formed branches of knowledge and techniques of education facilitate the physical, mental and emotional development of the learners. Schools have an unavoidable role in acquainting the students with the nature of changing field of education and in making necessary changes in the instructional techniques. In the modern world of technological innovations, all educational institutions are trying to improve their quality in terms of facilities and academic outputs.

Scientific knowledge is exploding every day. Knowledge available to mankind today is emerging in the form of science and technology. There is no limit or end to the accumulation of scientific knowledge. It also satisfies the intellectual thirst of human beings. Science education is a bridge between science and education, using psychology. It links the most powerful concepts of science to the growing minds of children through active experimental pedagogy. Science education plays a prominent role in Indian educational system. It has, as its objective, the aim of providing individual learners a firm grasp of the concepts and processes of science as also to impart the ability to use scientific method of problem-solving. As a result of it, every aspect of human civilization has been influenced to a very great extent.

The present world is the world of science and technology. Science is the most inexhaustible storehouse of knowledge. Continuous advances in scientific and technological research have led to the growth and greater application of science in contemporary society. The purpose of science education is to give individuals a firm grasps of the concepts and processes of science and to develop scientific attitude, scientific reasoning, problem solving ability and scientific temper and to impart them the ability to use the scientific method to other situations in life. Hence science education has been included in school curriculum at all levels. It is however necessary that science teaching be impressive so as to inculcate its values in young minds.

The most striking innovation in the field of educational technology is the use of computers. Computer is included in the hardware approach of educational technology. It is one of the machines of automation in teaching and learning and is used for presenting individualized instruction. The main objective of teaching through computer is to provide the needed flexibility for individualizing the educational process. It meets the specific needs of the student in a way in which is almost impossible to do in a face-to face student-teacher relationship.

Computers should have a major role in the teaching-learning process. Computers have become an essential class room tool for the acquisition, analysis, presentation, and communication of data in ways that allow students to become active participants in research and learning. The computers offer students very important resources for learning concepts through simulations, graphics, sound, data manipulation and model building. Computers can improve scientific learning and facilitate communication of ideas and concepts.

There are three roles for computer in education. First, it functions as a tutor for students by presenting material, evaluating responses, and depending on the basis of the evaluation, deciding what to present next. Second, it is a tool that helps students perform calculations, analyze data, keep records, or write papers. Third, it functions as tutee by having told what to do through programming.

A computer program can be designed to create models for experimental purpose. Students, that particularly in higher education, have the benefits of using computer as a computational tool. They learn a programming language and write a program to solve some of their course work problems treating the computer as an aid in much the same way as a slide rule or a set of mathematical tables. Computers are capable of giving almost instant feedback, tirelessly, no matter how many learners 'get it wrong' and it is equally well known that human tutors have limited value when it comes to learners repeatedly getting things wrong.

Review of Literature

Anboucarassy (2010) studied the effectiveness of Multimedia in Teaching Biological Science to IX Standard students. The results of the study revealed that experiment group performed better than the control group due to the exposure of multimedia based learning. Thus multimedia helps the students to sustain their interest and also their retention power compared to the traditional method of teaching. The constant use of multimedia will make students understand more and achieve more in their academic achievement. Hence it was concluded that the multimedia approach is considered to be one of the best techniques for biology teaching at IX standard level.

Ponraj and Sivakumar (2010) studied the effectiveness of Computer-Assisted Instruction in Teaching Zoology in Relation to Learners' Personality. The major findings of the study indicated that achievement scores of experimental group students were higher than the control group students after the treatment.

Yusuf, Mudasiru and Afolabi, Adedeji (2010) investigated the effects of computer assisted instruction (CAI) on secondary school students' performance in biology. The findings of the study showed that the performance of students exposed to CAI either individually or cooperatively were better than their counterparts exposed to the conventional classroom instruction. Based on the research findings recommendations were made on the need to develop relevant CAI packages for teaching biology in Nigerian secondary schools.

Objectives

1. To know the edu-digital skill among higher secondary students in Coimbatore district.
2. To find out the effectiveness of Multimedia Programme in teaching among higher secondary students.

Methodology

Research may be termed as a systemic inquiry of verified knowledge, it is an organized deliberate effort to collect information, to analyze it, to put it together and finally to evaluate it. This research paper on methodology describes elaborately, the sample that was chosen, research design, objectives of the study, data collection, statistical techniques used for data and analysis.

Population

Population selected for this study was 100 higher secondary students in a selected school at Coimbatore District.

Attitude Scale towards Multimedia Programme

The attitude scale was used to measure the level of attitude towards Multimedia programme. The scale was constructed and validated by the investigator.

The attitude scale towards multimedia programme, consisting of 40 items, was designed by the investigator and was given to experienced teachers who were handling Computer Science in higher secondary schools, professors of Computer Science and Education and Educational psychologists. On the basis of the suggestions of above experts, some items were restructured and some were eliminated. Finally 25 items were selected for this test. The scale for measuring the higher secondary student's attitude towards multimedia programme in the study is of the Likert type. This scale has as many as 25 statements of which 20 are favorable towards multimedia programme and the remaining are unfavourable towards it.

Scoring

In the Likert type of scale, against each statement, five alternatives namely "Strongly agree", "Agree", "Undecided", "Disagree", and "Strongly disagree" are given. The subjects have to indicate their choice by putting a tick-mark (√) under one of the five columns against each statement.

For favorable statement weight age of 4,3,2,1 and 0 were given from strongly agree to strongly disagree in that order. For unfavourable statements the scoring was reversed. Thus the strongly agree response will get 0 and the strongly disagree response will get 4. Here the weight age of 0,1,2,3 and 4 were given from strongly agree to the strongly disagree in that order.

Thus the score value lies between 0-100. The content validity of the tool was established based on the opinion given by the experts. The reliability of the tool was established by Split-Half method. It was found to be 0.83 which was significant.

Data Collection

Primary data, required for the present research work were collected by conducting direct interviews using questionnaire. All the respondents were given sufficient information about the Project work. These respondents were provided with the same questionnaires. They were also informed that they have to answer in the same fashion.

Hypothesis

There is no significant difference between the pre and post test mean scores of experimental group students in their attitude towards multimedia programme.

Administration of Retention Test

The Attitude Scale towards Multimedia Programme was constructed and validated by the investigator and was administered to the subjects of the experimental group. The pre test scores on attitude towards multimedia programme were collected. Thus pre test and post test scores on attitude towards multimedia programme were computed for analysis.

Analysis and Interpretation

To find out the significance of the difference between the pre and post test mean scores of experimental group students in their attitude towards multimedia programme the 't' test was used.

TABLE.26.1: Distribution of 't' Value between the Pre and Post Test mean Scores of Experimental Group Students in their Attitude towards Multimedia Programme

Group	N	Mean	S.D	't' value	Level of Significant
Pre test	50	42.08	10.42	24.47	p<0.05
Post test	50	93.58	2.57		

There is no significant difference between the pre and post test mean scores of experimental group students in their attitude towards multimedia programme.

The obtained 't' value is statistically significant since it is greater than the table 't' value 1.96 at 0.05 level of significance. Hence the null hypothesis is rejected. It shows that there is significant difference between the pre and post test mean scores of experimental group students in their attitude towards multimedia programme. It is therefore concluded that the experimental group students show more favorable attitude towards multimedia programme in the post test than the pre test.

TABLE.26.2: Showing the Stepwise Regression Analysis Predicting Factors Influencing Effectiveness of Edu-Digital Skill among Higher Secondary Students and Demographic Variables

Sl.No	Step/Source	Unstandardized Coefficients Beta	Std. Error	Standardized Coefficients Beta	Step t	P
1.	Gender	1.144	0.156	0.242	7.324	0.01
2.	Father education	1.254	0.359	0.163	3.495	0.01
3.	Mother education	2.615	0.462	0.361	5.661	0.01
4.	Monthly Income	2.175	0.402	0.280	5.410	0.01
5.	Father Occupation	1.022	0.513	0.137	1.992	0.01

* P < 0.01

Five variables viz Gender, Father Education, Mother Education, Monthly income and Father Occupation have significantly contributed for predicting the factors influencing effectiveness of edu-digital skill among higher secondary. The first variable Gender seems to be 7.324, Father education seems to be 3.495, Mother education seems to be 5.661, Monthly income seems to be 5.410 and Father occupation seems to be 1.992. The predictive value of these variables separately is 0.01.

TABLE. 26.3: Showing the Correlation between the Effectiveness of Edu-Digital Skill among Higher Secondary Students and Demographic Variables

Factors	Effectiveness of edu-digital skill among higher secondary students
Gender	0.920**
Father education	0.849**

Mother education	0.914**
Monthly Income	0.880**
Father Occupation	0.855**

* Significant at 0.01 level

Effectiveness of edu-digital skill among higher secondary students is positively and significantly related to Gender (0.920), Father education (0.849), Mother education (0.914), Monthly income (0.880) and Father occupation (0.855). So, the direct relationship between the effectiveness of edu-digital skill among higher secondary students and selected demographic variables.

CONCLUSION

Computer and multimedia technology for education offers a number of benefits. They allow the teacher to structure and present the information with varying special effects to the students. They can also be used for the storage of audio-visual information of various types. Multimedia programmes provide a lot of benefits. The benefits for learners include flexibility of scheduled instruction at a location convenient to learners, reduced student time, assured progress in skill development, increased achievement and increased retention and continuous report to the learners of progress and accomplishments, specified performance criteria, good response and feedback.

The application of multimedia programme would definitely create a good learning environment in classroom, sustaining attention and motivating the students to learn effectively. The application of multimedia may create a congenial learning climate in schools and can bring real life situations. The investigator has chosen the topic for the present study in order to address the problem faced by teachers, teaching science, to foster involvement in new teaching approaches, to get a feeling of satisfaction through learning in the classroom, to create joyful learning environment and to stimulate active information processing for effective learning,

In a vast country like India, enormous work is now being done in the field of education, but it is still not possible to equip each and every school with all the facilities for teaching science. Secondary schools need high quality teaching aids. Multimedia, as a teaching aid, is very much effective with colour, sound and graphics, which are found in the audio, video movie media. Any diagram can be explained in detail with 3D effects, which helps the students understand clearly. The students can get a live vision of life's aspects and scientific factors. Multimedia includes use of computer.

The present study has found out that the multimedia programme is very effective in higher secondary level. As the present teaching-learning process in higher secondary classes is very rigid, time bound and outmoded, it was proposed to use multimedia programme.

As multimedia programme develops a favourable attitude towards multimedia programme, motivates the students to involve in the process of learning, attracts students' attention in learning, accelerates the students' understanding of concepts of subjects, increases the retention power and that it is highly suitable for all categories of students ranging from low to high achievers, it is suggested that this multimedia programme be widely adopted and implemented in educational institutions as computer laboratory facilities are available in all the schools and colleges to enable the learners to learn the subjects of their choice according to their own pace and ability. Learning through multimedia programme is very easy, understandable and comfortable to all categories of students for all types of subjects.

❐

27

Educational-Digital Skill

There is a tremendous revolution in science and technology. Information in communication technologies have a deep cultural revolution changing. There is a need to make a realistic assessment of what technology cannot do to reach a plateau of productivity when the technology consistently delivers to realistic goals.

The impact of Science and Technology among Student

Digital skill is a vast technique used by all people. Educational technology and mobile learning, multi- media learning are all digital skill. Science is a boon. Man has discovered many wonderful things from the treasure of developing every day. It has made our life easier, happier and more secure. Science and technology has conquered time and space. It has made very good communication and made the transport easier. With the help of science and technology, modern medicine and medical treatments, the doctors save the life of sick people from the jaws of death. Many organs are now transplanted. It is used in the field of agriculture. The impact of science and technology among students in the field is both good and bad.

Science laboratory, space centre ISRO are taken in the highest form. Television, telecommunication, type- recorder, films, LCD projectors, digital and white board, e- learning, e-teaching, teleconferencing, teaching machine cell phones such as all types of multimedia are boons to us. But the students are affected by this because of misusing. So they blamed science. We cannot blame science. It is a wonderful boon.

Digital Skill in Website

By the wrong use of face book, web site, web-camera, especially cell phones, net connection, lab top etc. Science and technology become down. But once for all where we use science and technology in proper, correct and perfect way it is a boon to us otherwise it is curse and demon to us.

A secondary Information and Communication Technology curriculum should contribute to the building up of teams of professionals with these new competencies. The use of Information and Communication Technology cuts across all aspects of economic and social life. Technological developments in Information and Communication Technology are very rapid. Technology quickly becomes obsolete requiring new skills and knowledge to be mastered frequently. Adaptation is only possible when based on a sound understanding of the principles and concepts of Information and Communication Technology.

Review of Literature

Lei, Jing (2010) studied on Quantity versus Quality: A New Approach to Examine the Relationship between Technology Use and Student Outcomes. It is found that that to examine the relationship between technology use and student outcomes, the quality of technology use--how, and what, technology is used--is a more significant factor than the quantity of technology use--how much technology is used. This argument was exemplified by an empirical study that used both angles to examine the association between technology use and student outcomes. When only the quantity of technology use was examined, no significant association was observed. However, when the quality of technology was examined by investigating the specific types of technology uses, a significant association was identified between technology use and all student outcomes. Furthermore, different types of technology use showed different influences on specific student outcomes. General technology uses were positively associated with student technology proficiency, while subject-specific technology uses were negatively associated with student technology proficiency. Social-communication technology uses were significantly positively associated with developmental outcomes such as self-esteem and positive attitude towards school. Entertainment/exploration technology use showed significant positive association with student learning habits. None of these technology uses had significant influence on student academic outcome.

Chen, Rong-Ji (2010) studied on Investigating Models for Preservice Teachers' Use of Technology to Support Student-Centered Learning. The study addressed two limitations of previous research on factors related to teachers' integration of technology in their teaching. It attempted to test a structural equation model (SEM) of the relationships among a set of variables influencing preservice teachers' use of technology specifically to support student-centered learning. A review of literature led to a path model that provided the design and analysis for the study, which involved 206 preservice teachers in the United States. The results show that the proposed model had a moderate fit to the observed data, and a more parsimonious model was found to have a better fit. In addition, preservice teachers' self-efficacy of teaching with technology had the strongest influence on technology use, which was mediated by their perceived value of teaching and learning with technology. School's contextual factors had moderate influence on technology use. Moreover, the effect of preservice teachers' training on student-centered technology use was mediated by both perceived value and self-efficacy of technology. The implications for teacher preparation include close collaboration between teacher education program and field experience, focusing on specific technology uses.

Eisenberg, Mike; Johnson, Doug; Berkowitz, Bob (2010) studied on Information, Communications, and Technology (ICT) Skills Curriculum Based on the Big6 Skills Approach to Information Problem-Solving. There is clear and widespread agreement among the public and educators that all students need to be proficient technology users. Technology literacy is among the attributes that appear in nearly every set of "21st Century Skills." However, while districts spend a great deal of money on technology, there seems to be only a vague notion of what technology literacy really means. Defining and describing technology skills is only a first step to assure all children become proficient information and technology users. Other critical elements will include a teacher-supported scope and sequence of skills, well designed projects, and effective assessments. Equally essential is fruitful collaboration among classroom teachers, teacher librarians, and technology teachers in order to present students with a unified and integrated approach to ensure that all children master the skills they will need to thrive in an information-rich future. This article presents the "Information, Communications, and Technology (ICT) Skills for Information Problem Solving" curriculum which defines technology capabilities and identifies associated skills based on the Big6 Skills Approach. The Curriculum describes levels of technology proficiency, and in so doing, promotes the skills and concepts basic to information and technology. In an information society, it is essential that students are technologically productive and able to solve information problems effectively and efficiently. This curriculum requires more than teaching computer skills, technology hardware, and software programs in an isolated approach. An effective technology curriculum must be integrated across content areas and grade levels to improve the learning process. Technology is successfully integrated when it seamlessly supports curricular goals. Students learn and refine their technology skills when they work on projects that require them to solve problems and make decisions.

Savage, Robert S.; Erten, Ozlem; Abrami, Philip; Hipps, Geoffrey; Comaskey, Erin; van Lierop, Dea (2010) studied on ABRACAD-ABRA in the Hands of Teachers: The Effectiveness of a Web-Based Literacy Intervention in Grade 1 Language Arts Programs . Each teacher chose to use the program in qualitatively distinct ways that corresponded to the first three stages of Sandholtz, Ringstaff, and Dwyer's (1997) technology integration model, namely: "Entry," "Adoption" and "Adaptation." Growth in literacy between pre- and post-test revealed significant differences associated with technology integration style across all measures of literacy and related language skills. The largest and most-widespread effects were evident for the "Adaptation" group that linked technology content to wider learning themes in the classroom. In terms of overall growth in standardised literacy scores across all six such measures used, Adaptation proved to be 60% more effective than Adoption. Results suggest that explorations of exactly how teachers use technology have important implications for practice as well as for the interpretation of field-based studies of the effectiveness of educational technology.

Jun, Han; Zhuzhu, Wang (2010) studied on Capability Building in Educational Technology for Teachers in China. This paper gives a brief introduction to the project called Education Technology Capacity Building Plan for All Primary and Secondary Teachers now being implemented in China. Because information and communication technology skills training cannot match the demand of teachers' professional development, the Chinese Ministry of Education established the education technology standard for teachers and launched the project. This paper introduced the features of standard training and testing, and discusses the output and influence of the project.

McGarr, Oliver (2010) studied on Education for Sustainable Development in Technology Education in Irish Schools: A Curriculum Analysis. This paper explores the integration of Education for Sustainable Development (ESD) in technology education and the extent to which it is currently addressed in curriculum documents and state examinations in technology education at post-primary level in Ireland. This analysis is conducted amidst the backdrop of considerable change in technology education at post-primary level. The analysis of the provision of technology education found, that among the range of technology related subjects offered, the study of Technology and Society is only addressed in one in a comprehensive manner. The paper discusses the implications of this limited integration, examines the factors inhibiting greater integration of ESD and outlines opportunities for future development.

Waring, Scott M. (2010) studied on The Impact of a Technology Coordinator's Belief System upon Using Technology to Create a Community's History. As it has been shown that teachers of social studies content are less likely than teachers of other content areas to utilize technology in their classroom, this study focuses on one instructional technology coordinators' beliefs towards technology, instruction, and students and how these beliefs impacted how technology was utilized during a technology-enriched community history project with a group of fourth-grade students. It was determined that the instructional technology coordinators' beliefs included the following: (a) technology should serve as a tool and should be seamlessly integrated into the curriculum; (b) the teacher should construct meaningful experiences that allow students to become engaged in the learning process; however, before guiding student discovery, the teacher needs to explicitly teach basic technological skills; (c) and all students are able to learn and are capable of engaging in independent problem solving and critical thinking at some level. Her beliefs manifested themselves daily, particularly in the way that she approached instruction and integrated technology seamlessly into the curriculum. Through this study, it was found that the technology coordinator's beliefs toward technology, instruction, and her students directly impacted how technology was used in her classroom.

Jun, Han; Zhuzhu, Wang (2010) studied on Capability Building in Educational Technology for Teachers in China. This paper gives a brief introduction to the project called Education Technology Capacity Building Plan for All Primary and Secondary Teachers now being implemented in China. Because information and communication technology skills training cannot match the demand of teachers' professional development, the Chinese Ministry of Education established the education technology standard for teachers and launched the project. This paper introduced the features of standard training and testing, and discusses the output and influence of the project.

Ruzic-Dimitrijevic, Ljiljana; Dimitrijevic, Maja (2010) studied on Challenges IT Instructors Face in the Self-Education Process. We find that the earlier the instructors graduated, the smaller is the chance they studied the technologies similar to the ones they teach. We found that none of the surveyed instructors who graduated before 1979 teach a technology they studied. The analysis of the survey also supports the second hypothesis. The results show that 70% of the IT instructors have to change the course syllabus every 2-3 years due to the technology changes. We also found that the majority of the instructors primarily use textbooks and online tutorials to self teach new technologies, which supports the third hypothesis. By comparison, they take courses given by others and work on real life projects far less often. In contrast, most instructors agree that taking courses and working on projects would greatly help them in their self-education. Most instructors (16 out of 20) assert that the lack of time stops them from doing so, which according to the survey is found to be one of the major challenges they face in the process of self-education, supporting the fourth hypothesis. Considering the results of our research, as well as our own experience, we have identified a list of activities that make the process of self-education more efficient and/or effective for IT instructors. These activities include taking on-line tutorials, creating software programs using the environment/ language/tools covered in the courses, working on real life projects, taking organized courses, attending IT/CS conferences, seminars, and workshops, collecting experience from industry people, and using the help of advanced students. However, in order to create the time for IT instructors to apply the self-learning methods and stay on top of the new technologies, we conclude that it may be necessary that the university policy include the time for self-learning as a significant part of IT instructors' everyday duties, i.e., as a part of their "job description".

Larson, Lotta; Kuhn, Cyndi Danner; Collins, Royce Ann; Balthazor, Gerri; Ribble, Mike; Miller, Teresa Northern (2009) studied on Technology Instruction: Fixing the Disconnect. High school students spend much of their educational journeys immersed in "old" literacies of paper, pencil, and print books. But outside of the classroom, they are exposed to information and communication technologies--such as blogs, wikis, Internet browsers, multimedia, social networking sites, and a wide range of software--each of which demand new literacies. This disconnect is a serious problem for schools because it reflects a decline in school's relevancy to students' futures, and the gap between how schools teach and how students learn will only grow over time. The first step in updating a school's technology and instruction is to revisit and revise current vision statements by facilitating conversations with all stakeholders about expectations for student skills upon graduation. Vision setting must include the new literacies. Teachers and education leaders must model expectations and support visionary teaching and learning through technology. To make that happen, they need instructional technology specialists who not only have a strong knowledge of hardware, networks, and equipment maintenance but also understand the art of teaching and how to enhance and enrich the daily curriculum by integrating technology. To do this, instructional technology staff members and those creating the curriculum must engage in ongoing dialogue to ensure that computer language is translated into the language of teaching and is directly related to what teachers want to do in their classrooms. For schools to successfully integrate technology, leaders must encourage and support strong relationships between teachers and technology support staff members. Schools must also provide easy access to technology in classrooms so that teachers can effectively integrate technology into the curriculum. Limited resources and complicated check-out procedures often contribute to lack of use. In addition, frustrations over blocked sites or limited access to online resources prevent teachers from integrating technology. Leaders, teachers, and technology staff members need ongoing communication with one another to share needs, frustrations, and solutions. Schools must move ahead quickly. It may be understandable for teachers and leaders to be a bit behind in the use of technology, but it is no longer adequate or appropriate to hold students back. Students today will be leaders in a global society, and technology can connect them to that world in ways that were unimaginable 10 years ago. School leaders need to join students in their world--which includes all of the new literacies--so that everyone can function and contribute to the future.

Objectives

1. To study the level of teachers attitude towards using new technology in teaching
2. To find out whether there is any significant relationship between teachers attitude towards the use of new technology and their interest in teaching.

Methodology

The methodology adopted for the study is explained in detail. The sampling technique, size of the sample, variables of the study, description of the tool used and administration of tool are elaborated.

Sample

The study was conducted on 100 school teachers, Coimbatore district, Tamil Nadu.

Data Collection

Primary data, required for the present research work were collected by conducting direct interviews using questionnaire. All the respondents were given sufficient information about the study. These respondents were provided with the same questionnaires. They were also informed that they have to answer in the same fashion.

Analysis and Interpretation

Gender and Attitude towards the use of New Technology

Null Hypothesis No. 1

There is no significant difference between male and female teachers attitude towards the use of new technology.

TABLE. 27.1: The Significance of the Difference ('t' value) between mean Scores of Male and Female Teacher's Attitude towards the use of New Technology

Gender	N	Mean	SD	't' value	Level of Significance (0.05)
Male	50	100.30	11.81	4.89	Significant
Female	50	107.30	12.57		

It is evident from the table the calculated 't' value is 4.89 is significant at 0.05 level. Hence, the framed null hypothesis is rejected and research hypothesis is accepted. It is inferred that there is significant difference found between male and female teachers attitude towards the use of new technology.

Qualification and Attitude towards the use of New Technology

Null Hypothesis No. 2

There is no significant difference between undergraduate and post graduate teachers with respect to their attitude towards the use of new technology.

TABLE. 27.2: The Significance of the Difference ('t' value) between Undergraduate and post Graduate Teachers with Respect to their Attitude Towards the use of New Technology.

Qualification	N	Mean	SD	't' value	Level of Significance (0.05)
Under graduate	35	103.64	11.44	0.28	Not Significant
Post graduate	65	103.23	13.53		

It is evident from the table the calculated 't' value is 0.28 which is not significant at 0.05 level. Hence, the framed null hypothesis is accepted. It shows that there is no significant difference between undergraduate and post graduate teachers with respect to their attitude towards the use of new technology.

Locality of the School and Attitude towards the use of New Technology

Null Hypothesis No. 3

There is no significant difference between rural and urban school teachers attitude towards the use of new technology.

TABLE. 27.3: The Significance of the Difference ('t' value) between Rural and Urban School Teachers Attitude towards the use of New Technology

Locality of the school	N	Mean	SD	't' value	Level of Significance (0.05)
Rural	65	103.42	11.23	0.06	Not Significant
Urban	35	103.33	14.15		

It is evident from the table the calculated 't' value is 0.06 which is not significant at 0.05 level. Hence, the framed null hypothesis is accepted. It shows that there is no significant difference between rural and urban school teachers attitude towards the use of new technology.

Type of School and Attitude towards the use of New Technology

Null Hypothesis No. 4

There is no significant difference between private and government school teachers attitude towards the use of new technology.

TABLE. 27.4: The Significance of the Difference ('t' value) between Private and Government School Teachers Attitude towards the use of New Technology

Type of School	N	Mean	SD	't' value	Level of Significance (0.05)
Private	65	104.79	11.54	1.26	Not Significant
Government	35	102.78	13.01		

It is evident from the table the calculated 't' value is 1.26 which is not significant at 0.05 level. Hence, the framed null hypothesis is accepted. It shows that there is no significant difference between private and government school teachers attitude towards the use of new technology.

Level of Teaching and Attitude towards the use of New Technology

Null Hypothesis No. 5

There is no significant difference between secondary and higher secondary school teachers attitude towards the use of new technology.

TABLE.27.5: The Significance of the Difference ('t' test) between Secondary and Higher Secondary School Teachers Attitude towards the use of New Technology

Level of teaching	N	Mean	SD	't' value	Level of Significance (0.05)
Secondary School	60	102.12	12.12	1.85	Not Significant
Higher secondary School	40	104.82	13.03		

It is evident from the table the calculated 't' value is 1.85 which is not significant at 0.05 level. Hence, the framed null hypothesis is accepted. It is inferred that there is no significant difference between secondary and higher secondary school teachers attitude towards the use of new technology.

Teaching Experience and Attitude towards the use of New Technology

Null Hypothesis No. 6

There is no significant difference among teachers who have different years of teaching experience with respect to their attitude towards the use of new technology.

TABLE. 27.6: The Significance of the Difference ('F' test) among School Teachers with respect to their Attitude towards the use of New Technology

Teaching Experience	Sum of Squares	Mean Squares	df	'F' Value	Level of Significance (0.05)
Between Groups	2281.690	1140.845	2	7.48	Significant
Within Groups	45273.227	152.435	97		
Total	**47554.917**	-	**99**		

It is evident from the table the calculated 'F' value is 7.48 which is significant at 0.05 level. Hence, the framed null hypothesis is rejected and research hypothesis is accepted. It is inferred that there is significant difference among teachers who have different years of teaching experience with respect to their attitude towards the use of new technology.

TABLE. 27.7: The Significance of the Difference ('t' test) between Teachers who have dDifferent Years of Tteaching Experience with Respect to their Attitude towards the use of New Technology

Teaching experience	N	Mean	SD	't' value	Level of Significance (0.05)
Below 10 years	49	109.33	11.05	3.06	Significant
10-20 years	20	103.03	12.80		
Above 20 years	31	101.67	12.47	4.16	Significant
Below 10 years	49	109.33	11.05		
10-20 years	20	103.03	12.80	0.81	Not Significant
Above 20 years	31	101.67	12.47		

From table, it is revealed that there is significant difference between teachers who have below 10 years of teaching experience and 10-20 years of teaching experience and teachers who have above 20 years of teaching experience and below 10 years of teaching experience. Whereas no significant difference is found between teachers who have above 20 years of teaching experience and 10-20 years of teaching experience.

Correlation Analysis

Correlation Analysis between teachers attitude towards the use of new technology and interest in teaching.

One of the important objectives of the present investigation is to study the significant relationship between teacher's attitude towards the use of new technology and interest in teaching. For this purpose, the investigator applied the co-efficient of correlation ('r'). The computed values are given in the table. The investigator also framed a null hypothesis for testing the relationship between teacher's attitude towards the use of new technology and interest in teaching.

Null hypothesis No. 8

There is no significant relationship between teacher's attitude towards the use of new technology and interest in teaching.

TABLE. 27.8: Co-Efficient of Correlation between Teacher's Attitude towards the use of Mew Technology and Interest in Teaching

Correlation	N	'r' value	Level of Significance at 0.05 level
Teacher's attitude towards the use of new technology and interest in teaching	100	0.56	Significant

It is evident from the table the computed correlation coefficient 'r' for entire sample is 0.56, which is significant at 0.05 level. Hence, the framed null hypothesis is rejected. It is inferred that there is significant relationship found between teacher's attitude towards the use of new technology and their interest in teaching.

Suggestions

The present study gives a clear-cut view about the present position of teachers attitude towards the use of new technology and their interest in teaching. Based on the important findings stated earlier the following recommendations are suggested.

Teachers must be provided with adequate opportunities to enhance their knowledge in new technologies and equipments. The government should provide more effective environment through schools for them to improve their skills in application of new technologies in teaching.

Periodical in-service training programmes should be organized to keep their interest and quest in teaching.

The finding of the present study reveals that the teachers have neutral attitude towards the use of new technology in teaching and low interest in teaching. This indicates that the Heads of the institutions must look into the varied problems that influence the interest of teachers and find amicable solutions to their difficulties.

More activities should be planned in the curriculum to bring forth different modes of creative expressions which will provide competition and generate interest of teachers in teaching.

Sincere work and involved performances of teachers must be recognized and honoured by the authorities. And application of innovative methods and technologies in instruction must be encouraged.

In addition with the above recommendation the government and all the other concerned authorities should realize the problems of experienced teachers and provide conductive environment of growth and mutual help of teachers should be ensured.

CONCLUSION

The present study is conducted on teachers attitude towards the use of new technologies in teaching and their interest in teaching. The findings of the present study revealed that the teachers have neutral attitude towards the use of new technology and low interest in teaching. Therefore, the authorities and government should find suitable measures to improve the interest of teachers in teaching and the application of innovative technologies in Teaching Learning Process.

❐

Bibliography

1. Cruse, Alan D. (2000). Meaning in Language: An Introduction to Sematics and Pragmantics. United States: Oxford University Press Inc.
2. Quattrini,J.A.(1985).Brushing Up Your Writing Skills. 215 Park Avenue South, New York, N.Y.10003: Arco Publishing, Inc.
3. Montiel, C.J. and Estuar, M.R.(2006), Revolutionary Text: Social Psychology of Cellphone Texting during People Power II. Ateneo de Manila University.
4. Shidle, N.(1965).The Art of Successful Communication, USA: McGraw-Hill, Inc.
5. Edwards, Corban. (2009).Text Messaging Effects on Writing. Retrieved December 31, 2010 from htt://personal.georgiasouthern.edu/ce00988/.
6. Guerra, Nicole.(2007) Texting Affects Student Writing: R U Concerned?. Rettrieved January 6, 2011 from http://gnovisjournal.org/blog/text-based-short-hand-affecting-teens-writing-r-u-concerned.
7. Myhra, John.(2010).Negative Effects of Texting in the Classroom. Retrieved January 21, 2011 from http://www.56wrtg1150.wikidot.com/negative-effects-of-texting-in-the-classroom.
8. Glee Harrah Cady and Pat Mc Gregor (2005) "Internet is a network of network and the internet mostly connects network of computers". Journal of research in science teaching.
9. Barry (2006) "Relationship between students perceptions of their science class room learning environment and attitude", Journal of Educational Research.

10. Schafer (2007) vargo students science attitudes and self concept in science as a function of rose specific pupil/teacher interpersonal compatibility", San Francisco, California, National association for research in science teaching.
11 Williams (2008), "Attitude of high school pupils towards general science and its relationship with achievement and its subjects". Journal Community and Guidance.
12. Martis Anandi (2009), in test on scientific attitudes (TOSA), taking the point of view that attitudes must be inferred from the behavior of students, Journal of All India Association for Educational Research, Vol.17, Nos. 1 & 2, March & June.
13. Mohanty Ajay Kumar (2010), Attitudes towards education, critical thinking ability and specific effective behavious, Journal of all India Association for Educational Research, Vol.14, Nos.3 & 4.
14. Bharat, B.D. and Sharma, S (1992). Educational Technology, Karisha Publishing House, New Delhi.
15 Chaube, S.P. Akhilesh Chaube (1982). Philosophical and Sociological Foundation of Education, Vinod Pustak Mandir, Agra – 2.
16. Jagannat Mohanty (1994). Education for All (EFA). Deep & Deep Publications, New Delhi.
17. Kochhar, S.K. (1979). Teaching of Social Sciences, Sterling Publishers, PVT Ltd.
18. Kothari, C.R. (2004). Research Methodology, New Age International PVT Publishers, New Delhi.
19. Lay, E.J.S. (1990). Encyclopedia of Modern Methods of Teaching, Anmol Publications, New Delhi.
20. Malla Reddy Mamidi and S.Ravishankar (1962). Curriculam Development and Educational Technolgoy, Sterling Publishers Private Limited, New Delhi.
21. Neelam Yadav, (2003). A Handbook of Educational Technology, Anmol Publication Pvt Ltd. New Delhi.
22. Rameshchanta, and Dash, B.N. (2005). Foundations of Education, Neelkmal Publications Pvt. Ltd., Hyderbad.
23. Rao V.K. and Reddy R.S. (1992). The Nature of Educational Technology Common Wealth Publishers, New Delhi.
24. Winket and Lewis, R. (Ed.) (1987). CAL in the humanities and Social Sciences, Black well Scientific Publications, Great Britian.
25. Yogendra, K. Sharma (2001). History and Problems of Education (Volume-2) Kanisha Publishers, New Delhi.

26. Achuthan Sarla, et al, (1993), Computer Technology for Higher Education. Delhi: association of Indian Universities.
27. Aggarwal, J.C. (1995) *Essentials of Educational Technology Teaching Learning.* Vikas Publishing House Private Ltd, New Delhi.
28. Alexiaq Leon & et al (1999) Fundamentals of Information Technology, UBS Publishers Ltd., New Delhi.
29. BECT (2000) Inclusion and Special needs <http:// www. Becta. Org. uk/ inclusion/> Mcfarlane, A. (1997) Information technology and authentic learning: realizing the potential of computers in the primary school. London, Routledge.
30. Crook, C (1996) Schools of the future. In T, Gill (ed) Electronic children information revolution.
31. Koehler, M.J, Mishra. P. (2005) *What happens when the teacher design Educational Technology?* The development of technological pedagogical content knowledge. Journal of Educational Computing Research, 32(2)/131-152.
32. Lokesh Koul (2002) Methodology of Educationa Research, Second Edition, New Delhi, Vikas Pubish in House, Pvt. Ltd.
33. Mandha, V.K (1998). Modern Techniques of Teaching Vol. I, New Delhi: Anmol Publications Pvt., Ltd.
34. Mcfarlane, A.(1997) Information technology and authentic learning realizing the potential of computers in the primary school. London, Routledge.
35. Paul F. Morrill, et al. (1986) Computers in Education, New Jersey Prentice Hall. Englewood Cliffs.
36. Sampath. K., Panneerselvan. A and Santhanam. S. – 1998 – Introduction to Educational Technology – sterling Publishing Pvt.Ltd., NewDelhi.
37. Sampath et al., (1984). Introduction to Educational Technology, New Delhi: Sterling Publishers Pvt. Ltd.
38. Siddhqui, M.A. (2004), *Challenges of educational technology,* APH, Publishing Corporation, New Delhi.
40. Skemp(1976)Relational understanding and instrumental understanding Mathematics Teaching, 77,20-26.
41. Suja (2004), Computer Awareness among Higher Secondary School Teachers o fTrichy. Unpublished M.Ed., Dissertation. Bharathidasan University, Tiruchirappalli.
42. Tay, Vaughan. (2004) *Multimedia: Making It Work.* Tata Mc Graw-Hill Publishing Company Limited, New Delhi.

43. Understood, J, Cavendish, S. Lawson, (1996) Are integrated learning systems good for teachers too? Journal of Information Technology for Teacher Education 5(3), 207-218.
44. Vanaja. M and Rajasekar (2006). Educational Technology and Computer Education, New Delhi; Neel Kamal Publications Pvt. Ltd.
45. Agarwal. Binod Symes, Larry R. (Ed) 1994). Future of Computerization in Institutions of Higher Learning, New Delhi: Concept Publishing Company.
46. Alexiaq Leon & et al (1999) Fundamentals of Information Technology, UBS Publishers Ltd., New Delhi.
47. Best John. W. (1997). Research in Education. Fourth Edition, New Delhi: Prentice Hall of India (P) Ltd.
48. Dannis P. Curtain & et al., (1988) Information Technology, Tata Mc Graw Hill Edition, Tokyo.
49. Dignmatti Bhaskara Rao (2001). Information Technology. New Delhi: Discovery Publishing House.
50. Harrychand (1990) Techniques of Teaching, New Delhi: A shish Publication House.
51. Johnself (1985). Micro – computers in Education. Kent (UK): The harvester press.
52. Kothari. C.R. (1994). Research Methodology, Methods and Techniques. New Delhi: Willey Eastern Company.
53. Mandha, V.K (1998). Modern Techniques of Teaching Vol. I, New Delhi: Anmol Publications Pvt., Ltd.
54. Noushad Husain (2010). Computer-Based instructional Simulations in Education: Why and How. EDUTRACKS, Vol.10 - No.3, 22 - 26.
55. Panch. Ramalingam (2006) Education and Information Technology, ASC, Pondicherry.
56. Paul F. Morrill, et al. (1986) Computers in Education, New Jersey Prentice Hall. Englewood Cliffs.
57. Rafeedali, E. (2009). Computer-based Technology and its pedagogical utility. EDUTRACKS, Vol.9 - No.2, 37 - 39.
58. Sampath et al., (1984). Introduction to Educational Technology, New Delhi: Sterling Publishers Pvt. Ltd.
59. Sr. Nirmala Sundararaj. (2005). Attitude towards Computer Education of the B.Ed Trainees of Tamil Nadu Open University. Journal of Educational Research And Extension,Vol.47 (4),35-48
60. Suja (2004), Computer Awareness among Higher Secondary School Teachers o fTrichy. Unpublished M.Ed., Dissertation. Bharathidasan University, Tiruchirappalli.

65. Teresa, A. (1990) Effects of experimental learning style on Co-operative computer – aided instruction: Learning Disk Operating System. DAI: 52(5), 1991 1719-A.
66. Vanaja. M and Rajasekar (2006). Educational Technology and Computer Education, New Delhi; Neel Kamal Publications Pvt. Ltd.
67. Vimal kishor & Neha Mahant. (2010). Attitude of Tribal and Non-Tribal High School Students towards Studies. Experiments in Education, Vol. XXXVIII No.2, 25 – 26.
68. Best,J.W, (2003). *Research in Education,* Prentice – Hall of India (P) Ltd., New Delhi.
69. LokeshKoul.(2005). *Methodology of Educational Research,* Vikas Publishing House (P) Ltd, New Delhi.
70. Singh.Y.K,(2005). *Instructional Technology In Education,* P. P. H Publishing Corporation, New Delhi-110002.
71. Sareen.N, (2005). *Information and Communication Technology,* Anmol Publication Pvt.Ltd, New Delhi-110002.
71. Agostinho, Hedberg and Lefoe (2008), "Advanced Educational Technology", New Delhi :Knishka Publishers distribution.
72. Beerman, K., Brown, G., & Evans, M. (2011). Interactive CD study modules in food science and Human Nutrition: Assessing Technology-Enhanced study programs. *Journal of Educational Multimedia and Hypermedia,* 7(4): 365-374.
73. Coneia (2010), "Computer and language learning", International Journal, page no 15-68.
74. Fetterman (2008), Asia and the Pacific programme of educational in Innovation for development (APEID), page 15-82 UNESCO Regional offices for education in Asia and the Pacific.
75. Huang, S. D., &Aloi, J. (2010). The impact of using interactive video in teaching general biology. *The American Biology Teacher,* 53(5): 281-284.
76. Jamtshio (2008) "Living in the information age" Vadodara: Premise and Implication for school education programme, Challenges in School Education.
77. Johnson (2009), "Education, Its Philosophy, Psychology and Technology" Thrissur : Breeze publications.
78. Jonasson (2008), "Mastering the Internet", USA: International Journal of Information Technology and Communication.
79. Kalimuthu, T. (2010). Developing a video programme on environmental pollution in biology for higher secondary students. *Fifth Survey of Research in Education,* Vol. II, p.1377.

80. Koeppen and Andre (2011), "Quantitative Techniques and Operations Research" USA: Yamuna publications.
81. Kumar (2007) "A Study of Utilisation of Internet by the Students of Higher Education", M.Ed Dissertation, Annamalai University.
82. Lee (2009), "Third survey of researcher in education and development", Baroda.
83. Medina (2011) "Cognitive and Affective Attitude of Teachers towards Computer", Experiments in Education, 30 (2), pp.7-12.
84. Rama and Kumar (2007) "Cognitive and Affective Attitude of Teachers towards Computer", Experiments in Education, 30 (2), pp.7-12.
85. Singh (2008) "Introduction to educational technology, Sterility Publishers", New Delhi: Private Limited.
86. Stefansdottir (2007) "The Internet Complete Reference; Second Edition",New Delhi: Tata McGraw-Hill Company Limited".
87. Teles and Rylands (2011) "Living in the information age" Vadodara: Premise and Implication for school education programme, Challenges in School Education.
88. Wagh, S. K. (2011). Development of a multimedia instructional system for remedial measures in fractional numbers. *Fifth Survey of Research in Education,* Vol. II, pp.1299.
89. Achuthan Sarala, et al (1993), Computer Technology for Higher Education, Vol.1, 2 &3. New Delhi: Concept Publishing Company.
90. Akkinson, R.C and Wilson, H.A. (eds). (1969), Computer Assisted Instruction, New York Academic Press.
91. Best, J.W., (1983) Research in education, Fourth Edition, prentice Hall of India, New Delhi.
93. Chauhan, S.S (1973), A text book on Programmed Instruction, New Delhi, Sterling Publishers.
94. Douglas E. Comer (1996) Computer Net works and Internets, Second Edition.
95. Ferguson, George A., (1976) Statistical in psychology and Education, Fourth Edition Mc Graw- Hill Kogkusha Ltd., New Delhi.
96. Goyal, D.R. (1988), Teacher preparation for Computer Education. New Delhi: Sonal Printer.
97. Kothari, C.R., (1994) Research Methodology, Methods & Techniques, Willey Eastern Limited, New Delhi.
98. Lewis. R and TAGG, E.D (Eds) (1987), Trends in Computer Assisted Education, London: Black Well Scientific Publication.
99. Palaniappan, V.P. (1988) Computer and Educational Technology, December 98 Sona Printers, New Delhi.

100. Teresa, A (1990), Effective of experiential learning style on cooperative computer – aided instruction: Learning Disk Operating System, DAI, 52(5), 1991, 1719-A.
101. Barbour Michael, et al, (2012), *Online and Blended Learning: A Survey of Policy and Practice of K-12 Schools Around the World,* available at http://www.inacol.org/cms/wpcontent/uploads/2012/11/iNACOL_IntnlReport2011.pdf
102. Rogers Carl (1983), *The Interpersonal Relationship in the Facilitation of Learning,* London: Rutledge
103. The Oxford Group (2013), *Blended Learning—Current Use, Challenges and Best Practices,* report 2013, available at http://www.kineo.com/m/0/blended-learning-report-202013.pdf (accessed July 2013)
105. Ramesh Chandra (2004). Impact of Media and Technology in Education, Kalpaz Publications, New Delhi.
106. Rao, V.K.(2005). Instructional Technolgy, APH Publishing Corporation, New Delhi.
107. Rawat, S.C. (2004). Essentials of Educational Technology, R.Lall Book Depot, Meerut.
108. Zaidi, S.M.(2004). Educational Technology, Anmol Publisher Pvt. Ltd., New Delhi.
109. Anboucarassy, B. (2010). Effectiveness of Multimedia in Teaching Biological Science to IX Standard students. EDUTRACKS, 9(5): 37-38.
110. Dalacosta, K., Kamariotaki-Paparrigopoulou, M., Palyvos, J.A., & Spyrellis, N. (2009). Multimedia application with animated cartoons for teaching science in elementary education. Computers & Education, 52(4): 741-748. Retrieved March 20, 2010 http://www.linkinghub.elsevier.com/retrieve/pii/S0360131508001905
111. Jian Hu, Hao Yu, Jun Shao, Zhiyong Li, Jiawei Wang &Yining Wang (2009). Effects of dental 3D multimedia system on the performance of junior dental students in preclinical practice: a report from China. Advances in Health Sciences Education, 14(1): 123 – 133. Retrieved March 20, 2010 http://www.springerlink.com/content/c0n8075m367131x1/
112 Kanmani, M., &Radha, M. (2009). "Effectiveness of CAI package in basic electronics teaching", Journal of All India Association for Educational Research, 21(1): 47-50.
113. Korakakis, G., Pavlatou, E.A., Palyvos, J. A., &Spyrellis N. (2009). 3D visualization types in multimedia applications for science learning: A case study for 8th grade students in Greece. Computers & Education,52(2): 390-401. Retrieved March 21, 2010

114. Ponraj, P., &Sivakumar, R. (2010). Computer-Assisted Instruction in Zoology in Relation to Learners' Personality. EDUTRACKS, 9(6): 34-37.
115. Yusuf, Mudasiru O., &Afolabi, Adedeji O. (2010). Effects of Computer AssistedIinstruction (CAI) on Secondary School students' performance in biology. TOJET: The Turkish Online Journal of Educational Technology, 9(1): 62-69. Retrieved March 21, 2010.
116. Beavis C. (2006), popular culture, textual practice and identify and identify: literacy and the new technologies, in the middle years
117. Berry l. And Chapman e, (2006); Effect of Background Information and Audiovisual Presentation Modes on Students' Attention style and enjoyment listening to Unfamiliar Music.
118. Best, (1982); J., Johnson R., Warren W. (2006), A hand book of Education Technology.
119. Blackmork j., Johnson R., Warren W. (2006), A handbook of Education Technology.
120. Coyne, Margaret Ann (2006), Emerging Literacy: Assisting Parents to scaffold the emerging literacy skills of their preschool aged children through the use of electronic story books.
121. Joseph Kacharayll (2006); Educational Technology Year Book, 1998.
122. Lanksherar, C and Knoble, M (2003); New literacies: changing Knowledge and classroom learning. Philadelphia: open University press.
123. Lewis, C and Finders, M. (2004); implied adolescents and implied teachers; A generation gap for new times. D.E Alvermann (Ed.), Adolescents and literacies in adugital world (pp.101-113).New York: peter Lang publishing.
124. Aggarwal,Y.P., "Statistical Methods", New Delhi: Sterling Publication, Pvt. Ltd., 1986.
125. Ahuja, G.C and Pramila Ahuja., "How to increase your reading speed", London: Cambridge University Press, 1987.
126. Baurah.T.C., "The English Teacher Handbook," New Delhi: Sterling Publishers, Pvt. Ltd. 1991.
127. Best J.W and Khan J.V., "Research in Education", New Delhi: Prentice Hall Publishers, Pvt. Ltd. 2010.
128. Bharathi.T, "Personaity Development and Communicative English", New Delhi: Sterling Publishers, Pvt. Ltd. 2004.
129. Bindhu David, Sumod S.,"Reading Comprehension in English in relation to Achivement Motivation, Edutracks, 2011.
130. David Crytal, "A dictionary of Linguistics and Phonetics", London: Cambridge University Press, 1988.

131. Edmund Murphy, "A Practical English Grammar Book", New Delhi: Black Swan Publication, 2007.
132. Fredeick T. Wood, "An outine history of the English Language", Chennai: Macmillan India Ltd., 2008.
133. Hariprasad.M and Prakasan.V, "Communicative English", New Delhi: Neelkamal Publication, Pvt. Ltd. 2005.
134. Kohil.A, "Techniques of Teaching English", New Delhi: Dhanpat Raj Publication, Pvt. Ltd. 2005.
135. Krishna Mohan and Meera Benerji, "Developing Communicative skills", New Delhi: Macmillan India Ltd., 2009.
136. Kundu.C.L and Tutoo.D.N, "Educational Psychology",New Delhi: Sterling Publishers, Pvt. Ltd. 2004.
137. Lokesh Koul, "Methodology of Educational Research", New Delhi: Vikas Publishers, Pvt. Ltd. 2003.
138. Mangal S.K., "Methodology of Educational Psychology", New Delhi: Prentice Hall Publishers, Pvt. Ltd. 2007.
139. MLA of America, "Handbook for Writers of Research Papers", New Delhi: East-West Press, Pvt. Ltd. 2009.
140. Mowla, "English Language Teaching", New Delhi: Neelkamal Publication, Pvt. Ltd. 2008.
141. Sorakim, "On Improving English Communication", New Delhi: Journal of Media Communication, 2010.
142. Talawar M.S. and Benakanal V.A, "Advanced Educational Psychology", New Delhi: Sterling Publishers, Pvt. Ltd. 2009.
143. Tarafder S.K., "How to Learn Flawless English", Chennai: A.P.H.Publishing Corporation, 2005.
144. Wrenn.C.L., "The English Language", New Delhi: Vikas Publication, Pvt. Ltd. 2001.
145. Anand.S.P (2005), ABC'S of educational psychology 3edition, Magamaya a publishing house, New Delhi.
146. Best, J W (1998) Research in Education, New Delhi: Prentice Hall of India private LTD.
147. Dipak kumar Bhattacharyya, (2006) Research methodology 2nd edition, excel books - New Delhi.
148. Doug Lennick Fred Kiel (2005) Moral Intelligence. Enhancing business performance and leadership success. Pearson education publication south Asia.
149. Gold Fried, M.R and D'zurilla, J.J. "Predication of academic competence by means of the survey of study habits and attitudes", Journal of educational psychology, 1973.

150. Haris Mary B and Ream Fred. "A program to improve study habits in schools", vol. 9, July 1972.
151. Jamur K.K. "Study habits and achievement" psychological studies vol. 3, 1958.
152. John.W.Best. (2004). Research in Education. New Delhi, Pearson Prentice Hall.
153. Khan, S.B. "Affective correlates of academic achievement", Journal of educational psychology, 1969.
154. Mangal. S.K. (2003), Advanced educational psychology 2nd edition, Hall of India private ltd New Delhi.
155. Robert & Baron, (2006), Psychology 5th edition. Hall of India Pvt. Ltd. New Delhi.
156. Bakia, M. (2002). *The costs of computers in the classroom:* data from developing countries. TechKnowLogia
157. Becker, H. J., Ravitz, J. L., & Wong, Y. T. (1999). *Teacher and Teacher-Directed Student Use of computers and Software.* (Teaching, Learning, and Computing: 1998 National Survey.
158. Becta.(2002). *The Impact of Information and Communication Technologies on Pupil Learning and Atainment.* (ICT in Schools Research and Evaluation Series – No.7): DfES.
159. Coughlin, E. C., & Lemke, C. (1999). *Professional competency continuum: professional skills for the digital age classroom.* USA: Milken Exchange on Educational Technology.
160. Cradler, J., & Bridgforth, E. (2002). *Recent research on the effects of technology on teaching and learning.* [Online]. WestEd. Retrieved 25/10/2002, 2002, from the World Wide
161. Cradler, J., & Bridgforth, E. (2002). *Recent research on the effects of technology on teaching and learning.* [Online]. WestEd. Retrieved 25/10/2002, 2002, from the World Wide Web:www.wested.org/techpolicy/research.html
162. E.L. Baker and H.F. O'Neil (Ed.), T*echnology assessment in education and training.* Hillsdale, NJ: Lawrence Erlbaum.
163. Hannafin, R. D., & Savenye, W. C. (1993). *Technology in the classroom:* The teacher's new role and resistance to it. Educational Technology, 33(6), 26-31.
164. Rao V.K. (2003), *Educational Technology,* APH, Publishing Corporation, New Delhi.
165. Siddhqui, M.A. (2004), *Challenges of educational technology,* APH, Publishing Corporation, New Delhi.

166. Stephen, M. A., & Stanely, R.(1985). Computer Based Instruction; Methods and Development. New Delhi: Prentice Hall of India, Pvt. Ltd.
167. Agarwal. Binod Symes, Larry R. (Ed) (1994). Future of Computerization in Institutions of Higher Learning, New Delhi: Concept Publishing Company.
168. Aggarwal, Y.P (1988). Statistical Methods: Concepts, Application and Computation, New Delhi: Sterling Publications Pvt. Ltd.
169. Bloom, B. S., and D. R. Krathwohl (1956) Taxonomy of Educational Objectives: Handbook 1
170. John W. Best and James V. Kahn (1986) "Research in Education" (Fifth Edition) Prentice – Hall of India Pvt.Ltd., New Delhi.
171. Lokesh Koul (2002) Methodology of Educational Research, Second Edition, New Delhi: Vikas Publishing House, Pvt. Ltd.
172. Baker, A. J., Kessler-Sklar, S., Piotrkowski, C. S., & Parker, F. L. (1999). Kindergarten and firstgrade teachers' reported knowledge of parents' involvement in their children's education. *The Elementary School Journal,* 99(4), 367-383.
173. Christenson, S.L. (1995). Families and Schools: What is The Role of the School Psychologist? *School Psychology Quarterly,* 10(2), 118 - 132.
174. Chavkin, N. F. (2000). Family and community involvement policies: Teachers can lead the way. *The Clearing House*, 73(5), 287-290.
175. Decker, L. E., Decker, V. A., Boo, M. R., Gregg, G. A., & Erickson, J. (2000). *Engaging families and communities. Fairfax,* VA: National Community Education Association.
176. Henderson, A. T., & Berla, N. (1994). *A new generation of evidence: The family is critical to student achievement.* Columbia, MD: National Committee for Citizens in Education.
177. Kirschenbaum, H. (2000, January). The principal's view. *The High School Magazine,* 7(5), 26-29.
178. Langdon, C. A., & Vesper, N. (2000). The sixth Phi Delta Kappa poll of teachers' attitudes toward the public schools. *Phi Delta Kappan, 81*(8), 607-611.
179. Office of Educational Research and Improvement. (1990). *A profile of the American eighth grader.* Washington, DC: U.S. Department of Education, OERI.
180. Ramirez, A. Y. (1999). Survey on teachers' attitudes regarding parents and parental involvement. *School Community Journal,* 9 (2), 21-39.
181. Rose, L. C., Gallup, A. M., & Elam, S. M. (1997). The 29th Annual Phi Delta Kappa/Gallup Poll of the public's attitudes toward the public schools. *Phi Delta Kappan,* 79(1), 41-56.

182. Rumberger, R. W., Ghatak, R., Poulos, G., Ritter, P. L., & Dornbusch, S. M. (1990). Family influences on dropout behavior in one California high school. *Sociology of Education*, 63, 283-299.
183. Shores, E. F. (1998). A call to action: Family involvement as a critical component of teacher education programs. Tallahassee, FL: South Eastern Regional Vision for Education.
184. Trusty, J. (1996). Relationship of parental involvement in teens' career development to teens' attitudes, perceptions and behavior. *Journal of Research and Development in Education*, 30(1), 63-69.
185. White-Clark, R., & Decker, L. E. (1996). *The "hard to reach" parent: Old challenges, new insights.* Fairfax, VA: National Community Education Association.
186. Larson, Lotta; Kuhn, Cyndi Danner; Collins, Royce Ann; Balthazor, Gerri; Ribble, Mike; Miller, Teresa Northern (2009) Technology Instruction: Fixing the Disconnect. Principal Leadership, v10 n4 p54-58.
187. Chen, Rong-Ji (2010) Investigating Models for Preservice Teachers' Use of Technology to Support Student-Centered Learning. Computers & Education, v55 n1 p32-42.
188. Eisenberg, Mike; Johnson, Doug; Berkowitz, Bob (2010) Information, Communications, and Technology (ICT) Skills Curriculum Based on the Big6 Skills Approach to Information Problem-Solving. Library Media Connection, v28 n6 p24-27.
189. Jun, Han; Zhuzhu, Wang(2010) Capability Building in Educational Technology for Teachers in China British Journal of Educational Technology, v41 n4 p607-611.
190. Lei, Jing (2010) Quantity versus Quality: A New Approach to Examine the Relationship between Technology Use and Student Outcomes. 2010.
191. Lesisko, Lee J.; Wright, Robert J.; O'Hern, Brenda (2010) Technology Integration: A Best Practice Perspective. Online Submission, Paper presented at the Annual Meeting of the Eastern Educational Research Association (Savannah, GA, Feb 10-13, 2010).
192. McGarr, Oliver (2010) Education for Sustainable Development in Technology Education in Irish Schools: A Curriculum Analysis. International Journal of Technology and Design Education, v20 n3 p317-332.
193. Ruzic-Dimitrijevic, Ljiljana; Dimitrijevic, Maja (2010) Challenges IT Instructors Face in the Self-Education Process. Journal of Information Technology Education, v9 pIIP-35-IIP-48.
194. Savage, Robert S.; Erten, Ozlem; Abrami, Philip; Hipps, Geoffrey; Comaskey, Erin; van Lierop, Dea (2010) ABRACADABRA in the Hands of Teachers: The Effectiveness of a Web-Based Literacy Intervention in

Grade 1 Language Arts Programs . Computers & Education, v55 n2 p911-922.

195. Shapley, Kelly; Sheehan, Daniel; Maloney, Catherine; Caranikas-Walker, Fanny (2010) Effects of Technology Immersion on Teachers' Growth in Technology Competency, Ideology, and Practices. Journal of Educational Computing Research, v42 n1 p1-33.
196. Waring, Scott M. (2010) The Impact of a Technology Coordinator's Belief System upon Using Technology to Create a Community's History. Computers in the Schools, v27 n2 p76-98.
197. Anboucarassy, B. (2010). *Effectiveness of Multimedia in Teaching Biological Science* to IX Standard students. EDUTRACKS, 9(5): 37-38.
198. Balasubramanian, N., & Jayaraman (2001). Relative Effectiveness among Different Modes of Computer Based Instruction. *Experiments in Education,* 29 (2): 9-13.
199. Chang, Chun-Yen (2002). The impact of different forms of multimedia CAI on students' science achievement. *Innovations in Education and Teaching International,* 39 (4): 280-88. Retrieved March 20, 2010
200. Dawson, M. E., Skinner, S., & Zeitlin, A. (2003). Rules of Engagement: Proceed with Caution when Integrating Multimedia learning Tools into Existing Course Formats. *Electronic Journal of Science Education,* 7(4). Retrieved March 21, 2010
201. Garnett, P., Hackling, M., & Oliver, R. (1997). An Interactive Multimedia Package Designed to Improve Beginning Students' Understanding of Chemical Equations. *UniServe Science News,* Vol. 8, pp. 18-21. Retrieved March 21, 2010
202. Kadhiravan, S., & Suresh, V. (2001). Effect of Computer-assisted Instruction on Self-regulated Learning. *Perspective in Education,* 18(3): 161-169.
203. Kanmani, M., &Radha, M. (2009). "Effectiveness of CAI package in basic electronics teaching", *Journal of All India Association for Educational Research,* 21(1): 47-50.
204. Korakakis, G., Pavlatou, E.A., Palyvos, J. A., & Spyrellis N. (2009). 3D visualization types in multimedia applications for science learning: A case study for 8th grade students in Greece. *Computers & Education,* 52(2): 390-401. Retrieved March 21, 2010
205. Liao, Yuen-kuang& Chen, Yu-wen (2007). The Effect of Computer Simulation Instruction on Student Learning: A Meta-analysis of Studies in Taiwan. *Journal of Information Technology and Applications,* 2(2): 69-79. Retrieved March 21, 2010

206. O'Day, Danton H. (2007). The value of Animations in Biology Teaching: A Study of Long – Term Memory Retention. *Journal of CBE - Life Science Education,* (3): 217-223. Retrieved March 20, 2010
207. O'Day, Danton H. (2007). The value of Animations in Biology Teaching: A Study of Long – Term Memory Retention. *Journal of CBE - Life Science Education,* 6 (3): 217-223. Retrieved March 20, 2010
208. Ponraj, P., & Sivakumar, R. (2010). Computer-Assisted Instruction in Zoology in Relation to Learners' Personality. EDUTRACKS, 9 (6): 34-37.
209. Pryor, Caroline R., & Bitter, Gary G. (2008). Using multimedia to teach in-service teachers: Impacts on learning, application, and retention. Computers in Human Behavior, 24 (6): 2668-2681. Retrieved March 20, 2010
210. Rotbain, Y., Marbach-Ad, G., &Stavy, R. (2008). Using a computer animation to teach high school molecular biology. *Journal of Science Education and Technology,* 17(1): 49 – 58. Retrieved March 21, 2010
211. Segers, E., &Verhoeven, L. (2002). Multimedia support of early literacy learning. *Computers and Education,* 39(3): 207-221. Retrieved March 20, 2010
212. She, Hsiao-Ching& Chen, Yi-Zen (2009). The impact of multimedia effect on science learning: Evidence from eye movements. *Computers & Education,* 53(4): 1297-1307. Retrieved March 20, 2010
213. Thilaka Suresh (2000). Instructional strategy change on the achievement in biotechnology and attitude towards science among higher secondary school students. *Journal of All India Association for Educational Research,* 12(3 & 7): 14-19.
214. Vernadakis, N., Zetou, E., Tsitskari, E., Giannousi, M., & Kioumourtzoglou, E. (2008). Student attitude and learning outcomes of multimedia computer-assisted versus traditional instruction in basketball. *Education and Information Technologies,* 13(3): 167-183.
215. Victor, AdeosunOlufemi (2008). Relative effects of three Multi-Media Instructional Packages on Nigerian student's achievement in Social Studies. *Pakistan Journal of Social Sciences,* 5 (5): 415 – 420. Retrieved March 20, 2010
216. Yusuf, Mudasiru O., &Afolabi, Adedeji O. (2010). Effects of Computer AssistedIinstruction (CAI) on Secondary School students' performance in biology. *TOJET: The Turkish Online Journal of Educational Technology,* 9 (1): 62-69. Retrieved March 21, 2010.

217. Anand.S.P (2005), ABC'S of educational psychology 3edition, Magamaya a publishing house, New Delhi.
218. Best, J W (1998) Research in Education, New Delhi: Prentice Hall of India private LTD.
219. Dipak kumar Bhattacharyya, (2006) Research methodology 2nd edition, excel books - New Delhi.
220. Doug Lennick Fred Kie1 (2005) Moral Intelligence. Enhancing business performance and leadership success. Pearson education publication south Asia.
221. John.W.Best. (2004). Research in Education. New Delhi, Pearson Prentice Hall.
222. Mangal S.K. (2003), Advanced educational psychology 2nd edition, Hall of India private ltd New Delhi.
223. Robert & Baron, (2006), Psychology 5th edition. Hall of India Pvt. Ltd. New Delhi.
224. Agarwal and jain "Study habits as a function of needs and achievement", Asian journal of psychology and Education, India. 1969.
225. Beyar,Steven Larson. Factors in the school environmental associated with student achievement in Science, Dissertation Abstracts international, June, Vol.52(12) Page 319. 1991
226. Brown, C.S."Study habits of failed and successful students in first tow, years of colleges" Journal of experimentation in Education, vol.9 page 205-268. 1941.
227. Best John, Wand Kahn James: Resear.ch in education, prentice Hall India private limited, New Delhi, 1989.
228. Carter:"Method of learning as a factor in the production of school success", Journal of educational psychology, Baroda, Indian, 1974.
229. Chatterjee, B.B. "Trends in the study habits of teachers under training", Journal of Education and psychology, Delhi, 1995,2(1),11.
230. Clark Thayer, Susan. Dissertation Abstracts International, Oct 1987 vol.48, No 4 page 872.
231. Desai, S.D. "A study of classroom ethos pupils, motivation and academic Achievement", PhD in education M.S University of Baroda; 1979.
232. Haris Mary B and Ream Fred. "A program to improve study habits in schools", vol.9, July 1972.
233. Kan Swal, M.R. "Progress of education reading habits and skills" Indian educational Abstracts, vol.17 July - Sep, 1971
234. Aggarwal, Y.P. Statistical Methods Concepts Application and Compotation, Sterling Publishers (P) Ltd., New Delhi – 110016

235. Allport, G.W. 1929: Pattern of Growth in Personality, Henry Holt and Co., Inc., New York.
236. Asthana, Anju: A study of social maturity among school going children in the city of Lucknow, PhD., Education, university of Lucknow, 1989.
237. Beyar,Steven Larson. Factors in the school environmental associated with student achievement in Science, Dissertation Abstracts international, June, Vol.52(12) P.319. 1991
238. Bhargava (1986), Values in relation to religious and moral education, Journal of Indian Education, Vol.13, No.2. pp. 15-17.
239. Chatterjee, B.B. "Trends in the study habits of teachers under training", Journal of Education and psychology, Delhi, 1995,2(1),11.
240. Gosh, Suresh Chandra, The History of Education in Modern India 1757 – 1986, Orient Longman, New Delhi, 1995.
241. Henderson, A. T., & Berla, N. (1994). A new generation of evidence: The family is critical to student achievement. Columbia, MD: National Committee for Citizens in Education.
242. Keetz Mary, A. "Social position and family correlation of study habits", Journal of Psychological Research, vol 23, 1979.
243. Khandeker, M. (1974). A study of dropouts. TISS, Bombay, Buch., M.B., Second Survey of Research in Education (1972-73).
244. Malathy, R. Women's Employment, ed., Gupta Sunich and Gupta Mukta, Anmoal Publications Pvt. Ltd., New Delhi, 1996.
245. Ramirez, A. Y. (1999). Survey on teachers' attitudes regarding parents and parental involvement. School Community Journal, 9(2), 21-39.
246. Ramprasad, (2007), An analytical Study of the attitudes of B.Ed. Students towards value oriented education. M.Ed. Dissertation, Dept. of Education, S.V. University, Tirupati
247. Vathsala, S. (1981). Potential dropouts at middle school level. Ph.D., Edu. Madras U., Buch M.B., Third Survey of Research in Education (1978-83).
248. White-Clark, R., & Decker, L. E. (1996). The "hard to reach" parent: Old challenges, new insights. Fairfax, VA: National Community Education Association.
249. Young C.N. "Scholarship and Social Adjustment" School and Society 43, 607-688. 1936.
250. Glee Harrah Cady and Pat Mc Gregor (2005) "Internet is a network of network and the internet mostly connects network of computers". Journal of research in science teaching.
251. Barry (2006) "Relationship between students perceptions of their science class room learning environment and attitude", Journal of Educational Research.

252. Schafer (2007) vargo students science attitudes and self concept in science as a function of rose specific pupil/teacher interpersonal compatibility", San Francisco, California, National association for research in science teaching.

253. Williams (2008), "Attitude of high school pupils towards general science and its relationship with achievement and its subjects". Journal Community and Guidance.

254. Martis Anandi (2009), in test on scientific attitudes (TOSA), taking the point of view that attitudes must be inferred from the behavior of students, Journal of All India Association for Educational Research, Vol.17, Nos. 1 & 2, March & June.

255. Mohanty Ajay Kumar (2010), Attitudes towards education, critical thinking ability and specific effective behavious, Journal of all India Association for Educational Research, Vol.14, Nos.3 & 4.

256. Hammet Gandhi, H. & Varma, M. (2008). Elucidating Mathematical problem solving through met cognition. Journal of Indian Education, 30(3).

257. Kaholan & Vinod uppal, (2007) Womens attitude and achievement in relation to achievement motivation, Journal of Education and Psychology, Vol. xxxviii, No 3: 198-201.

258. Live, Carl (2008) Formative Assessment Pre- Test to Identify College students' Prior Knowledge, Misconceptions and Learning Difficulties in Biology. International Journals of Science and Mathematics Vol.4.

259. LongDon, Bernard (2013) Genetics - Are there inherent learning difficulties?

260. Lovelace, M. K. (2005). Meta-Analysis of Experimental Research Based on the Dunn and Dunn Model. Journal of Educational Research, 98(3), 176-183.

261. Malini, Sujatha (2006) The Attitude of special and Normal School Teachers towards children with Disabilities.

262. Mary Lou Koran, John J. Koran (2006) Individual and teacher/class effects in aptitude treatment studies, American Educational Research Journal, Vol.17, No.3: 291-302.

263. Mary Lou Koran, John J. Koran (2006) Individual and teacher/class effects in aptitude treatment studies, American Educational Research Journal, Vol.17, No.3: 291-302.

264. Robert B. Burns, (2012) The relation of aptitude to learning at different points in the time during instruction, Journal of Educational Psychology, Vol. 72, No.6: 705-789.

265. Dan Sullivan (2014-01-14). "Cost of the Cloud: A Developer's Guide to Reducing Your AWS Bill". PragTech Publishing. Retrieved 2014-11-27.
266. "Cloud Computing: Clash of the clouds". The Economist. 2009-10-15. Retrieved 2009-11-03
267. Semple, Bryan. (2011-07-14) "Five Capacity Management Challenges for Private Clouds," Cloud Computing Journal.
268. Cloud Computing Grows Up: Benefits Exceed Expectations According to Report. Press Release, May 21, 2013.
269. Anboucarassy, B. (2010). Effectiveness of Multimedia in Teaching Biological Science to IX Standard students. EDUTRACKS, 9(5): 37-38.
270. Kanmani, M., & Radha, M. (2009). "Effectiveness of CAI package in basic electronics teaching", Journal of All India Association for Educational Research, 21(1): 47-50.
271. Korakakis, G., Pavlatou, E.A., Palyvos, J. A., & Spyrellis N. (2009). 3D visualization types in multimedia applications for science learning: A case study for 8th grade students in Greece. Computers & Education, 52(2): 390-401. Retrieved March 21, 2010 http://portal.acm.org/citation.cfm?id=1480558
272. Ponraj, P., & Sivakumar, R. (2010). Computer-Assisted Instruction in Zoology in Relation to Learners' Personality. EDUTRACKS, 9(6): 34-37.
273. Yusuf, Mudasiru O., & Afolabi, Adedeji O. (2010). Effects of Computer AssistedIinstruction (CAI) on Secondary School students' performance in biology. TOJET: The Turkish Online Journal of Educational Technology, 9(1): 62-69. Retrieved March 21, 2010
274. Larson, Lotta; Kuhn, Cyndi Danner; Collins, Royce Ann; Balthazor, Gerri; Ribble, Mike; Miller, Teresa Northern (2009) Technology Instruction: Fixing the Disconnect. Principal Leadership, v10 n4 p54-58.
275. Chen, Rong-Ji (2010) Investigating Models for Preservice Teachers' Use of Technology to Support Student-Centered Learning. Computers & Education, v55 n1 p32-42.
276. Eisenberg, Mike; Johnson, Doug; Berkowitz, Bob (2010) Information, Communications, and Technology (ICT) Skills Curriculum Based on the Big6 Skills Approach to Information Problem-Solving. Library Media Connection, v28 n6 p24-27.
277. Jun, Han; Zhuzhu, Wang(2010) Capability Building in Educational Technology for Teachers in China British Journal of Educational Technology, v41 n4 p607-611.
278. Lei, Jing (2010) Quantity versus Quality: A New Approach to Examine the Relationship between Technology Use and Student Outcomes. 2010.

279. McGarr, Oliver (2010) Education for Sustainable Development in Technology Education in Irish Schools: A Curriculum Analysis. International Journal of Technology and Design Education, v20 n3 p317-332.

280. Ruzic-Dimitrijevic, Ljiljana; Dimitrijevic, Maja (2010) Challenges IT Instructors Face in the Self-Education Process. Journal of Information Technology Education, v9 pIIP-35-IIP-48.

281. Savage, Robert S.; Erten, Ozlem; Abrami, Philip; Hipps, Geoffrey; Comaskey, Erin; van Lierop, Dea (2010) ABRACADABRA in the Hands of Teachers: The Effectiveness of a Web-Based Literacy Intervention in Grade 1 Language Arts Programs . Computers & Education, v55 n2 p911-922.

282. Shapley, Kelly; Sheehan, Daniel; Maloney, Catherine; Caranikas-Walker, Fanny (2010) Effects of Technology Immersion on Teachers' Growth in Technology Competency, Ideology, and Practices. Journal of Educational Computing Research, v42 n1 p1-33.

❑❑❑